D1521603

Urban Education

A REFERENCE HANDBOOK

CONTEMPORARY EDUCATION ISSUES

Urban Education

A REFERENCE HANDBOOK

Kathy L. Adams and
Dale E. Adams

A B C CLIO

Santa Barbara, California • Denver, Colorado • Oxford, England

Library of Congress Cataloging-in-Publication Data
Adams, Kathy L.
  Urban education : a reference handbook / Kathy L. Adams and
Dale E. Adams.
    p. cm. — (Contemporary education issues)
Includes bibliographical references and index.
  ISBN 1-57607-362-9 (hardcover : alk. paper); ISBN 1-85109-520-9 (e-book)
  1. Education, Urban—United States—Handbooks, manuals, etc.
2. School improvement programs—United States—Handbooks, manuals, etc.
I. Adams, Dale E. II. Title. III. Series.
LC5131.A33 2003
370'.9173'2—dc22

                                                              2003020127

08 07 06 05 04 03   10 9 8 7 6 5 4 3 2 1

This book is also available on the World Wide Web as an e-book.
Visit www.abc-clio.com for details.

ABC-CLIO, Inc.
130 Cremona Drive, P.O. Box 1911
Santa Barbara, California 93116-1911

This book is printed on acid-free paper.
Manufactured in the United States of America

*This book is dedicated to our son, TJ,
and our grandchildren,
and to our parents,
who could not give us much materially
but gave us a hard work ethic and
the belief that we could do anything.*

*Mostly this book is for the teachers who have reported
to class to love and make an impact on urban children
despite mediocre pay, run-down facilities, incompetent
administrators, an overpowering bureaucracy, and the
frustration of being under constant attack by media and
politicians who seem incapable of taking the time to
find out what is actually happening in urban schools.*

☙ Contents

◆◇ Series Editor's Preface

The Contemporary Education Issues series is dedicated to providing readers with an up-to-date exploration of the central issues in education today. Books in the series will examine such controversial topics as home schooling, charter schools, privatization of public schools, Native American education, African American education, literacy, curriculum development, and many others. The series is national in scope and is intended to encourage research by anyone interested in the field.

Because education is undergoing radical if not revolutionary change, the series is particularly concerned with how contemporary controversies in education affect both the organization of schools and the content and delivery of curriculum. Authors endeavor to provide a balanced understanding of the issues and their effects on teachers, students, parents, administrators, and policymakers. The aim of the Contemporary Education Issues series is to publish excellent research on today's educational concerns by some of the finest scholar/practitioners in the field while pointing to new directions. The series promises to offer important analyses of some of the most controversial issues facing society today.

Danny Weil
Series Editor

⬤⬥ Preface

The importance of our urban education system cannot be overstated. Urban education acts as a barometer that indicates the soundness of not only our entire education system but also our society as a whole. The problems with urban public education, real and perceived, need to be solved through the collaborative efforts of educators, parents, elected officials, and of course the students.

In this book we have attempted to present a balanced view of the issues that surround urban education. Both of us have spent several years teaching in an urban public school district and thus are familiar with the challenges involved in teaching the students who need our help the most.

The conservative forces see urban education as a quagmire of wasted funding and efforts. The education forces see urban education as a misunderstood entity that is not nearly as badly off as others believe. The truth lies somewhere in between. A good deal of work and reform needs to take place, but the situation is not hopeless.

One of the barriers to applying the correct fix is that the parents of the children who attend these schools do not have the political power that their numbers would imply. Statistics show that the majority of parents of urban public school students live at or below the poverty line. And it is an accepted fact that the same demographic of people do not consistently exercise their right to vote. Given the fact that they cannot hire lobbyists, their political clout is diminished. In other words, the politicians who create state and local educational policies are not answerable to the population they are sworn to serve. If the same conditions permeated some of the more affluent districts, parents would be up in arms, demanding that the politicians fix the schools; but, alas, these problems are mostly confined to the inner cities.

The education community needs to accept part of the blame as well. More research needs to be conducted to ascertain the causes of and possible solutions to these challenges. And, equally important, the results of this research need to be disseminated to a wider audience. The general public needs to be aware of the overall situation as well as the needed reforms.

Parents of urban students also need to accept some of the blame. We have witnessed neglect on a much wider scale in the urban setting than in other types of districts. All parents need to ensure that their children believe in the promise and value of education. Without such an emphasis at home, the value of education is sometimes lost on students.

Teachers and administrators also need to accept some blame. The challenges of teaching urban students, though overwhelming at times, are still worthy of our best efforts. Urban educators need to be objective in choosing reforms that will help their students, and teaching strategies need to fit the needs of the students. Additional training can help to implement programs that will have the best effect on the students.

Finally, students themselves need to accept some of the blame for the conditions of their schools. Urban students face more challenges than their suburban counterparts, but these challenges should not be used as excuses for lack of effort. Some of our most inspirational citizens have come from an urban background. Barriers need to be seen as challenges that need to be overcome.

Kathy L. Adams and Dale E. Adams

Urban Education

●◆ A REFERENCE HANDBOOK

Chapter One

◆ **Introduction**

In 1974, Tyack wrote a book, *One Best System: A History of American Urban Education,* and he ended the book with this quote: "To create urban schools which really teach students, which reflect the pluralism of the society, which serve the quest for social justice—this is a task which will take persistent imagination, wisdom, and will" (p. 291). This search for one best system of urban schools continues today. There is no doubt in anyone's mind that urban education, schools, teachers, and students are under close scrutiny in the twenty-first century.

What are urban schools? Some define them as schools that are located in a central city of a metropolitan area; others, as schools that contain students who are socially or academically at risk. The U.S. Department of Education's National Center for Education Statistics reported that, as of 1997, 75 percent or more of American households are served by a central city of a major metropolitan area and 575 of these cities consist of districts that contained at-risk children. The U.S. Census Bureau defines an at-risk student as one whose family has the following characteristics:

- ◆ The student is not living with both parents
- ◆ The student's parent or the head of the household is a high school dropout
- ◆ The family's income is below the poverty level
- ◆ Family members have no steady full-time employment
- ◆ The family may be receiving welfare
- ◆ The family has no health insurance for the student

Urban schools have the highest dropout rates of all public school systems. They educate 40 percent of this country's low-income students and 75 percent of its minority students. Urban districts have the largest number of students with physical, emotional, and mental disabilities. In many cases, urban teachers teach in dilapidated buildings with insufficient resources and have little control over curriculum and pedagogical decisions.

This chapter provides both an overview and a history of urban education, because it is important to put into context what the reality of urban schools is in the twenty-first century.

OVERVIEW OF URBAN EDUCATION

Curriculum

What is the curriculum in urban schools? There are major debates over this issue, but as urban schools seek true equality of education there appears to be a movement toward more and more outside control and a structured curriculum with strong white middle-class values. Curriculum is largely affected by the whim of those who control the funding in urban schools and, as such, can be only as good as the resources available.

Chapter 3 addresses this issue in discussions about product versus process, planning, and controlled, hidden, and mandated curricula. It also provides information on school designs and programs available in urban schools. There are as yet no final answers to the questions regarding urban curriculum because little research has been conducted on whether different curriculum models and designs are even effective. In addition, teachers who may hold the key to true equality of education are still largely ignored in the curriculum process, even though they are the ones teaching the material, observing students, and utilizing teachable moments.

Assessment, Accountability, and Standards

Assessment, accountability, and standards greatly affect urban schools, but do these factors lead to true equality? Some believe that high-stakes accountability will solve some of the seemingly overwhelming problems regarding perceived achievement. Others feel that high-stakes testing acts as a deterrent to authentic assessment and well-written, locally controlled, nonbiased standards—two factors that could potentially level the playing field for all children, even the urban poor.

In Chapter 4 you will read about the increased pressure on urban schools and how these issues are impacting curriculum; about inequities in an urban district and what students and teachers face during the school day; and about authentic assessment and the support for and opposition to standards.

Teaching and Teachers

It is hard being a teacher, and even harder being an urban teacher. There are no typical days but lots of unpredictable ones. Dealing with students from different backgrounds, making immediate decisions, balancing several tasks at once, and continuing to labor at a thankless and very public job can be overwhelmingly stressful. Having few resources and little control over curriculum and pedagogical decisions, and working in dilapidated buildings with mold, leaking water, no air conditioning, and, in some cases, no heat—these circumstances can take a toll. Equally stressful are the day-to-day bureaucracy of urban schools, the teachers' concern for the welfare of their students, and the teacher-bashing that takes place (even among urban teachers' suburban counterparts). The difficulties are never-ending, making this an almost impossible job.

In Chapter 5 you will read about teaching in urban schools, including such topics as recruitment, retention, career ladders, and teacher-led schools. You will also read about what it takes to be a great urban teacher and how a new teacher, a teacher who left the profession, and a retired urban teacher felt about urban schools.

Politics and Funding

Chapter 6 covers politics and funding in urban schools. You will read about busing, levies, property taxes and bond issues, court battles over funding, and unfunded mandates and choice programs, as well as about how these factors affect urban schools. You will also read about the challenges to create true educational equality, which may not be met through charter schools, vouchers, or states taking over schools. Rather, these challenges require equitable resources, economic assistance, and attention to other societal issues.

Further research on urban schools is also crucial. This research needs to be disseminated to elected officials and the general public so that they have a better picture of the causes of the problems facing urban education and, ultimately, can support better solutions.

Current Trends and Issues

The problems faced by urban districts are enormous and will not be solved with any single effort. Even an increase in funding will not solve all of them. The deeper problems of poverty hamper especially those programs whose aims are increased achievement, attendance, and graduation numbers.

Truly effective school reform must address socioeconomic status before improvements can be realized. All of the players—students, teachers, parents, administrators, and politicians—need to come together in the common cause of creating an educational environment that advances true equality for all.

In Chapter 7 you will read about the impact on urban schools from the reports titled *A Nation at Risk*, *America 2000*, and *Goals 2000* as well as the recently passed No Child Left Behind Act. In addition, you will read about standardized tests, for-profit educational corporations, school choice, and the changing face of high schools.

Resources

Chapter 8 refers the reader to selected print and nonprint resources that are available for further reading and study. Chapter 9 contains a list of organizations, associations, and government agencies. And the appendices include a glossary of terms, information on a teacher leader program, transcripts of interviews with an urban teacher and principal, and an article about the effects of high-stakes assessment on students.

Conclusion

In the case of *Abbot v. Burke*, the New Jersey supreme court made it clear that disadvantaged students in urban schools need more than just equity in funding and program quality. They also require supplemental and compensatory assistance. This ruling should help all to realize that true equality in education will never be realized without additional assistance from services and resources such as preschool, full-day kindergarten, fully funded Head Start, reduced class sizes, field trips, instructional intervention (including culturally responsive curriculum and teaching), school-to-work-and-college programs, safe schools, full-service schools, special education including specialists in brain research, sociologists, and psychologists, and finally, high-quality, fully certified teachers. In attempting to address some of these issues, the No Child Left Behind Act offers hope for the future. But without the services and resources listed above, the emphasis on test scores, coupled with unfunded mandates and indifference to the challenges of poverty and societal issues, will ultimately leave urban schools right where they are.

A SHORT HISTORY OF
U.S. URBAN PUBLIC EDUCATION

Compulsory urban public education is a system that has undergone several transformations leading up to its current form. The current U.S. system is a result not only of the efforts of several different groups of people, from Puritans to European immigrants of the late nineteenth century, but also of interpretations by the U.S. Supreme Court. This system has been influenced by various European countries, but its current makeup is much different from what one would find in Europe. American society started out as an agrarian culture, and as we developed as a nation the population slowly moved from the farms to the cities. We have gone from a segregated system based on race, social class, and religion to one that accepts all students regardless of background. The present section charts this process.

Early Colonial Education

The early rural schools were attended by students on a voluntary basis throughout the thirteen colonies. The number of students in class depended upon the season. The spring and fall were the busiest times of the year because of planting and harvesting and were therefore the lowest times of attendance. During these periods the needs of the family were considered more important than the academic progress of the child. This agrarian approach to public education is still somewhat in effect inasmuch as most public schools operate nine months a year with a short spring break and summers off. Longer school years did not come about until the American population started to shift from the farm to the factory and from the village to the city.

Except in Massachusetts, education was not mandatory and often exceeded the means of common people in the early days of the colonies. Wealthier families might have hired a tutor for the children. Latin Grammar schools were created to educate the upper social classes in the middle colonies, mostly to prepare students for college. Boys from the middle and upper social classes were allowed to attend school, but poor boys, girls in general, and, of course, slaves were not allowed. Education was far from compulsory.

Early American education was also deeply steeped in religion. As far back as the Reformation, Martin Luther believed that people should be literate in order to read the Bible for themselves. This religious influence weighed heavily upon the early American settlers, most of whom were Protestant.

In fact, Puritans were one of the first groups of people to make school attendance mandatory. In the Massachusetts colony, Puritan children often learned how to read and write by using a Horn Book—a device made from the horn of an ox that was fashioned into a flat surface. Lessons were placed under the semi-transparent horn. On these Horn Books, scripture was written to be read and memorized.

As early as 1642, education laws were passed in the colony of Massachusetts. One such law, the Old Deluder Satan Act, required that towns hire a schoolmaster to teach the children how to read and write. The idea was that if children could read the Bible, then the devil could not corrupt them.

Despite the religious emphasis on early public education, there were controversies. The majority of immigrants to the original thirteen colonies were Protestant. Schools used the Bible to teach the children to read and write, and the King James Version of the Bible was the chosen text. This adopted text upset the Catholic populations in the colonies since Catholics did not recognize the King James Version of the Bible as the true word of God.

The issue of which religious text to use rose to prominence after independence. In New York State, Catholic organizations came into direct confrontation with state governments over the use of the King James Bible. In 1840, New York governor William Seward asked the state legislature to create more schools to deal with the increase in immigration (Watras, 2002). Catholic leaders asked for some of this funding to support parish schools that did not use the King James Bible as a primary text. The government refused to give the additional funds and also refused to remove the King James Bible as a school text.

Since the Catholics were in the minority they could not change the school policies or replace the King James Version, so they started their own schools. These schools taught basic educational skills and were designed to be kept in line with Catholic doctrine. This was the start of the parochial school movement in the United States.

EARLY GOVERNMENT ACTIONS (AND INACTIONS)

The origins of the U.S. education system did not come from the federal government. There is no provision for public education within the framework of the Constitution, the Declaration of Independence, or the Articles of Confederation. In fact, education largely was, and still is, considered a reserved power of the states. This fact alone makes the U.S. system different from the European one: We have fifty separate state constitutions that dictate how public education is to be carried out. Even among the original thirteen colonies themselves, and later among the fifty states, there were differences in quality and availability of public education.

The founding fathers started to address the issue of education only after the United States became a free country. Steps were taken in individual states to create educational systems. For example, one of the founding fathers made an attempt to create a statewide public educational system: Thomas Jefferson, then governor of Virginia, proposed that a public school system be created and that the top 10 percent of school pupils be given a free scholarship to attend the College of William and Mary.

In 1779, in his preamble to a bill, Jefferson wrote in support of a more general diffusion of knowledge

> able to guard the sacred deposit of the rights and liberties of their fellow citizens, and that they should be called to that charge without regard to wealth, birth or other accidental condition or circumstance; but the indigence of the greater number disabling them from so educating, at their own expense, those of their children whom nature hath fitly formed and disposed to become useful instruments for the public, it is better such should be sought for and educated as the common experience of all, than that the happiness of all should be confided to the weak or wicked. (quoted in Alexander and Alexander, 1992, p. 25)

Despite this progressive attempt at educational reform, the idea was shot down by the Virginia legislature.

The first federal document that even mentioned public education was the Northwest Territories Act. This act was created during the time that the Articles of Confederation were the law of the land. It not only provided a blueprint for territories to eventually achieve statehood but also offered a way to provide public education to the children of these new states by stipulating that every township had to provide land that was to be set aside and sold to fund schools and teachers.

Charity and Sunday Schools

During the early stages of the Industrial Revolution a migration started from the farms to the cities. The cost of educating the new influx of children to the cities was too expensive to provide for all. Free education was not available. Therefore, Charity schools were created by groups of concerned citizens. Often founded by a society or funded by a philanthropist, Charity schools were designed to provide a free education to the poor. For some they represented the only option for free education. Charity schools were intended to solve the problem of educating the newly urbanized children, but they were overmatched. There simply was not enough money to provide education for the masses in the urban areas.

As mentioned previously, one of the main reasons for learning to read, and thus for attending school, was to receive religious instruction. Martin Luther's belief in the importance of reading was shared by the early American settlers. And one of the early attempts at providing this service was the Sunday school. Sunday schools were created to provide basic education for urban children because, with industrialization, the village church had lost some of its influence on the population. The church also provided this schooling as a way to bring the family into the church itself. The power of the church, and of religious instruction overall, lessened during the Industrial Revolution with the vast migration of people to the cities and into the factories.

Sunday schools were also created to bring in younger children and provide them with a basic education. Sunday was the best day of the week to try and teach children because the other six days were spent working in the factories. Sunday school curriculum was based on religious morals with a smattering of general knowledge. The teachers were volunteers with little or no formal training as educators. More often than not, they were not up to the task. The education that the children received was basic at best.

Due to the industrialization, there was a vast migration of people moving toward the urban centers. Urbanization happened so quickly that the population of some U.S. cities doubled almost every year. During the early phase of the Industrial Revolution, most cities were not ready for the large influx of people because their infrastructure did not provide for the services that this movement required.

The family unit itself was being challenged due to the conditions in the cities and factories. Men and women worked in the factories, as did children when they became old enough. In some cases, parents and children worked different shifts. Due to the lack of parental supervision, there were large numbers of children in the streets. Schools were now seen as a way to get control of unsupervised children.

Factory owners also saw a need for education of the masses. The factories needed not just general laborers but skilled workers who were capable of fixing the machines. Schools were seen as a way to provide literacy as well as instilling a work ethic in these new workers.

Sunday schools were more popular than private schools and even the early public schools because they permitted children to get enough of an education to read and yet still help with the family income. Sunday schools shifted their focus to include more religious studies when child labor laws started to come into effect. With mandatory public education the task of providing basic literacy fell eventually to the public school systems.

The Lancaster System, Monitor Schools, and Common Schools

During the early stages of the Industrial Revolution, some children entered into apprenticeships. Under the terms of these apprenticeships, parents signed contracts with craftsmen so the children could learn a trade. The children lived in the craftsmen's houses until they learned the trade well enough to become craftsmen themselves.

Girls were often sent off to learn the skills of a domestic. They were neither expected nor encouraged to learn any skills other than those that would serve them in the working world and in their marriages. The apprenticeship system was not capable of serving the educational needs of the community, nor was it large enough to accommodate the large numbers of children entering the cities. In addition, industrialization tended to smother the need for fine skills.

One attempt at providing basic and low-cost education was the Lancaster system. Joseph Lancaster started his schools in England during the height of the Industrial Revolution. The Lancaster schools provided education for a large number of children at a substantial savings compared to traditional private schools. The idea was tempting, especially because of the low cost involved.

The Lancaster system—eventually known as the Monitor system—was organized around one single teacher. This teacher was responsible for a huge number of students. For example, in 1806, the Free School Society started a school in New York City where each teacher was put in charge of about 1,000 students.

Obviously one teacher could not supervise, much less teach, that many students. He therefore enlisted the help of higher-achieving students to "monitor" the other students. In this way, instruction flowed down an educational chain of command. The teacher would teach the basic lesson of the day to the monitor students, who would then teach and supervise the other children in the lesson. The quality of the education from Monitor schools was questionable. There was a shortage of qualified teachers, and the number of students they had to deal with was simply too large. Lancaster eventually tried to open several schools in the United States. All of these schools failed, but the Monitor system remained in effect in one form or another.

Common Schools—a name associated with almost any school that did not charge tuition—were advocated by early education reformers such as Horace Mann. In 1848, in his Twelfth Report to the Massachusetts Board of Education, Mann wrote: "Without undervaluing any other human agency, it may be safely affirmed that the Common School, improved and energized, as it can easily be, may become the most effective and benignant of all the forces of civilization" (quoted in Alexander and Alexander, 1992, p. 26). Common Schools allowed students from all backgrounds to attend and were funded by taxes, mostly property taxes. They were not popular with wealthier citizens, who complained about having to pay taxes to support schools that did not provide for their children.

In New York, a committee headed by Horace Greeley drafted a letter to the state legislature. In this letter the committee argued that all property within the state should be taxed to pay for free public education. The reasoning behind this proclamation was that everyone profited from the maintenance of schools. Greeley believed that schools would spread conventional morals, provide a ladder on which aspiring children could climb, and protect the wealth of established classes (Watras, 2002).

The Common Schools were primarily elementary schools. Few high schools were designated as Common Schools in the early stages of the movement because the need for secondary education was not thought to be a priority.

The Common Schools eventually gave way to public schools, forming the foundation of the public school system. The idea of a school that accepted students regardless of class or religion was appealing to many, especially given the large influx of immigrants who needed a way to help transform their children into Americans.

Immigration

The first immigrants to the colonies were primarily farmers. They came in search of a place where they could actually own land. Most came from Western Europe with the dream of owning a farm to pass down to their sons, settling east of the Appalachian Mountains.

During the mid-1800s more and more immigrants came to the United States. Many of this new group were from Eastern and Southern

Europe, but they, too, were farmers. These people moved to the newly opened up interior of the country. However, there were also many new Americans who stayed in the cities to work in the factories. Leaders in the United States were concerned about the large influx of people who carried with them their own beliefs, cultures, and religions (Lee, 1957). It was decided that these new people should be "Americanized," that an institution was required to conduct this process, and that the public school system was the best vehicle for doing so since it was already in place.

Schools taught English to those who could not read, write, or speak the language. They also taught students to say the Pledge of Allegiance, and to become familiar with other "American" customs. The students learned about government, the blessings of democracy, and the basics of capitalism because all of these themes were different from what they were accustomed to in their mother countries.

Indeed, it was the public school system that carried out the ideals of the great American Melting Pot. When the new Americans had learned the English language, the factory foremen could give orders more efficiently, and shipping products became easier when the workers could read the orders.

Compulsory School Attendance and Early Public Education

Mandatory school attendance was not uniformly accepted in the United States until World War I. The size of the school year differed from state to state, and to a small degree it still does. States were simply required to have the children in school for a fixed number of days a year.

Mandatory school attendance was especially important in creating child labor laws. However, the laws regarding days and years of attendance were left up to a particular state. Rhode Island was the first state to create a child labor law that prevented children from working unless they had completed a minimum level of education.

Public education differed greatly from state to state. The National Education Association (NEA) tried to create a standardized pattern for school attendance. In 1892, it established the Committee of Ten. The members were college presidents, professors, and teachers. The goal of the committee was to create a high school that had different subjects and contained harder courses in preparation for college attendance. The outcome was a standardized curriculum that was geared toward college preparation. Not much thought was given to students who would not go on to college or to the social classes of the students themselves.

The public school movement was largely due to the work of people like Horace Mann of Massachusetts. Public schools were permitted, but not necessarily required, in all states. Local schools were initially watched over by state and local governments, and legislatures dictated what was to be taught. Massachusetts was the first state to create local school boards to watch over the schools. The local board was charged with hiring and firing teachers and overseeing curriculum decisions, but the state retained control over all of the school systems by appointing a chief state school officer.

Although citizens started to control the school systems, they still needed someone to take care of daily operations. A head or "principal" teacher was given this responsibility. When the school systems became larger, it was hard for school boards to make all of the necessary decisions. Thus the office of superintendent of schools was created.

Eventually states began to create state-level boards of education. These boards dictated curriculum as well as standards to be followed. States differed as to how the members were selected. Some were appointed while others were elected. The procedure for choosing school board members has become one of the largest political issues over the years since these boards deal with sensitive issues such as the teaching of evolution versus creationism, sex education, and funding.

At first, the U.S. government tried to stay out of the educational debates between states. Other than the Morrill Act of 1862, which helped states to create land grant colleges, and the Morrill Act of 1890, which encouraged colleges to provide agricultural instruction, the business of education was strictly a state affair.

This strict state control started to change during the New Deal. One of Franklin Delano Roosevelt's ideas was the establishment of the National Youth Administration (NYA). The NYA helped to provide funds for students to attend school during the Depression.

During the 1950s and the 1960s the federal government became involved in education with such issues as integration, the GI Bill (which provided federal money for World War II veterans to attend college), and the National Science Foundation. During the 1970s, there was significant federal involvement in the treatment of handicapped students.

Public Law (PL) 94-142, created for the treatment and education of those facing physical and mental challenges, mandated the Individual Education Plan (IEP). The goal of the IEP was to place students with challenges in the "least restrictive environment." PL 94-142 resulted in a great financial burden on public education in general, and urban education specifically. There was, and still is, a larger percentage of students with physical or mental challenges in urban schools than in suburban or rural schools. The federal government did not provide adequate funding to make the changes or mandates required by PL 94–142.

Owing to the larger number of children with special needs in urban schools, the implementation of the law caused greater expenditures on special education. Today more money is spent per student in urban schools than in suburban schools. Many states provide funding for special education programs, but some are better at it than others.

In the past the federal government has used several different cabinet positions to deal with education. The NEA has lobbied for years for the creation of a cabinet-level Department of Education. The belief was that if the department existed at the cabinet level, education would become more important on the federal level.

Under the Carter administration the Department of Education came into being. It was not exceptionally popular with political traditionalists, who did not see the need. In fact, Ronald Reagan, while president, tried to eliminate the position, although he eventually appointed a head to the department. The prominence that the position holds in U.S. education depends upon who is in power. Under the Reagan administration it was believed that the federal government should have a limited role in U.S. education. Under President Clinton's administration the Department of Education became more active in public school reforms.

African Americans

Unlike the early immigrants of the colonies, Africans did not come to the United States by choice. Slavery emerged early in the colonial period. At Jamestown, it began when a Portuguese ship arrived with African slaves. Having used up a good deal of the available Native Americans, the plantation owners were in desperate need of labor. Although there was a moderate population of African Americans living in the cities of the North, the majority of the population inhabited the South both prior to and immediately after the Civil War. In the South it was rare for slaves to be educated.

In 1831, Nat Turner, a southern slave, led an uprising against the white population. Although the uprising failed and Nat Turner was put to death, it was considered a bad idea to educate slaves. Indeed, after the Nat Turner Uprising, it became illegal to educate slaves in many southern states. In 1832, for example, South Carolina passed a law that made it illegal to teach slaves to read and write. White citizens who violated this law were fined up to $100 and jailed up to six months. Slaves who broke this law were subject to as many as fifty lashes with a whip. Free blacks could be punished by fine, jail, and corporal punishment.

Several other laws that restricted slaves were created both before and after the Civil War. After the war, when white southerners reclaimed state governments, these laws were called Black Codes.

During and after the Civil War, efforts were made to educate the newly freed slaves. Volunteers from New England came down south and established schools during the conflict and after the fighting had stopped. The National Freedmen's Aid Society and the American Missionary Society provided many teachers for these schools.

During Reconstruction several attempts were made to help former slaves become literate. On the federal level, the Freedmen's Bureau was established as part of the Reconstruction reforms. The bureau was responsible for helping former slaves adjust to freedom by providing vocational training and education. These noble efforts would eventually stop after 1878, when President Grant stated that the period of Reconstruction was over. The costs of maintaining the Freedmen's Bureau as well as other Reconstruction programs had become too expensive for the federal government to maintain.

With the end of Reconstruction, former white southern politicians came to power in the South. Jim Crow laws came into effect, discouraging voting, among other activities, by African Americans throughout most of the South. Education, though no longer illegal for African Americans, was neither encouraged nor properly funded.

The African American population had started to shift to the North prior to the Civil War, partly owing to the movements of runaway slaves. Yet after the Civil War the majority of the African American population was still located in the South. The largest migration of African Americans to the North occurred during World War I.

While Europe was engaged in the early stages of World War I, the need for military goods was great. Britain and France sought these goods in the United States. Northern factories had a hard time keeping up with orders due to the limited labor pool. Northern labor agents went to African American communities in the South with the promise of good factory jobs in Cleveland, Detroit, and Chicago. Even African American newspapers displayed ads that depicted the good life in the North. Groups of African Americans flocked north in large numbers.

Unfortunately, African Americans were not welcomed into the northern cities. City infrastructures were overwhelmed, leading to shortages of food, housing, and schooling. One effect of these shortages was the creation of ghettos with schools that catered to the African American society and resembled the inadequate schools in the South.

Things became worse after World War I when factory orders fell off and African Americans started to lose their jobs. Segregation became the norm for most African Americans in the North as well as in the South. The separate schools that had started in the South started to spread to the North. African Americans attended all-black schools due to their geographical location as well as by law in some places. Efforts to desegregate the schools were defeated in court and culminated with the Supreme Court case of *Plessy v. Ferguson* (1898).

In this case, the Court ruled that separate schools based on race were constitutional provided that they met the guidelines of "separate but equal." This clause was accepted in name but not in practice. The black schools were almost always inferior to the white schools in terms of teachers, curriculum, funding, and the quality of buildings.

The segregation of schools did not change until the Supreme Court case of *Brown v. Board of Education*. The lead lawyer, Thurgood Marshall, successfully argued that the system was unfair because the schools were indeed not equal.

Brown v. Board of Education overturned the effects of *Plessy v. Ferguson*. The judges, having decided that African American students developed feelings of inferiority as a result of being segregated, concluded that separate education was unequal.

Southern states did not embrace this decision. State legislatures found loopholes to get around it, and Senator Strom Thurmond of South Carolina tried to get the southern states to stand together and defy the decision.

White Southern society was even more outraged at the decision. In some cases outright intimidation was used to prevent the desegregation of schools. For example, in 1957, the Arkansas National Guard had to help an African American girl enter a predominantly white school while white citizens shouted obscenities at the young student.

The Civil Rights Movement's Effect on Urban Education

Even with the *Brown* decision, desegregation was not a reality. By 1963, only 9 percent of schools were desegregated. It would take actions on the civil rights front to create real change in education—actions like the Montgomery Bus Boycott, the Birmingham demonstrations, and the March on Washington. Images of peaceful demonstrators being attacked by police dogs in Birmingham, coupled with peaceful demonstrations in Washington and with Dr. Martin Luther King's "I have a dream" speech, started to change the public's stance on segregation.

Resistance was still apparent in the South, but better tactics achieved success. For example, the National Association for the Advancement of Colored People (NAACP) had to sue individual school districts in order to desegregate. Due to numerous appeals the process was slow and expensive, and true segregation was not a reality. The federal Department of Health, Education, and Welfare (HEW) changed the minds of district administrators when it imposed financial sanctions on districts that did not comply with the law. In a five-year period HEW initiated six hundred administrative proceedings against segregated school districts (Watras, 2002).

During the days of segregation many attempts were made to improve education for African Americans. Some African Americans, such as Booker T. Washington and William Edward Burghardt Du Bois, believed that education could improve race relations. In 1881 Washington created a school—the famous Tuskegee Institute—that provided industrial training to African Americans. The Alabama Legislature gave the young school $2,000 for teachers' salaries (Watras, 2002). Washington was praised at first, but some started to criticize his school as a poor educational model.

Du Bois disagreed with Washington regarding what form education should take. He believed that higher academic learning should come before a program that taught only industrial and agricultural arts, and was concerned that college opportunities would be compromised if the country adopted the industrial training for African Americans. Du Bois also believed that segregation in schools would lead to segregation throughout a lifetime.

The integration of schools by minority children occurred amid controversies that still exist today. One of the most controversial methods to desegregate schools was busing. The idea here was to bus white children to mostly black schools and black children to mostly white schools. In 1980, only about 7 percent of white parents disliked the prospect of sending their children to schools with black children. However, 77 percent of the same parents opposed the idea of busing because they felt that sending their children out of their neighborhood was unacceptable (Rossell, 1990).

Even some African American leaders objected to the idea of forced integration. These included Stokely Carmichael and Charles Hamilton, who called for Black Power. Members of the Black Power movement were concerned with several issues that affected African Americans, especially education. They were somewhat against moving black children out of black neighborhoods on the grounds that black communities had some power over the schools their children attended because they had some say in hiring teachers, selecting materials, and setting policies.

Desegregation also caused an increase in Catholic school attendance. For example, as the urban schools desegregated in Boston, over 2,000 more students enrolled in Catholic schools (Watras, 2002). Even some Catholic systems practiced a form of segregation. In Dayton, Ohio, for instance, there were Catholic schools whose population was mostly African American while other schools in the suburbs were almost completely white. This is still the case today in some areas.

Urban Schools and Poverty

As many have perceived, we have a culture of poverty in the United States. What this means is that people who are born in poor neighborhoods rarely leave these neighborhoods for a more prosperous life. The ability to break the cycle of poverty has been the focus of many programs designed to meet the unique needs of the urban child. The effectiveness and purpose of such programs have been subjects of debate from the 1950s to today.

In 1964, President Johnson declared war on poverty. His administration spent over a billion dollars on educational programs that were created to close the gap between poor and rich, black and white.

James Conant, a former president of Harvard University, was one of the first people to study the differences between suburban and urban schools. In influential suburbs he found wonderful homes and modern, well-staffed schools. But in the poorer sections of urban areas he found tenement buildings and schools that were underfunded and poorly staffed.

The problems in the urban schools were many. One was that very few parents of urban schoolchildren had completed high school. In addition, because school buildings were old, they required a greater amount of money for upkeep and maintenance. This extra expenditure limited the money that could be spent for things like curriculum and lower class sizes to better equalize education. And since the income level of urban parents was far below that of suburban parents, there was less money available for urban districts. These districts simply could not raise the money needed to improve the condition of the schools or to provide equalizing resources and experiences.

Another problem had to do with a separate culture in the slums. The definition of education was different there. Vocational and practical education seemed to be more valued than academic education. Poor children were simply not expected to attend college. Indeed, it was believed that the teachers who tried to instill the value of higher education in these children were either failing to communicate with them or setting them up for failure.

The federal government tried to close the educational gaps with various programs. Some of these programs were fought against and are still somewhat controversial. Title I—also known as Better Schooling for Educationally Deprived Children—was a federal program that gave money to schools with a large percentage of children who lived below the poverty line. It got off to a rocky start because some school districts did not know what criteria to use to decide whether they were eligible for Title I compensation. States were given some leeway in how they could spend Title I funds. For example, some districts spent the money on hiring extra teachers to reduce class size while others spent the money on specialist teachers for reading. Title I was considered a great success at first, but scientific studies yielded results that were less encouraging. The studies concluded that the plan to spend the monies was not sufficiently thorough or thought-out.

Title I underwent several changes during the 1980s. The number of students who qualified increased to include all children who needed help. Many of these children were temporarily taken out of the classroom to receive remedial instruction. Such removals came to be known as "pull outs," and children who were continually pulled out of classrooms were referred to as "at-risk" students.

Another federally funded program created to assist underprivileged children was Head Start, founded by Sargent Shriver. The director of the Office of Equal Opportunity under Johnson, Shriver believed that children living in poverty needed help before they reached school age. In essence, then, Head Start was created to prepare the underprivileged child for school. It had three broad goals:

- To include the family
- To focus on several aspects of child improvement
- To allow the child to experience success

The program had some growing pains, however. With no set curriculum there was a wide variety of thought on what the children needed to be taught. There seemed to be mass confusion, perhaps as a result of the large number of volunteers who staffed the project.

Studies on Head Start have highlighted many problems. One of the biggest is the fact that not all Head Start programs utilize the same curriculum, making it difficult to compare programs. Another is the lack of sufficient funding to help the neediest children. On the other hand, many of the studies have relied only on quantitative data such as standardized test scores, thus omitting positive effects such as parents getting training for jobs and, ultimately, getting their families out of poverty. For this reason, some people have questioned the accuracy of the studies conducted to assess the success of Head Start.

1980 to the Present Day

The conservative stance on education during the Reagan administration culminated in the report known as *A Nation at Risk*. Responding to the concern of college administrators, business leaders, and military leaders that they had to dedicate time to remediate workers in basic education skills, Secretary of Education T. H. Bell created a commission to look at the quality of education in the United States. The commission's report—*A Nation at Risk*—stated that education in the United States seemed to be inferior to that of other nations. One of the most controversial recommendations concerned the tightening of graduation requirements.

The National Commission on Excellence in Education (NCEE) contended that current U.S. students were scoring lower on standardized tests than students during the 1950s. The NCEE members blamed schools for presenting a diluted curriculum. It wanted better-trained teachers, merit pay systems, more homework, and standardized tests. Although the Reagan administration promoted all of these changes, it did not provide the federal funding to follow through on them. It was up to the states to fund these changes if they wished to do so.

Educators were quick to point out perceived flaws in the report. It seemed to them that government officials were blaming current economic conditions on the nation's schools, especially urban schools, and that there were errors in the way the commission had gathered evidence. These critics were mostly ignored, however, and 120,000 copies of the report were printed, in addition to the copies that appeared in newspapers and periodicals.

Urban schools were hit the hardest by the information in *A Nation at Risk*. Reformers wanted urban schools to perform as well as their suburban counterparts—"or else." The "or else" part came in places like Milwaukee, Wisconsin, where a program of educational vouchers was put in place that allowed parents, specifically those with children in failing schools, to take some of the funding directed to failing schools and use it to place their children in private schools.

Proponents of educational vouchers contend that the increased competition will force failing public schools to improve in order to survive, whereas critics argue that the movement of motivated children will further weaken the public schools. Critics are also concerned that, because most private schools are parochial, vouchers may violate separation of church and state as interpreted with respect to the establishment clause of the U.S. Constitution. In addition, they fault the use of standardized tests to measure the effectiveness of urban schools.

Proficiency tests have been created in several states over the last twenty years. These tests have become the principal measure of accountability for individuals, schools, and districts. Critics contend that the tests are racially biased and written in the language of upper-middle-class white people. Proponents argue that some urban children have achieved diplomas for simply showing up at school rather than for their academic achievement. Some states have taken these tests a step further by making them "high stakes" for students, teachers, schools, and districts. What this means for students is that, based on a test score, they could be denied a diploma or held back a grade. Teachers and principals have been surplussed from schools, schools have been redesigned, and whole schools and districts have been taken over or rewarded based on test scores.

Some educators are very worried about the resegregation of urban schools. A great deal of white flight occurred in the 1980s, and between 1994 and 1999 federal court orders released public school districts from having to implement desegregation plans. Observers have also noted a resurgence in tracking since the utilization of test scores and teacher judgments to place students, especially in desegregated schools. In some instances, students are removed from their regular classroom during the weeks before testing and required to undergo intensive test preparation—thus missing out on the learning taking place in their original classroom.

Proposals were also made to improve public education during George H. W. Bush's administration. Bush initiated the *America 2000* program, and, based on a forum with state governors, his administration outlined reforms. However, like his predecessor, Ronald Reagan, he did not provide the funding to back up these proposals. Bush simply stated that he did not want to "throw money at the problem."

One of the most controversial aspects of *America 2000* was the idea of national standards. Republicans and Democrats alike thought that schools should be locally controlled. The idea of national standards upset those who thought local control would be overruled by federal regulation. Other controversial aspects included school prayer and vouchers.

When Bill Clinton took office in 1992, he retained most of the *America 2000* reforms. Clinton created *Goals 2000,* which was very similar to the *America 2000* program. The only major omissions were school prayer and vouchers. Despite the philosophical differences between Clinton and Bush, their beliefs about educational reform were very similar. For example, both supported standardized testing and both believed in school choice (although Clinton's preference was for public school choice whereas Bush supported the use of educational vouchers). In addition, both campaigned on reforming education, but neither of them seemed to have any solid plans to help urban schools.

With the proliferation of standardized tests, urban public schools came under constant attack. An educational voucher program was started in Cleveland, Ohio, as well as throughout the state of Florida. In Cleveland, the board of education was taken over by the state.

White flight, which had started during integration, accelerated when school districts were rated by the states. Other choice programs such as charter and magnet schools became more popular. In 2002, the administration of George W. Bush was able to establish a system that required all states and all schools to conduct standardized testing. Even perceived political liberals such as Senator Ted Kennedy signed on to the reforms of this second Bush administration.

The enactment of the No Child Left Behind Act will have far-reaching effects on education, and many changes will be required around the nation. This act represents the largest involvement of the federal government in public education in several decades.

Teachers have also been included in these reforms. Many are now required to pass standardized tests in order to receive a teaching certificate or license. In addition, early and frequent observations are now being included in the requirements for maintaining a teaching license. School accountability programs have taken over the curriculum in most schools, especially urban schools.

The future of urban public education is further brought into question by the 2002 Supreme Court ruling on educational vouchers. Specifically, the Court found that the Cleveland educational voucher system did not violate the separation of church and state. Some educators are concerned that educational vouchers will spell the end to urban schools as we know them. They fear that urban schools will become a dumping ground for special education students, poorly motivated students, and students whose parents are not concerned with achievement. Others, however, believe that the recent Supreme Court decision will have little effect, given that statewide educational voucher initiatives have failed in several states over the last ten years in California and Michigan. The future of urban public education and the effects of educational vouchers remain unsettled.

The challenges faced by today's urban educators and students are being felt throughout the nation. There is hope that initiatives such as the No Child Left Behind Act will ensure that all urban students achieve at the same level as students from more affluent schools, but many urban educators do not believe this will happen.

There is still the basic issue of funding. Despite the fact that more money is spent in some urban districts than in suburban districts, the necessary funding levels have not been realized. The costs of urban education, including those associated with salaries, upkeep of older buildings, security, and special education, are not as pressing in the suburban districts. And of course the problems faced by urban students even before they enter the school building are substantial.

Wholesale changes need to be made in the urban society as a whole before the dream of equal achievement can be realized. The problems associated with poverty such as poor nutrition, lead poisoning, exposure to drugs and crime, and a society that does not value education as highly as other pursuits must be overcome before universal achievement levels can be reached.

Education *can* be the great equalizer, as expressed by Horace Mann, but this dream cannot be attained by education alone. It will take the will of the entire population of this country to raise the standard of living and opportunities for all before serious inroads can be made in urban education.

REFERENCES

Alexander, Kern, and Alexander, M. David. *American Public School Law,* 3rd ed. St. Paul, MN: West Publishing Company, 1992.

Lee, Gordon C. *Introduction to Education in Modern America.* New York: Holt, 1957.

Rossell, Christine H. "The Carrot or the Stick for School Desegregation Policy: Magnet Schools or Forced Busing" (Eric Reproduction Service No. ED 366 687). 1990.

Tyack, David B. *One Best System: A History of American Urban Education.* Cambridge, MA: Harvard University Press, 1974.

U.S. Census Bureau. Available online at http://www.census.gov.

U.S. Department of Education, National Center for Education Statistics. 1997. Available online at http://nces.ed.gov.

Watras, Joseph. *The Foundations of Educational Curriculum and Diversity.* Boston: Allyn and Bacon, 2002.

Chapter Two

☙ Chronology

The urban education movement started during the 1700s, triggered by the migration of people from the farm to the cities. A large part of the urban public school movement was also influenced by the migration of Europeans to America. This migration highlighted a need to create a system to "Americanize" migrants into U.S. society. The system was designed to introduce these new Americans to democracy, the English language, and the free market system. The third major portion of the urban education system was the civil rights movement. Supreme Court cases such as *Plessy v. Ferguson*, which made segregation legal, and *Brown v. Board of Education*, which made segregation illegal, used public education to bring integration into other parts of American society.

1600–1800: THE COLONIAL PERIOD

There was no uniform public education system in the thirteen colonies. The majority of the population was agrarian and Protestant. School attendance was voluntary and affected by the seasons. What education did exist was available mostly through private schools (such as Benjamin Franklin's academy) or private tutors. An emphasis on religion and morals was part of the curriculum. The most common texts in New England were the Bible and the Horn Book. Massachusetts passed laws designed to save children from sin. The first was the Massachusetts School Law of 1642, which charged local magistrates with ensuring that children attended school. This law helped establish the control of education at the local level and was one of the first attempts to make school attendance compulsory. The law of 1642, also known as the Old Deluder Satan Act (see Chapter 1), required every town of fifty or more families to hire a teacher. The use of the King James Bible gave rise to one of the first education-related controversies in history (one that continues to this day), inasmuch as the Catholic population did not want their children to study a Protestant text. This controversy led to the development of the first parochial schools.

The U.S. Constitution and the Articles of Confederation made no mention of education rendering the responsibility of educating America's youth as a reserved power of the states.

Even the founding fathers had little luck creating a free public school system. Thomas Jefferson tried to do so while serving as the governor of Virginia, but he was unable to convince the state legislature.

The Northwest Territory Ordinance was the first law to create funding for education.

In 1751, Benjamin Franklin established the Franklin Academy. Although the tuition was too high for most families, he set a precedent for recognizing the importance of secondary education.

In 1774, a school was started by the Abolitionist society in Philadelphia for African American children. Similar schools followed.

1800–1900:
INDUSTRIAL REVOLUTION, IMMIGRATION, BLACKS, AND SECONDARY SCHOOLS

Education reformers such as Horace Mann started common schools in New England. The idea of free schools through high school, and of local boards of education, was part of this reform. Free and common schools were not widespread throughout the nation at this time. The cities, especially, were in need of free education for the growing young populations.

Faced with the lack of city infrastructures, influential and wealthy citizens saw the need for educating the city's youth and attempted to create Charity schools. These schools failed due to lack of adequate funding and qualified teachers. The church created Sunday schools to try and fill the gap. Sunday schools were academic schools that were attended on Sunday, the only day that the children did not have to work in the factories. However, Sunday schools were inadequate due to a lack of qualified teachers. Joseph Lancaster created the Factory or Monitor schools to fill the void. Monitor schools were initially popular because they were a low-cost way of educating children. But they, too, were ineffective, due to the basic design of the schools and the lack of qualified teachers.

Immigrants of the late 1800s and early 1900s were different from those who had come to America during colonial times in that they were mostly from Eastern and Southern Europe. These new Americans were not familiar with the concepts of self-government or capitalism, so publicly funded schools were started as a means of "Americanizing" them and helping them learn the skills needed for the new technology in the factories.

Schools were also seen as a way to keep children out of trouble. Due to conditions in the factories, the traditional family unit was challenged. City youth were often left unsupervised. The belief was that schools would keep the children off the streets.

In 1824, free education for black children became available in New York.

In 1840, the parochial school movement in New York created a huge presence in urban schools, but white and black students were still separated.

By 1860, about 50 percent of the children were enrolled in public schools—an indication that most states had formalized their free school systems.

In 1861, during the Civil War, teachers were sent from the North to the South to teach.

In 1862, the First Morrill Act was passed, enabling public money to be utilized to establish land grant universities.

In 1866, former confederate states enacted black codes to maintain the racial status quo.

In 1867, a National Board of Education was established, at which point the patterns of American education were essentially in place.

In 1868, the Fourteenth Amendment granted citizenship to blacks.

In 1870, the Freedman Bureau was abolished and the Fifteenth Amendment passed, giving blacks the right to vote.

In 1874, the Kalamazoo case (*Stuart v. School District No. 1 of the Village of Kalamazoo*) set the precedent for state legislatures' right to levy taxes to support schools, resulting in a boom in the number of secondary schools and students.

In 1890, the Second Morrill Act provided land grant institutions for both black and white systems.

In 1896, *Plessy v. Ferguson* set the standard of "separate but equal," which allowed legal segregation to continue in the United States.

In 1918, the National Education Associations Commission on the Reorganization of Secondary Education specified seven specific goals for public schools. Known as the "Cardinal Principles," these led to the comprehensive high school. It was also at this time that compulsory attendance laws became more prevalent, requiring school attendance until the age of sixteen.

1928–1945: DEPRESSION AND WAR

There was little visible change between the schools of the early 1900s and those of the 1930s, but education was harder to fund with so many people out of work and moving around the country. Some of the New Deal programs, such as the Civilian Conservation Corps, were designed to create jobs for the youth of America. Attempts to include a heavy educational base with these organizations were mostly ineffective. The American high school experience changed with the coming of World War II now that young men, whether they had graduated or not, were enlisting in the armed services. The war also affected women in the teaching profession and other fields: Though traditionally paid less than men, during World War II they began receiving high-paying factory jobs when orders for war goods increased. For the first time, school boards felt the pressure to pay female teachers on the same level as male teachers.

By 1940, almost 75 percent of five- to twenty-year-olds were in school.

1916–1950: MIGRATION OF AFRICAN AMERICANS TO THE NORTH AND EAST

Prior to the Civil War the overwhelming majority of African Americans lived in the South. With the exception of a few escaped slaves and free blacks, the African American was in slavery. After the Civil War the vast majority of African Americans still lived in the southeast section of the United States. Reconstruction programs such as the Freedmen's Bureau provided some educational opportunities for blacks, but these opportunities stopped with the end of reconstruction. With the start of World War I, factory orders for war goods skyrocketed in the industrial North. Labor agents actively recruited blacks from the South with the promise of high wages and good schools. A large number of African Americans decided to migrate north for the industrial jobs created by the European conflict.

The infrastructures of urban cities like Cleveland and Chicago were not equipped for the increase in population. African Americans who came north in the hopes of a better way of life for themselves and their children continued to experience segregation. African Americans mostly moved into poorer sections of the cities. Blacks experienced a lower standard of living than white residents of the cities. This included inadequate and unequal urban schools. Efforts to stop segregation were defeated by the U.S. Supreme Court. In 1932, the *Journal of Negro Education* was founded at Howard University.

The following year saw publication of *Miseducation of the Negro*, a book that stressed the teaching of European mainstream history while also teaching the life, history, language, philosophy, and literature of African people.

1950–1970: THE CIVIL RIGHTS MOVEMENT

The National Association for the Advancement of Colored People (NAACP) challenged the "separate but equal" aspect of public education. It was proven that public education was indeed separate, but not equal. With the Supreme Court case of *Brown v. Board of Education*, segregation was outlawed.

Although *Brown* represented a great victory, segregation and inequality did not change overnight. Southern governors, such as George Wallace of Alabama, refused to integrate the state universities, and local and state governments resisted efforts to desegregate. For example, Governor Faubus of Arkansas used the Arkansas National Guard to block African American students from entering a Little Rock high school. The federal government had to step in and force the hand of school boards and government officials to comply with the Supreme Court ruling. The Civil Rights Act of 1964 forced school boards to comply.

In 1966, busing became the primary solution to school segregation after the issuance of the Coleman Report. This report, which compiled data from thousands of students and teachers across the United States, found that academic achievement was related to the social composition of the school, the verbal skills of the teacher, and the student's family background. The media took this to mean that black children who attended integrated schools would receive a better education if they attended schools where most of their classmates were white. The Coleman Report concluded in 1975 that busing had failed since it led to white families fleeing urban schools for suburban ones.

1958–1980: ATTEMPTS TO IMPROVE URBAN EDUCATION

In 1958, in response to Sputnik, the National Defense Education Act was passed, providing federal funds to improve the quality of education. These funds were used to purchase large-scale curriculum reform projects in math and science, increase funding for education of gifted students, and provide summer workshops for teachers.

In 1964, President Johnson declared war on poverty. Johnson's administration spent over a billion dollars on educational programs that were intended to close the achievement gap between poor and rich, black and white. These educational programs included Head Start, which provided preschool assistance and nutrition to children in poverty. The perceived failure of these programs is partially due to outside influences such as parents' income, parents' lack of college education, and all of the other problems associated with poverty.

In 1967, criticism of urban schools became an important issue with the publication of Jonathan Kozol's book *Death at an Early Age* and Herbert Kohl's book *36 Children*.

In 1970, funding inequities came to the fore when *Robinson v. Cahill* went to trial. This lawsuit was filed to demonstrate that the constitutional mandate had still not been realized.

In 1973, *San Antonio Independent School District v. Rodriguez* was the most significant case to reach the Supreme Court. The Court had overruled the federal court in San Antonio, Texas, which found that the current school funding system violated the Fourteenth Amendment's equal-protection clause. This outcome was important because in *Brown v. Board of Education* the courts had ruled that education was a highly important government function whereas in the San Antonio case they ruled that nothing in the Constitution said that schools have to be comparable to one another. This funding controversy has continued into the twenty-first century.

In 1975, Public Law 94-142 was created to ensure the best public education for children with mental and physical challenges. PL 94-142 was important because the percentage of students with challenges was, and still is, much higher in urban districts.

In 1979, President Carter raised the Department of Education to the cabinet level.

Desegregation became a big issue in cities such as Boston, where mandatory court-ordered busing forced white students and black students to attend public schools away from their neighborhoods. Busing was used as a form of integration, but as it received more and more public outcry there was a movement toward magnet schools. Magnet schools, which are public schools of choice, became popular because they both complied with court-ordered desegregation and helped stop white flight.

Magnet schools were formed within urban districts and utilized a different curriculum in an attempt to integrate schools without busing. However, these magnet schools eventually experienced problems associated with the districts' central office administration, entrance tests, and increased costs of operation.

1980–2003:
URBAN PUBLIC EDUCATION UNDER ATTACK

Despite well-intentioned efforts during the latter portion of the twentieth century, the problems of improving urban public education have not been solved. During the Reagan administration a committee was set up that criticized public education in general and urban public education specifically. In 1983 the National Commission on Excellence in Education published a report called *A Nation at Risk* in which U.S. public education was unfavorably compared to other industrialized nations. Urban schools, in particular, were described as failing due to low test scores, high dropout rates, and low graduation standards. All attempts at increasing funding for public education were criticized by the conservative forces in American society. "Throwing good money after bad" became a rallying cry for the proponents of educational vouchers and charter schools.

After the release of A *Nation at Risk* many states began to create new laws that focused on accountability, class size, instructional resources, intervention programs, computers, calendars, parental involvement, graduation and athletic requirements, promotion and retention, training, basic skills, grading, teacher and school incentives, career ladders, merit pay, alternative certification, staff development, and tests. In some cases, state spending was increased along with state mandates.

Goals 2000 was an outline by the first Bush administration to try to fix the problems of urban public education. It has been criticized for being underfunded and for containing controversial steps such as vouchers and a high reliance on standardized testing.

In 1981, in New Jersey, the funding case *Abbott v. Burke* was filed because local property taxes were still being used to fund public schools.

In 1990, *Abbott v. Burke* was again before the New Jersey supreme court, which ruled that funding efforts needed to be focused on schools in the poorest districts because disadvantaged students in urban schools need not just equity in funding and program quality but also supplemental and compensatory assistance. The battle over funding is still continuing today in many states.

During the years 1994 to 1999, federal courts ordered the release of public school districts from having to implement desegregation plans, but tracking based on test scores and teacher judgment still segregates minority and poor students once they are in nonsegregated schools.

In 1995, school psychologists Berliner and Berliner published *Manufactured Crisis,* claiming that the evidence does not support the conservative attack on U.S. public schools.

In 1996, a $17 million grant was given to seventeen states, Puerto Rico, and the District of Columbia to help with start-up and development of charter schools.

During George W. Bush's tenure as president he signed the Leave No Child Behind Act in 2002. Portions of this bill have been criticized due to the possible lack of money resulting from potential economic downturns. In addition, there is a perceived overreliance on the use of standardized tests to prove or disprove the effectiveness of urban schools.

Also in 2002, one of the most anticipated Supreme Court rulings on the constitutionality of educational vouchers was settled by a 5–4 vote. The Court ruled that educational vouchers are constitutional. This decision hugely affects the future of urban public education.

Chapter Three

✦ Curriculum in Urban Schools

Many believe that education and schools hold all of the answers to the world's problems. For urban schoolchildren this belief is the great hope for true equality and opportunity. With this hope comes change upon change in curriculum. Yet searching for the best curriculum can actually cause more problems. This chapter will present information on curriculum in school design, programs, and urban schools.

DEFINITIONS AND TYPES OF CURRICULUM

Curriculum was originally known as the course of study or whatever textbook was in use. Some people, including many noneducators, believe this is still the definition of curriculum; in reality, however, several definitions have evolved as time has passed and social forces have been at work.

One definition is that curriculum is a list of a sequence of courses (Zais, 1976). Another definition is that curriculum is a plan for instruction, such as may be found in a program of study. About the time of the Progressive Education movement of the 1920s to 1940s, the curriculum definition reflected the current thinking that curriculum means planned experiences (Saylor and Alexander, 1966; Thompson and Gregg, 1997). In the 1980s the shift in definition came to reflect the growing belief that curriculum was based on social factors or represented a way toward growth and equality (Tanner and Tanner, 1980; Gay, 1990). The definition is important because the beliefs held about curriculum influence the power it wields. This is especially true in urban schools. An understanding of curriculum today, if all of these definitions were combined, would be as follows:

> Curriculum is everything that goes on in a school and outside the school in the learners' lives, whether it is planned or unplanned. This includes the resources the students have or do not have and includes the quality of the teacher and resources such as a piece of chalk, computers, etc. . . . or lack thereof. It includes the experiences the students experience,

whether planned or hidden. It depends on the student as the learner including their culture, background knowledge, learning style, and multiple intelligence strength and weakness [and on what] is taught and not taught including the books and resources used or not used, content used or not used, subjects taken and not taken, the sequence of courses, objectives, standards, and interpersonal relationships.

With this definition you can see why curriculum is critical and can be used to enhance or hurt a student. This is especially true in urban schools.

Product versus Process

Palmer (1998, p. 94) states that "good education is always more process than product. If a student has received no more than a packet of information at the end of an educational transaction, that student has been duped. Good education teaches students to become both producers of knowledge and discerning consumers of what other people claim to know." There are differences between the process and the product of curriculum. Some believe curriculum is an end in itself, while others hold that the process or the plan for learning is the most important part. This is an important distinction because the focus will change the curriculum that the student experiences. For example, if the focus is on passing a standardized test, then the outcome becomes the most important part and the curriculum begins to look like short snippets of information passed on to students quickly just to be learned for a test. There is no in-depth search for answers, problem solving, or critical thinking. On the other hand, if the process becomes the focus, then these elements will become part of the curriculum. The coverage of subjects becomes slower, more in-depth, and more integrated into real-life problem solving. This is a critical distinction in urban schools because many reforms are based on trying to make up the perceived lack of middle-class knowledge that the student possesses, so the teaching becomes focused more on skills and outcomes than on process.

Curriculum Planning

Planning of curriculum can be internal (in schools) or external (outside of schools). For instance, teachers may be handed a curriculum prepared by a district or a state and then plan from the curriculum based on their students' needs. Tanner and Tanner (1980) wrote that teachers and curriculum planning can occur at three levels:

Imitative-Maintenance: The teacher will maintain and follow the current curriculum, including just using textbooks, workbooks, and routine activities. The focus will be very skill based.

Mediative: The teacher will integrate curriculum but will utilize conditions such as teachable moments and students' own interests, will use other resources outside of the school, and will work on improving his or her own teaching.

Creative-Generative: At this level of planning the curriculum is examined in its entirety by the teacher and school staff. This group questions priorities and relationships, uses broad concepts, seeks to establish relationships with other teachers so they can experiment in their classrooms and share, gets help integrating across subject areas, seeks out research findings for improvement, tries to be more involved in curriculum at the school-district level, and, finally, looks outside the district for a wide range of resources.

Some urban schools are attempting to reach the creative-generative level but, by and large, are at the imitative-maintenance level. The reason may very well be that these urban schools and teachers suffer from pressures, insufficient resources, and lack of support and thus become overwhelmed with day-to-day existence and just cannot get past survival. This leaves them stagnating at the imitative-maintenance level. In addition, as of 2003, the real and perceived pressures on teachers and schools from high-stakes accountability have created a culture of fear that prevents urban schools and teachers from truly changing and growing and seeking out the creative-generative level.

Externally, curriculum planning can occur at the whim of outside forces such as tradition, social and political power, and economic prosperity and downfall. In an effort to seek answers to the poverty and inequality inherent in urban schools, these outside forces are very apparent in urban schools in the United States. Such forces, especially high-stakes accountability, can create more problems than solutions. One answer forced upon urban schools has been controlled or prepackaged curriculum.

Prepackaged or Controlled Curriculum

Apple (1979) wrote that prepackaged or controlled curriculum is based on the belief that if curriculum is controlled, then the curriculum is teacher-proofed so that all students can do well. This teacher-proofed curriculum is prevalent in urban schools as they search for answers to equality of education. According to Kohn (1999), this controlled curriculum is increasing. For example, during the 1996–1997 legislative year, state legislators introduced sixty-seven phonics bills and ten states passed laws requiring phonics to be taught.

Here is an example of a prepackaged reading program from Adams (2001):

> The curriculum looked cultish with rituals of hand signals, use of timers, the same language and same materials irrespective of the classroom. The students move together at the sound of a bell, as one observes in a factory. The teachers and students are bombarded with reading curriculum propaganda. The prescribed reading curriculum permeates the environment, climate, and everything the teachers do. The halls are lined with the mandated postings of students' work, required charts, etc. It is meaningless. All students' work begins to look the same such as in a factory of producing the same goods and the charts become just like pieces of furniture that are not used or noticed anymore. The students in the fourth grade follow a five-day cycle of the same activities in the same order on each day but with a different story or book. Just as Apple (1992) wrote, the students are tested weekly and the teacher follows a script that tells them what to do and say for each part.

Here is an example:

TEACHER INSTRUCTIONS:

Teacher introduction: "Have you ever had to get the hint? Have you ever given someone a hint?"

What the teacher is to say is in quotation marks.

(If necessary, provide students with the following examples. Have students discuss their experiences with getting the hint.)

Hinting at a gift you would like to receive for your birthday.

A person who wants a favor but doesn't want to ask for it might give someone a hint that they need help.

"In these situations, the person who realized something or got the hint was actually doing something called making an inference."

"When we make inferences we use what we see and hear combined with what we already know to make a decision about something."

"When the person got the hint and decided to do what they did, they were combining what they saw or heard with what they already knew to make their decision."

"Do you think it is more fun to try to figure out how to do something or to be told exactly how to do it?" (*Students will probably say that they feel good when they figure something out on their own.*) (in italics)

"When we are reading, we need to make inferences. Authors know that it is fun to figure things out. So they don't always tell us everything directly. Most of the time, authors leave us clues in their writing. We have to pick up these clues and use them to make inferences. Authors depend upon us to make inferences all the time as we read about story characters and events. When they let you figure things our for yourself, it makes reading a story more interesting."

"Since authors often suggest things without directly stating them, we need to be able to make inferences. Inferences help us to understand what we are reading by helping us to think about the characters. Inferences also help us to relate causes to effects, draw conclusions and make predictions."

"Today we are going to practice identifying inferences that can be made about a selection. Let's try a few examples."

It goes like this throughout the five-day lessons, day after day and over and over. The curriculum tells the teachers what to say and what responses should be expected from the students. It gives the impression that the teacher is not a professional or doesn't have enough knowledge to make good pedagogical choices. I observed the teachers reading this with a monotone voice, rolling their eyes at me and generally giving the impression that they were aware that this was a ridiculous way to teach. I observed no meaning and enthusiasm in the teaching. This curriculum was controlled by an observer. They would come in at any time, sit down with their checklists containing the list of required posted charts and daily activities, observe and time the teachers to make sure they were doing what they were told in the specified required time frame. . . . [T]he teachers refer to this checking as a visit from the "Gestapo."

What the teacher says and how the student is to respond are all written out. The teachers and students are timed to make sure they are on the correct activity on the correct day. There are worksheets and tests that are teacher-proofed. The overpowering control comes from an observer, usually an administrator, who will actually write up teachers if they are not doing exactly what they are supposed to do. Outside of the individual classrooms, in the schools, the curriculum is controlled by mandated lesson planning and checklist evaluation. In some urban schools, teachers are experiencing severe reprimands for deviating from this controlled curriculum and are being told that there are no longer any teachable moments. In classrooms where students are taught in this manner, it is like a robot teaching a bunch of robots. When you observe in these schools, you are bombarded by slogans and propaganda. This fear is cultivated, leaving one with the feeling of entering a cult.

Some will ask what is wrong with controlled or prepackaged curriculum. The answer is that when curriculum is controlled, students' cultural and individual learning needs are not met, powerful teachable moments are lost, and real-life learning and the research on effective teaching are ignored. In addition, what sometimes happens is that many important curricular topics are never covered, so the question becomes whose knowledge is valued and perpetuated? More important, this curriculum will not prepare students for real-world learning and work in the future. Finally, the voices of teachers, students, parents, and other stakeholders are not valued or heard. As teachers and students become disillusioned with this controlled curriculum, the loss of quality teachers and student scholars is a real possibility.

Hidden Curriculum

There is planned and unplanned curriculum. Curriculum has evolved as a plan of study, but when children are brought together you also get unplanned or hidden curriculum. The hidden curriculum deeply impacts urban schools.

Hidden curriculum involves:

- What is valued and not valued by the school culture and the community
- What is taught and not taught
- Who is teaching the students
- How students think about themselves and their culture, including whether they fit in
- What beliefs are perpetuated, including self-fulfilling prophecies and expectations for students' futures
- The condition of the school building
- The environment and the culture of the school, including whether there is overpowering control and obedience

All of these factors reflect the charge by some that the failure of urban schools is due to the curriculum. In urban schools, curriculum that is based on white, middle-class values is not culturally responsive. Dilapidated facilities and beliefs, including the failure of school personnel to believe that students can succeed, perpetuate the notion that urban students' buildings and even themselves as students are not valued. When the students then feel that they and their culture are not valued, they become disillusioned with school and education, and many drop out or feel pushed out.

State-Mandated Curriculum and Accountability

As the concern for performance of educational programs and schools has brought an emphasis on accountability, state-mandated curriculum and high-stakes tests have increasingly become the norm. State-mandated curriculum is hitting urban schools hard. This test-preparation curriculum has narrowed the curriculum to only the knowledge and skills deemed essential by state legislatures and, in some cases, by some educational bureaucracies. Consisting of a list of objectives or standards that are often at the low level of Bloom's taxonomy, this curriculum has led to a continuation of teaching that is not culturally responsive for urban students. The curriculum is controlled by requiring the posting of objectives, the turning in of lesson plans, and teacher evaluations and report cards that are tied directly to the test objectives. Contrary to research findings, subjects are separated into single facts with no connections to other subjects. Some teachers have even begun teaching single subjects as early as first grade to meet the objectives for these subjects. Doing so ignores the connections to other subjects and the relationships with teachers that are needed to assist minority and at-risk students. Some argue that teachers within their classrooms have creativity to present the curriculum in any way they deem necessary, but others counter that this rigidity of curriculum has influenced teachers on how its gets taught because there is a connection between what is taught and how it is taught. Furthermore, the test preparation materials are becoming the curriculum. In one neighborhood school the fourth-grade social studies book is a test preparation workbook filled with worksheet activities that the students fill in day after day in preparation for tests (Adams, 2001). And many of the tests themselves are created without involving stakeholders or having a planned curriculum or materials for the curriculum. Teachers have been scrambling to prepare curriculum and resources to match the test objectives. As a matter of fact, in 2002, New York City's United Federation of Teachers spent $2 million to provide curriculum guides and training for teachers at each grade level to help the teachers prepare their students for a test given later that year.

The newest buzzword under accountability is *alignment*. Advocates of curriculum alignment point to students traveling from school to school or district to district and not having consistency in the curriculum. However, the other side is best summed up by one teacher's question: "Isn't this just teaching to the test?" Curriculum alignment has also come to mean college preparation courses, despite the fact that not all students plan on attending college or have the intellectual capacity to do so. This has included a shift from instruction in all academic subjects to college preparation curriculum, even at vocational education schools.

Unfair Resource Equity

Curriculum can involve everything from the actual teacher to a pencil, paper, materials, and other resources. This is where the problem lies. In urban schools the teacher, the materials, and other resources are not equal to those available in suburban or rural schools—or in urban schools with more money available.

There are reports of students sharing books and of having no books to take home to study. The books that schools do have are often old and outdated. In some cases, school libraries have to close because the school cannot afford a librarian; in others, teachers are using thousands of dollars of their own money to buy basics such as copies, paper and pencils, and, believe it or not, even toilet paper.

Even though computers and technology are readily available and a requirement for many work positions, a digital divide still exists in urban schools. There is simply no money for replacement of computers, repairs, tech support, supplies, or training of teachers on how to use them. Meanwhile, suburban and other middle-class students have computers at home. The digital divide will continue until urban disadvantaged students have access to computers at home and urban schools have full funding of resources.

There are state mandates to improve instruction, such as small class sizes and full-day kindergarten, but no extra money is given to fund these mandates. Urban schools must then make hard choices based on their limited resources. So they do things like place fifty or sixty students in a classroom, place two teachers in the room because there are no extra classrooms, or use closets and shower rooms for makeshift classrooms. They also put off repairs to 100-year-old schools to fund extra teachers or do away with nonacademic subjects.

In recent years, money has increasingly been spent on test preparation materials. At one neighborhood urban school, $50,000 was spent on a reform design and $10,000 on other test preparation materials, leaving only $8,000 to be spent among forty teachers for copies and other basic supplies (Adams, 2001). Sadly, many art, music, library, and PE classes are gone, along with counselors and after-school programs, because under academic accountability they are considered frills. Some after-school programs have been created, but only for test preparation and tutoring.

One form of assistance for additional funding has come from the business community. Businesses have formed partnerships with many urban schools to increase the materials and resources available. Unfortunately, this assistance sometimes comes with a price, requiring a certain curriculum to be taught or certain products to be sold and advertised. At some urban schools, for example, teachers are given packets of teaching material that carry the business's agenda and interests; at others, only one name-brand soda or other food product can be sold or bought in return for money and supplies.

SCHOOL PROGRAMS AND DESIGNS

This section provides information about school programs and designs that vary across classrooms, schools, and even entire districts. The search for solutions has evolved as historical, societal, and political needs and agendas have changed. However, in the quest for the best way to efficiently educate a mass number of poor and minority children, the bureaucracy often gets in the way of true reform by ignoring research and, in some cases, wasting money on poor solutions.

Curriculum Designs

Most curriculum designs are categorized as subject-centered, broad-fields, core, spiral, problem-solving, or, more recently, technology-based. Each of these designs has both merits and pitfalls.

Subject-Centered Curriculum

The *subject-centered curriculum* is based on the separating of subjects by content to be learned. The learning and teaching that take place are thus very sequential. The benefit of this curriculum is that it is easy for students to transfer from school to school and from district to district. In addition, a great deal of content can be covered quickly. However, dividing subject matter in this manner is unsupported by research, focuses on facts to be recalled, and does not reflect real-life learning.

Broad-Fields Curriculum

The *broad-fields curriculum* expands the subjects into broad categories. For example, instead of just history or civics, the area of study becomes social studies so that subjects are no longer separated as they would be in a subject-centered curriculum. This curriculum helps to teach generalizations, concepts, and principles within a broad-field area, thus supporting inquiry and discovery learning. It has been criticized for its dependence on the teacher for the delivery of instruction; some fear that some generalizations, concepts, or principles may be missed.

Core Curriculum

The premise of the *core curriculum* is that there is general knowledge that all students should possess to be successful. This is a helpful design for beginning teachers and for consistency across schools within a district. It has been criticized for its difficulty in integrating subjects and activities for applying knowledge across disciplines.

Spiral Curriculum

The *spiral curriculum* revisits the curriculum at different points to ensure that students, once they have background knowledge in a subject, are better able to understand what they may not have understood before or are more developmentally prepared for it. This curriculum has been criticized for being very repetitive and unnecessary in some subjects.

Problem-Solving Curriculum

The *problem-solving curriculum* involves giving students problems to solve. Students then demonstrate that they have the background knowledge needed to apply what they have learned to solve a new problem. The positives of this curriculum include the integration of subjects across disciplines, the in-depth coverage and understanding of subject content, and the utilization of authentic problems like those encountered in real life. The criticism is that some facts and essential knowledge may not be taught if the instructor does not very carefully document the covered objectives.

Technology Curriculum

The *technology curriculum* is delivered almost exclusively through instruction by computer programs. These programs provide all the information students need by means of ongoing practice and pre- and post-tests. One benefit of this curriculum is its emphasis on the mastery of skills; another is the fact that students can work at their own pace. It has been criticized on the grounds that there is little, if any, teacher interaction and that it lacks the dimensions of socialization.

These designs are found in all schools in one form or another. In an attempt to create whole-school reform, many think tanks, university-

and government-sponsored groups, and private corporations began creating and disseminating whole-school designs in comprehensive packages. One such group that consolidates researched designs is known as the New American Schools. Below are examples of these designs.

New American Schools

The New American Schools organization was based on the belief that a comprehensive school-improvement plan can lead to improved student achievement. The New American Schools organization helps to support proven programs. Proven programs are defined as programs that are research-based and proven to be effective when implemented correctly. Although each of the proven programs' designs has unique features, most are characterized by a change in governance of the school, a change in curriculum, and parent and community involvement.

It is important to note that in many urban districts some schools were ordered to take on a focus and were allowed to choose only from one of the New American Schools designs for their focus. In addition, Congress and many states designated a grant of around $50,000 for the start-up costs of comprehensive school redesigns only if one of the New American Schools designs were chosen. In 2002, nine design teams were recognized: the Accelerated Schools Project, ATLAS Communities, Conect Schools, Different Ways of Knowing, Expeditionary Learning Outward Bound, The Leonard Bernstein Center for Learning, Modern Red Schoolhouse, Turning Points, and Urban Learning Centers. They have also established a list of promising design teams that have not yet met the New American Schools guidelines.

Accelerated Schools Project

The Accelerated Schools Project encompasses the values of equity, communication, participation, collaboration, community spirit, reflection, risk taking, experimentation, discovery, trust, and schools as the center of expertise. The Accelerated Schools Project cites three guiding principles: empowerment with responsibility, unity of purpose, and building on strengths. When this design is first implemented in a school, all stakeholders in the school, including parents and the broader community, come together to form a vision of the school. The stakeholders also attempt to identify the causes of the school's problems and solutions for these problems. Then a leadership team is formed on site to continue professional development for the school's continued growth. The curriculum focuses on acceleration instead of remediation for students so that all students receive "motivating instructional experiences that are authentic, inclusive, learner-centered, interactive, and continuous, built around the instructional practices typically reserved for the gifted and talented population"(New American Schools, 2002).

Cited evidence of improvement includes reduced discipline referrals and retentions, increased parental and community involvement, higher test scores, and parents and teachers having greater decision making in the school's governance.

ATLAS Communities

This design involves teams of teachers utilizing local standards to develop curriculum and assessment that align with and flow from the elementary schools to the middle schools and then to the high school. These teams of teachers then collaborate with parents and administrators to implement the curriculum and assessment practices.

Cited evidence of effectiveness includes one example of a letter documenting the increased scores on the Iowa Test of Basic Skills.

Co-nect Schools

This design has been available since 1992. It promotes programs for technology integration, literacy, and project-based learning. The technology integration includes aligning curriculum, instruction, assessment, and resources to state standards.

According to cited evidence, independent studies confirm that there have been improvements in student achievement, school climate, and instructional practices since implementation of the design.

Different Ways of Knowing

This K–8 design includes a three-year course of study that integrates social studies with literature, and math and science with the arts. The expectation is that all stakeholders will participate fully in the implementation of this design.

Cited evidence at this time is based on written testimonials from several participants.

Expeditionary Learning Outward Bound

The teachers who utilize this design integrate the curriculum into expeditionary real-world projects. These projects consist of learning experiences involving hands-on activities over a span of six to eight weeks. The learning experiences themselves integrate standards that are connected to service and character development. Another component of this design is the "looping" of teachers with their students to the next grade, so that each teacher can stay with the same group of students for more than one year.

Cited evidence consists of reports from five independent organizations including the Rand Corporation and the University of Colorado Department of Education. This evidence indicates improvements in student achievement as established from portfolios and standardized tests, improved attendance rates and parent participation, and reduced disciplinary actions.

The Leonard Bernstein Center for Learning

This design utilizes the arts for more effective learning. First, students experience a master work of art. Then they discuss the important ideas associated with the work by making inquiries and utilizing continuous questioning. Next, the students create their own artwork of value, reflect on this work, and demonstrate that they understand its important components. The emphasis of this design is to improve understanding, retention, transfer, and application. The schools that utilize this design are expected to demonstrate transformative leadership by all of its stakeholders.

Cited evidence of effectiveness includes two school reports of improved reading and math scores. In addition, teachers reported observing increases in students' use of creativity, inquiry, and reflective thinking. They also reported that students displayed an increase in positive self-esteem and expressed an increased love of learning.

Modern Red Schoolhouse

This design is based on working with teams of teachers to design standards-driven curriculum. The stakeholders, along with facilitators from Modern Red Schoolhouse, utilize core curriculum, local standards, and the integration of technology to create a school-wide curriculum. The use of innovative teaching and student groupings is encouraged.

Cited evidence of this design's effectiveness includes testimonials from one parent and one principal.

Turning Points

This design focuses on the middle school years and involves the formation of teacher study groups. These study groups use peer observation to examine student work in teams. The design also utilizes shared governance processes as well as a common planning time for teachers to use to improve their teaching.

Cited evidence includes a study conducted in 1990 in thirty-one Illinois middle schools. Improvements were seen in student achievement, and the results were released in the *Phi Delta Kappan* in March 1997.

Urban Learning Centers

This design, which incorporates a K–12 model for urban schools, attempts to address the health and well-being of students and their families. The school's governance and management are restructured so that community members become involved in decision making.

Cited evidence of effectiveness consists of testimonials from two teachers and one principal.

The following passage describes the experience of one urban neighborhood school that implemented a New American Schools design:

> The urban district began pressuring neighborhood schools to pick a school focus. The focus could only come from one of the New American Schools designs. The schools were also reassured by the district that the funds needed to fully implement the focus would be available. A committee of teachers went to look at choices of the designs but the principal steered them to only one particular design. Pressure for choosing one of the designs started in the weekly staff meetings when the teachers and staff were warned that they would get something they didn't like if they did not choose quickly. A staff vote was held and the necessary two-thirds approval vote was received.
>
> The first conflict came when staff were told that they would have to attend training sessions on their own time in August. As implementation continued, some teachers were very vocal about the control from timed lessons and lesson plans that told exactly what the teacher was to say and how the students were to respond. They also became concerned when the principal and school implementation facilitator began to make observations to ensure that the program was being fully implemented. As time passed, the entire culture of the school changed. The halls became lined with propaganda about the design, and students' work all looked the same. When reading time was announced, students would groan. Teachers became increasingly frustrated by the pressure and loss of teachable moments. Teacher's attendance began to fall and as the year ended five teachers announced they were leaving due to the

changes. Things became worse. The school found out that the $50,000 grant mostly ate up the cost of the start-up materials, training, and implementation visits. When they sought additional assistance from the district, the school was told to make some hard decisions because they would not be receiving any additional funds and they could not stop the design because they had signed a contract. Since the program required at least three extra staff members at $60,000 each to minimally fund, hard decisions had to be made. Specialists were reduced, which included reduced art and music instruction, and the media center was now to be run by a teacher's aide instead of a certified librarian. Also, only one of the extra positions would be funded, effectively ceasing the full and correct implementation of the program. The school and the district both shared the blame for the failure of the design because it was never fully funded nor implemented. The harm to children and ignoring of research and the loss of the best teachers continued in this urban neighborhood school.

Many problems arise when major changes are implemented in urban schools. Unfortunately, sometimes the most effective research on how children learn is ignored. In addition, societal problems are sometimes just too great for one school to overcome without a great deal of outside assistance and resources. It should also be noted that parents and community members are often not consulted about what they truly want for their children before changes are made.

Problems with money and resources persist as well. The $50,000 grants given by Congress and some states often pay for just the beginning implementation and materials costs for many designs. And when the grants are discontinued in the third year, schools must find other outside sources to continue the programs or they are back where they started.

Magnet Schools

Some urban districts have attempted to seek improvement, prevent white flight, and satisfy court-ordered desegregation by creating a system of magnet schools with the utilization of different school designs and curriculum. Many schools also utilize individual programs or designs within different classrooms in schools and in some cases have separate schools within schools.

Magnet schools use many different designs and curriculum, but it's often the case that to enter and attend a magnet school the student must pass a test, have a referral, or undergo an audition. Parents must sometimes wait for hours in line to register their child; they must also meet race quotas and promise to participate in a school's activities. In addition, a student can be kicked out of a magnet program for nonattendance, low test scores, or inappropriate behavior. Some magnet programs utilize curriculum and designs that may include Montessori, Paideia, year-round schools, an arts focus, or a college preparatory curriculum.

Montessori

This curriculum is based on the work of Maria Montessori. There are four tenets in Montessori. The first is to help each individual child reach his or her potential through creativity. The second is to have a prepared, child-friendly environment so the child is free to explore and discover. The third tenet is to utilize teachable moments during children's developmental stages, when they are able to learn a task easily. The fourth tenet is to utilize multisensory Montessori materials that stimulate and isolate skills and allow for self-correction. Many Montessori curriculum schools have some entrance requirements such as required parental involvement and racial balance. The classrooms usually have small class sizes and utilize teacher's aides for further adult and child interaction.

Paideia

The Paideia curriculum is based on the writings of Mortimer Adler. This design incorporates a strong liberal arts course of study, which includes strong reading, writing, speaking, and listening skills. Students are expected to be active participants in the learning process. Different teaching methodologies including didactic, coaching, and seminars are utilized to explore different areas of knowledge.

Typically the students are taught by means of the traditional didactic lecture. In this format, the teacher introduces a subject or concept to the students and then assigns several practical exercises to ensure that the students understand the concept and can demonstrate this understanding to a set standard. Coaching is the second part of the Paideia system. The classroom teacher, who is sometimes helped by another teacher or "coach," assigns practical exercises and helps individual students who need assistance in understanding the concept. The third part of the Paideia system involves seminars. In this format, students are assigned a reading prior to the seminar. Typically the reading is meant to challenge the students' intellect. Students mark sections of the reading that they think are significant as well as sections that they do not understand. On the day prior to the seminar the students meet with the teacher to conduct a reading lab. Students take turns identifying words or sections that they do not understand. The reading lab is conducted as a class and all students are expected to participate. On the day of the seminar the teacher presents an open-ended question to the class. The students then take time finding passages in the text that either relate to or answer the question, after which they take turns explaining what the question means and pointing out whether the text provides any answers to the question. The teacher facilitates the discussion and keeps track of student participation. All students are required to participate with their own ideas in the discussion. Toward the end of the discussion the teacher will offer another open-ended question that may shed some light on the intent of the author of the concept that the teacher wants the students to understand. Again, discussion takes place. The teacher records individual students' efforts and the students are given a grade based on their participation.

Year-Round Schools

Year-round schools utilize many different designs and curriculums and are created for many different reasons. These schools are touted as the answer to overcrowding, funding shortages, and to improving the educational process, especially for disadvantaged students. Although research is mixed, proponents claim that year-round schools minimize learning loss by decreasing the long summer vacation and thus increasing achievement. Critics of year-round schools claim that they are disruptive to family life, provide little or no academic benefit, and save little or no money or may even cost more. One year-round school teacher, after her urban magnet school closed, said: "We were a dumping ground for other schools and some parents who did not want their children at home and for other magnet schools that would recruit the parents of low-achieving and behavioral-problem students to come to our school." The year-round design is sometimes seen in individual schools but may also occur throughout a whole district.

Integrated Arts

This curriculum, which stresses academics through the creative arts, is enriched by dance, art, drama, music, and creative writing. Many schools implementing an arts-enriched curriculum require auditions, teacher or principal recommendations, and videos or portfolios of students' experience for entry. Sometimes mentorships with adults who have careers in the arts, partnerships with the local arts community, and resources are utilized.

One urban teacher was distressed when one of her gifted students did not get entry into an urban arts magnet school because of his behavioral problems. "I called the school," she said, "and was told that from the report card behavioral grades Randy would not be successful in their program. I was so upset because I felt his behavior came from him not being able to express his gifts in a neighborhood school."

College Preparatory

The college preparatory curriculum stresses academic subjects. This usually involves four years of English, three years of math, three years of social studies, two years of a lab science, and a foreign language. The English classes utilize a curriculum of standard American English and stress strong skills in expository writing, and students are expected to be able to analyze literature, including significant works of American and world literature. The math curriculum expects students to understand Algebra I, Geometry, and Algebra II. The science curriculum, which should enable a student to utilize scientific ideas with an inquiry analytical approach, expects students to have a strong knowledge of scientific vocabulary, to be able to read and understand magazines and books in scientific fields, and to be able to write scientific reports. Finally, the social studies curriculum incorporates ideas from American cultural heritage, so students are expected to understand democratic processes, institutions, and the free enterprise system, and to be able to utilize historical research to write reports.

Unfortunately, magnet schools are not always the answer for academic achievement within an urban system. For one thing, there are inequalities among magnet and neighborhood schools in some urban districts. Magnet schools may receive more funding and staff support, and can send problem students or students with low test scores back to neighborhood schools. And parents can choose to send their children, and to contribute time and resources, to magnet schools. Unfortunately, success stories about magnet schools make their way into the media without telling the whole story, making it appear as though the magnet schools' curriculum is the answer to academic achievement.

One story that *didn't* make it into the media described a period of time when magnet schools dumped all of their special education students after accountability was implemented with standardized test score reporting. At the beginning of the school year, special education students showed up at their neighborhood schools with no prior warning, and, thus, no support services were ready and available for them. The neighborhood schools then had to scramble to get these services and to address the overcrowding that resulted.

In the following passage, a teacher describes how a magnet school recruited its top-achieving students:

> [The Factory school was] so similar to my last teaching situation, where we were under constant pressure to teach the promotion standards, post them each day for each lesson, and make sure the students knew what promotion standard we were addressing. The school was in academic emergency, which meant that if we didn't raise our scores and have more students passing, we would go into redesign. (Everyone is let go and all new staff is hired for the coming school year.) We worked hard and met all of our quotas for students passing the test. One problem we had was the alternative magnet school in the area. They would wait for our test results, call the Board office [to] get the students who passed their proficiencies, and send letters to our top students, recruiting them to come to their school [and] touting their excellent academic record. Of course parents were impressed, pulled their students out of our school, and enrolled them in the alternative magnet school. This left the neighborhood school right back where it started every year, academically struggling, because our top students kept getting recruited, leaving the students in the factory to be more pressured to meet the specifications laid down.

Virtual and Alternate Behavioral Schools

Virtual schools have been formed in an attempt to keep students in school by offering classes at their homes as well as extended hours at a school site. The curriculum is delivered on the Internet or through various software programs. The curriculum is comprehensive, consisting of pretests, content, and posttests. The use of online learning requires self-motivated learners, time management, the ability to read from computer screens, and the ability to navigate through the online process. Advocates of virtual schools claim that students who may not attend school due to family situations will do so in a virtual environment. They also point to the fact that, in some districts, a virtual environment is the only way certain specialized classes (such as Russian language instruction) can be offered. On the other hand, critics of virtual schools worry about the loss of socialization and the lack of interactions with teachers and other students. There is little research on virtual schools at this time.

Although not strictly considered magnet schools, alternate behavioral schools have been formed in an effort to address the learning needs of students with severe behavioral problems and to prevent these students from disrupting the learning of others. These schools utilize small class sizes, individualized curriculum, and support services. Many times the schools are formed in conjunction with psychiatric services and programs.

SCHOOLS WITHIN SCHOOLS

The following designs occur within schools or are contained in whole schools. For example, some high schools have become smaller schools within the same school building, and some elementary schools have, say, a fourth- to sixth-grade Paideia program while at the same time offering regular fourth- to sixth-grade classrooms in the same building.

Some organizations are attempting to assist with more personalized schools. For example, the Bill and Melinda Gates Foundation, the Knowledge Works Foundation, the Ford Foundation, and the Ohio Department of Education are working together to assist urban high schools in Ohio to create more personalized and smaller schools. Selected schools are being given implementation grants to create smaller learning communities or small schools within high school buildings. In September 2002, $4.8 million was given in the form of planning grants and seventeen districts were awarded these grants, encompassing forty-seven schools. The schools that demonstrate the most effective programs have been promised implementation grants.

Academy of Mathematics and Science

In this program, curriculum emphasis is on the integration of math and science. The students recruited for this program are those who demonstrate strong academic ability in math and science and plan to go to college. The curriculum is comprehensive, rigorous, and involves hands-on learning. Students who enter the program have the same curriculum and subjects during the ninth and tenth grades. They then choose one of three different tracks during their junior and senior years of high school: Pre-Engineering, Technology, or Biophysics.

During their junior and senior years the students spend two bells (class periods) in both mathematics and science. The math curriculum is quite challenging in that it includes Algebra I, Geometry, Algebra II, and Pre-Calculus; some students even go on to Calculus. The science classes are also challenging. All students take Biology, Chemistry, and Earth Science, and some take two years of Physics while others take Advanced Biology and Environmental Science.

This curriculum is designed to provide the tools needed for difficult mathematics and science courses in college, and it prepares students for careers in math, science, and computer technology. In addition, internships and mentors are provided by area corporations.

Zoo Academy

The Zoo Academy is a unique and innovative program offered by the Cincinnati Public Schools in Cincinnati, Ohio. Initially, students study in the Cincinnati Academy of Mathematics and Science (CAMAS) program at Hughes High School in Cincinnati; then, during their junior and senior years, they study at the world-renowned Cincinnati Zoo and Botanical Garden, where they spend time at the zoo's aquarium, the bird, elephant, and primate houses, the wildlife canyon, and the jungle trails. The students' curriculum includes research projects and field studies, and among the teachers are zookeepers and horticulturists.

Teaching and Technology

To enroll in this school within a school, students must demonstrate a desire for a career in education. The curriculum involves four years of technology instruction, the opportunity to observe teachers in job-shadowing situations, and the opportunity to spend a senior internship in an actual teaching situation.

Communications

This program is intended for students who want a career in communications. The curriculum involves advertising, graphic design, photography, public relations, television production, and learning about professional journalism. Mentorships and internships with working adults are available.

Health Professions

This program prepares students for a career in medicine. Students get the opportunity to volunteer and observe in health settings and to serve internships with laboratory and field experiences.

CLASSROOM, SCHOOL, AND DISTRICT DESIGNS

The following designs and structures may be seen in a single classroom, in an individual school, or throughout a whole district.

Looping

Looping occurs when a single graded class of students stays with the same teacher for two or more years or grade levels. Once the students reach a grade where they are promoted to the next teacher, the previous teacher moves back to a lower level where he or she picks up a new group of students. Looping supports disadvantaged students' need for connections to one adult and produces in-depth relationships with peers. Teachers have the advantage of working with curriculum, as well as with students and parents, from one year to the next. McClellan (1995) reported that looping increased student attendance and that students felt less apprehensive about the start of a new school year. In addition, teachers experienced a gain in teaching time and felt more knowledgeable about their students' intellectual strengths and weaknesses.

Nongraded or Multi-Age Curriculum

In the United States, nongraded or multi-age education was the rule until the beginning of the twentieth century. Factors such as the influx of immigrants and the Industrial Revolution, which brought massive numbers of people to urban centers, put pressure on schools to educate many students. As Miller (1989, p. ix) writes, "The graded school system was driven by a need for managing large numbers of students rather than for meeting individual students' needs [and] the graded school has survived as the dominant organizational structure since its emergence 150 years ago."

Multi-age is defined as "a class grouping in which students of different ages and identified age levels are grouped together in a single classroom for the purpose of providing effective instruction" (Miller, 1995, p. 29). It typically involves ages five, six, and seven; six, seven, and eight; or eight, nine, and ten. The purpose of multi-age is to allow students to progress at their own individual rate rather than according to an arbitrary age formula. Students spend two to three years with the same teacher, and the curriculum focuses on developmentally appropriate practice and individualized instruction. There is usually either a small class size or a teacher aide to assist. The classroom is characterized by a family atmosphere with flexible groupings; students' interests are the priority. This program is expensive and requires time and continuity on the part of the teacher.

Proponents of the nongraded curriculum consider it beneficial because students are allowed to develop at their own rates without damage from retention. In addition, students and teachers get to spend more than one year together, enabling teachers to learn students' learning styles and allowing students to avoid having to adjust to a new teacher every year. Research has found that nongraded grouping leads to more positive student attitudes and behaviors than graded structures and that there is greater job satisfaction for teachers.

Opponents claim that the possibility of retention is motivating for some students, and that nongraded or multi-age education prevents students from experiencing competition for grades (which simulates the real world of work). In addition, the cost of small class sizes and instructor assistants is prohibitive.

Multiple Intelligences

The Multiple Intelligences design is based on Howard Gardner's work. Some schools are redesigning their curriculum, teaching methods, and assessments to incorporate the eight multiple intelligences: verbal-linguistic, visual-spatial, logical-mathematical, bodily-kinesthetic, musical-rhythmic, interpersonal, intrapersonal, and naturalistic.

- Verbal-linguistic intelligence is based on the ability to communicate through language, poetry, other languages, and storytelling.
- Visual-spatial intelligence is the ability to get visual images from information such as charts, graphs, and pictures.
- Logical-mathematical intelligence utilizes math and logic to think things through.
- Bodily-kinesthetic intelligence involves the use of all or part of the body to solve problems or to create.
- Musical-rhythmic intelligence is the ability to create and understand meaning from sound.
- Interpersonal intelligence is the ability to feel others' moods, to help others, and to enjoy small-group work.
- Intrapersonal intelligence is the ability to understand one's own feelings and to work alone.
- Naturalist intelligence is the ability to use features of the environment, whether manmade or natural.

Gardner is continuing to look at multiple intelligences. His belief is that all children possess these intelligences but have different strengths and weaknesses. Schools have historically been verbal-linguistic and mathematical-logical in their orientation, but we now know that all intelligences are of equal importance. Yet to be seen is what effect this finding will have on urban students' academic achievement.

Block Scheduling

Block scheduling of curriculum allows flexibility in instructional time and activities by organizing the teaching day into fewer, but longer, class periods. Teachers end up with more time to plan together and are encouraged to use the extra time for trying innovative teaching methods and providing hands-on activities and labs. Students experience improved academic performance because they are given time to explore subjects in greater depth. They are also able to retake a class without falling behind their peers because this schedule allows the opportunity to cover multiple sections in a year. In addition, time on task is increased: Students have less opportunity to be late to class, and transition activities such as taking attendance are fewer in number. Since this scheduling greatly reduces the number of students a teacher is responsible for, it enables teachers to get to know their students better. These outcomes—personalization of instruction and relationships, and reduction in retention—are especially important at urban middle and high school levels.

Accelerated Program

This curriculum design is not connected to the Accelerated American Schools Design but, rather, has to do with allowing students who are two or more years behind (due to retention, illness, or other causes) to catch up with their peers and pass on to the next grade level. This program has been implemented in a partnership between two teachers within a school building; it is also currently in place at a middle school in Cincinnati, Ohio. In some cases, students are brought to grade level and pass on to high school. Yet to be researched is whether they graduate and lead productive lives.

Some urban schools have also begun tutoring programs and mini-summer school during the year in an attempt to catch students up during the year, thus reducing retention, summer school attendance, and, ultimately, the overall dropout rate.

CHARTER SCHOOL CURRICULUM

Some charter schools have attempted to address the unique needs of urban minority students by utilizing culturally responsive curriculum and addressing the concerns of bilingual, Native American, Afrocentric, and Appalachian students.

Afrocentric curriculum is utilized in an effort to address African American students' unique schooling needs. This curriculum is based on integrating subject matter into the African world view and studying the peoples of African descent. In some cases, individual classrooms and even entire schools have attempted to implement and immerse this curriculum. Before- and after-school programs, cultural events, tutoring, and mentoring programs have also been developed to assist these students.

A unique Appalachian charter school in Cincinnati, Ohio, has been formed by parents and community members in an attempt to address the almost 100 percent dropout rate of urban, white Appalachian students. After years of planning, the school opened in the year 2000. Besides being the only urban school to address Appalachian culture specifically, it is a charter school that is sanctioned by a district. This sanctioning by Cincinnati's public schools gives the Appalachian charter school access to district resources and helps it stay in compliance with regulations. The school also gets supplemental money, is allowed to lease the district's building and to use the services of the district's maintenance and facilities workers, and is able to contract for psychological services. The curriculum it uses addresses state and district standards that are interwoven with Appalachian cultural heritage. Graduates of the school are increasing in number, and many students are going on to college or working after graduation.

It must be noted, however, that as of 2003, charter schools have shown no improvements over urban public schools in terms of academic achievement and test scores. In addition, some charter schools have been taken over due to fiscal irresponsibilities.

FOR-PROFIT CORPORATIONS

Private corporations and school management firms have attempted to take over single- and whole-district schools in order to make a profit while claiming to reform education. One such private corporation, Edison Project, is run for profit. This corporation utilizes an extended-day, year-round school, technology approach, whereas some New American Schools design curriculum within their schools. As of this writing, Edison Project is in severe financial trouble. In addition, some teachers are complaining that the curriculum is too test preparation–oriented and that their pay is not comparable to that provided by local schools.

FULL-SERVICE SCHOOLS

Some individuals and communities are attempting to get assistance for schools with urban socioeconomic problems by developing and supporting full-service schools. Full-service schools offer a host of services at the school site, ranging from medical and counseling staff to social services, parenting classes, extended-day activities, job training, and GED classes. These services allow students and their families to become more involved in the school, and attendance problems are reduced because students are able to receive needed medical and counseling services on-site. Since we now know that academic achievement is positively impacted by parental involvement, that many minority parents feel unwelcome at schools, and, most important, that it's hard to study when one is sick, malnourished, or in pain, full-service schools will be important to research in the coming years.

CONCLUSION

Whoever controls the curriculum has control over knowledge, and whoever controls teachers controls what is taught and in what manner. Those in power continue to try to address societal problems while trying to control curriculum, but they often ignore the bigger societal issues such as the lead poisoning, malnutrition, medical problems, and poverty of urban students. Urban schools are under a great deal of pressure because of the need to equalize education. What happens in response to this pressure is that teachers and students sometimes get experimented on while best-practices research is ignored. We have learned, though, that curriculum is largely at the whim of funding in urban schools and can be only as good as the resources available. Also, there is great value in getting teachers actively involved in the curriculum process, because they are the ones who will be teaching the material, observing students, and utilizing teachable moments. As yet, however, there are no true answers because little research has been conducted on whether different curriculum models and designs are even effective. Hopefully, the future holds the answer to truly equalizing schools.

REFERENCES

Adams, Kathy. "The Making of Robots: Control and De-skilling of Fourth Grade Teachers in an Urban Appalachian School after the Implementation of the Ohio Proficiency Test." Dissertation, University of Cincinnati, 2001.

Apple, Michael. *Ideology and Curriculum.* London: Routledge & Kegan, 1979.

_____. "The Text and Cultural Politics." *Educational Researcher* 21, no. 7 (1992): 4–11.

Gay, Geneva. "Achieving Educational Equality through Curriculum Desegregation." *Phi Delta Kappan* 72, no. 1 (September 1990): 61–62.

Kohn, Alfie. *Beyond Traditional Classrooms and Tougher Standards.* New York: Houghton Mifflin, 1999.

McClellan, Diane. "Looping through the Years: Teachers and Students Progressing Together. The MAGnet Newsletter on Mixed-Age Grouping in Preschool and Elementary Settings 4, no. 1 (Fall/Winter 1995): 1–3.

Miller, Bruce. "The Multigrade Classroom: A Resource Handbook for Small, Rural Schools" (Eric Reproduction Service No. ED 320 719). 1989.

_____. "Are Multiage Grouping Practices a Missing Link in the Educational Reform Debate?" *National Association of Secondary School Principals (NASSP) Bulletin* (February 1995), pp. 27–32.

New American Schools. 2002. Available online at http://www.naschools.org.

Palmer, Parker. *The Courage to Teach: Exploring the Inner Landscape of a Teacher's Life.* San Francisco: Jossey-Bass Publishers, 1998.

Saylor, J. Galen, and Alexander, William. *Curriculum Planning for Modern Schools.* New York: Holt, Rinehart and Winston, 1966.

Tanner, Daniel, and Tanner, Laurel. *Curriculum Development: Theory into Practice.* New York: Macmillan, 1980.

Thompson, Sue, and Gregg, Larry. "Reculturing Middle Schools for Meaningful Change." *Middle School Journal* 28, no. 5 (May 1997): 27–31.

Zais, Robert. *Curriculum Principles and Foundations.* New York: Harper and Row, 1976.

Chapter Four

☙ Assessment, Accountability, and Standards in Urban Schools

This chapter focuses on assessment, accountability, and standards as individual issues but also interchangeably because they are not easily separated. Assessment and accountability for schools have existed in the United States since the late 1800s, and standards, as well as curriculum (what is taught), have historically come under local control. Early on, in fact, teachers were accountable only to local trustees, parents, taxpayers, and the children. The teachers conformed to community expectations or lost their jobs. The original curriculum consisted of whatever textbook was provided and whatever subjects the local community wanted.

Assessment and accountability started with Horace Mann in Boston when he let it be known that he felt the Boston schools were substandard in comparison to what he observed on a recent overseas trip. He believed that discipline and teaching were not effective or appropriate. Mann then called for accountability. In response to this, he was charged with interfering with local educational control. Mann received support from Samuel Gridley Howe, friend and fellow reformer, who began to utilize written tests for school accountability. Top students in grammar school took the tests and these students were used as the norming group. The content of the tests came from the textbooks used in the schools. At the time, since the educational belief was that rote learning was most effective, the tests stressed memorization of facts. This is where the United States got its emphasis on skills, memorization, and hard data for assessment and accountability.

Pressure for assessment and accountability increased in the 1980s and 1990s, and critics claim that today it is alienating successful urban teachers and causing discrimination against minority and at-risk students. Some claim that assessment pressure is higher on urban schools—a situation that can be viewed as either good or bad. Advocates for equality of education say there is a need for this pressure, but others believe that this assessment and accountability are based on middle-class values and that the assessments are biased and, as such, a flawed method for accountability. In addition, many believe that the problems of urban schools are society's problems and not easily solved through education alone.

ASSESSMENT

To assess means "to sit beside," whereas to evaluate means "to place worth or merit on an object." It appears to some that, with increased high-stakes accountability, true assessment and assistance to students and teachers are declining (especially in urban schools) and have taken on an evaluation role instead of an assessment role.

In the twenty-first century the political and media pressure on urban schools and teachers has never been greater. This pressure influences public perceptions, including parents' beliefs that schools are failing. Critics contend that published reports comparing schools or suggesting the schools are failing just based on test scores, while not knowing the full facts, further damage true urban school reform. In addition, since the schools get a lot of negative press, no one gets to read or hear about all the great schools, teachers, and students in urban districts. For example, urban schools are often compared negatively with surrounding suburban schools. Yet even comparisons within urban districts of schools with more advantaged than disadvantaged students lead to further misinformation and conflicts. Unfortunately, these in turn can lead to the loss of true reform among educators, schools, and districts that truly want to make instruction and learning meaningful and create life-long learners and successful adults of urban students.

There are two main beliefs about meaningful assessment. One is that assessment requires changes in teacher practice; the other is that assessment should be aimed at improving teaching and learning (Delandshere and Jones, 1999). True assessment was historically meant to inform instruction; but in the twenty-first century, high stakes have become a way to control and manipulate teachers and teaching, because those who control assessment and the curriculum are also the ones who control teachers (Kohn, 1998, 1999). As one legislator put it when a teacher asked him about parents' responsibility for their children's education: "I can legislate teachers but not parents" (personal communication between a teacher and the author).

Elkind (1989, p. 117) reminds us: "Although some testing can be useful, it is currently so overused that many children and parents are more concerned about grades and test scores than about what a child has learned." Historically hard numbers have been viewed by the public and parents as the most objective measures of school success. Numbers are familiar because parents and other adults expect what they themselves experienced in school—namely, paper-and-pencil number-graded tests.

One urban teacher told the authors that her students had seven weeks of testing in a forty-week year, and this did not include the time to prepare the students for just the format of the tests. Biased tests containing questions about middle-class shopping at the mall and going on vacation—language that may not be understood by or culturally relevant to inner-city poor children—are unfair and do not give a true assessment of what urban students know and can do. For example, there are no questions about bus schedules in such tests, and often the test makers just change the name of the student in the problem or color in the faces of the children in illustrations and report that the tests are now nonbiased. The tests also do not allow for critical or diverse thinking. For example, on one question about the best route to get to a state capitol a student wrote that the "correct" (shortest) route was one he would not take because of current road construction that could add hours to the trip. This was a brilliant answer for a nine-year-old but the wrong answer according to the answer sheet. In another instance, a student did not pick the correct answer because it was spelled incorrectly, so he figured it couldn't be correct.

Curriculum and Assessment

Amrein and Berliner (2002) examined high-stakes tests in eighteen states and found that although test scores were increasing they found no evidence, except in one analysis, that these tests increased student learning. What they did find was increased test preparation, the possible exclusion of some students from the tests, and a narrowed curriculum that focused only on test preparation. In fact, the tests brought about other consequences such as increased dropout rates, possible cheating, and teachers quitting. Adams (2001) also observed teachers not teaching at certain grade levels because of the tests, using worksheets and test preparation books as the curriculum, and denying students recess, art, music, physical education (PE), and field trips. In addition, controlled curriculum was in use that involved timed lessons as well as teachers and students responding with set scripts. Such practices are anathema to urban students who need more rich, equalizing experiences—not fewer.

As one teacher put it while writing about the changes in curriculum because of these tests:

In many ways the curriculum is comparable to feeding the starving. In this comparison the student and the starving are the parties that need something; the starving need food and the students need knowledge. One would never take the starving person, tear off a morsel of bread, and tell him he is full. Changing curriculum to standardized testing is exactly like feeding the starving the morsel of bread. We are graduating students the state and our curriculum say are 'full' when in reality they are still starving. Until something is done about this we will continue to promote and graduate 'malnourished students.' A school's curriculum needs to allow each student to eat until they are full; then and only then can we solve this problem. (personal communication to the authors)

Some believe that if these practices continue, fair, reliable, valid, and culturally nonbiased assessment will be an illusion. Instead urban schools and districts may end up alienating excellent urban teachers and administrators who may have the true answer for disadvantaged at-risk students' success.

Unfortunately, urban teachers are also under attack and expected to take high-stakes tests themselves. Teaching to the test, bias problems, and the financial cost of these tests are prohibitive. This money could be better used to create rich, equalizing curriculum, smaller class sizes, and authentic, unbiased assessment and to address other problems that urban students bring to schools.

Authentic Assessment

Some believe authentic assessment may be the true equalizer of education. Rodriguez and Bellanca (1996) assert that authentic assessment is critical for assisting urban students. *Authentic assessment* is defined as assessment that utilizes products that closely resemble the real world. Also sometimes used in this context is the term *alternative assessment*, which is defined as assessment that involves something other than the traditional paper-and-pencil tests.

Some examples of authentic assessment products follow:

- Portfolios
- Projects
- Presentations
- Demonstrations
- Simulations
- Videotapes and audiotapes
- Group work

➥ Photographs, artwork, diagrams, graphs, and charts
➥ Software
➥ Slides
➥ Observational records
➥ Interviews
➥ Performances
➥ Role plays
➥ Teaching others

An authentic assessment product meets the requirements of an objective or standard and requires problem solving, creative, diverse thinking, and multitasking—just like in the real world. An important part of the product is the self-reflection that takes place both during the creation of the product and after its completion. Authentic assessment products can be scored by rubrics that provide clear criteria to meet the objective or standard and, again, involve the learner in the process.

Rubrics are scoring scales that assess a product based on set criteria. For example, a student's performance or product can be assessed against a preset criterion that contains different levels of performance. Rubrics can also contain descriptors, which spell out what performance the student is to achieve. There are various types of rubrics, including the analytic and the holistic. Analytic rubrics look at the level of performance on each criterion while holistic rubrics look at the whole performance and give an overall score. Educators who support the use of rubrics cite better feedback, clearer expectations, and objective and consistent assessment as motivating factors.

Supporters of authentic assessment claim that this type of assessment demonstrates growth, enables constructivism to work, provides better formative and summative feedback to the teacher and student, and provides the learner with more control. As students go through the process and product of the assessment, they are in fact reflecting and still learning; thus authentic assessment ends the problem of what constitutes an "A" and better meets the needs of individual learners.

What does authentic assessment look like? First, all stakeholders decide what students should be able to do and learn. Then performance assessments such as portfolios or videos are designed to demonstrate successful attainment of a standard or objective. Many schools already use authentic assessment in their writing curriculum, as do many state tests. One problem is that the state tests often ask students to write on topics that urban students know nothing about, such as vacations at the beach.

Those who object to authentic assessment products claim that objectivity, reliability, and validity come into question, that the costs associated with them can be prohibitive, and that they are time-consuming.

Many urban teachers express frustration over the fact that they want to utilize authentic or alternative assessment but they are required to give paper-and-pencil tests—and in the current high-stakes environment these tests are the only ones they hear about or see.

Supporters of true assessment believe that assessment is supposed to be used to help individual students and to inform instruction, not to pit school against school and district against district. The future calls for a balanced approach to assessment, along with assessment that enables self-evaluation and more formative assessment for teachers. We must have reliable, valid, culturally nonbiased assessment in order to ensure fair and true accountability in urban schools. So the question becomes what learners and adults do we want to create? No one believes that we want teachers only teaching to a test, first graders crying, fourth graders throwing up, or students who have overcome obstacles and poverty being prevented from graduating.

ACCOUNTABILITY

Originally teachers were accountable only to local authorities and parents. During the mid-1800s, however, accountability took on more outside control when Horace Mann in Massachusetts pushed for improvements in schools. Although the original purpose of accountability was to assess individual students, the state quickly began to use it to numerically compare and rank schools. Unfortunately, resources were given to schools that needed it the least—those with the highest rate of return on standardized tests—and this is still going on in the twenty-first century. Standardized tests have become the principal measure of accountability for individuals, schools, and districts. Critics contend that these tests are racially biased and written in the language of the white upper-middle class. Proponents argue that some urban children have achieved diplomas for simply showing up at school rather than for meeting promotion standards. Taking standardized tests a step further, some states have made passing them a requirement for going on to the next grade and getting a high school diploma. Thus these tests have taken on very high stakes.

Accountability and assessment have become interchangeable in the twenty-first century. Some charge that schools and teachers, especially in urban areas, do not want accountability. What teachers answer back is that they do not want accountability that is unfair, that leads to students' retention based only on a test score, and that closes down schools that have problems that are much greater than what test scores demonstrate. Even suburban and rural district teachers express shock at the teaching conditions in urban school districts, though some admit that they buy into the media reporting and perception that there is something wrong with urban teachers. For example, when they hear that urban students cannot read they assume it is because urban schools have poor teachers. There have even been examples in the media where suburban teachers brag about their schools' test scores even when they know they teach in high socioeconomic-level schools and schools where students have to test to get into their programs. For example, in a large midwestern Ohio urban school district, one school was a low-income neighborhood school during the previous year and in the following year became a magnet school. When the test scores came out, the new magnet school received an award from the state for increased test scores. However, no scores went up—just the population of students changed. When Hoover (2001) examined Ohio Proficiency Test (OPT) scores in every district in Ohio, he found that the higher the socioeconomic status of the students, the higher the OPT scores.

Description of an Unfair Accountability System in a Large Urban Midwestern School District

The urban district in this example was deeply impacted by the state's implementation of high-stakes tests and accountability. The district previously was well known for implementing its own reforms, including a world-renowned career teacher ladder and excellent magnet school programs. It had also begun to receive an annual state report card based on twenty-seven categories that included staff and student attendance, grade retention and dropout rates, and, mostly, ratings based on the state's test results. In response to this state report card the district began to individually rate its schools in one of five categories. In the highest category, *Incentive*, all staff in the awarded building received a check based on the performance level. If a school ended up with the lowest rating, *Redesign*, the school was closed and all staff members had to find other positions. The new school then received a whole new staff and curriculum focus. This redesign and curriculum focus usually involved controlled curriculum. The school ratings were seen to be extremely unfair and counterproductive because there were huge differences among the schools in this district in terms of allocated resources and support and the economic status and parental involvement of its students. One example concerns a system of magnet schools where students could not attend unless their test scores were high and they qualified for attendance on academic and ability criteria including parent involvement. In fact, poor attendance, behavior referrals, special education status, or low test scores could result in the return of magnet students to their neighborhood schools. Consider, for instance, the district's elite high school, Elm Hills, where students were admitted based only on high test scores and positive referrals. This school ended up on the *Incentive* level, of course, and all staff received bonus checks. It has become very clear from the yearly published ratings that magnet schools where students must test in and parents must wait for hours in line to get their children enrolled have the highest ratings whereas neighborhood schools have the lowest ratings.

One problem that has occurred over time involves outstanding teachers who transfer to magnet schools or leave the district because the embarrassment of teaching in an urban neighborhood school has been too stigmatizing. Unfortunately, this situation has left the neighborhood schools with brand new teachers and those who could not transfer out, despite the students' need for excellent teachers and staff. Sadly, in one of these neighborhood schools, none of the sixth graders ever go on to complete high school.

This district has gone from program to program and utilized controlled curriculum in its neighborhood schools but, unfortunately, never learns the lesson of true success for all of its students. Accountability looks at group bias and is impacted by socioeconomic factors, parental involvement, attendance, school resources, and other factors that are outside a school's control. Blame takes too much energy, time, and money when these things could be better spent on true reform. If people continue to believe that standardized test scores equate to learning and school effectiveness, true equality and future student potential and success may be out of reach.

Description of a Typical Day under High-Stakes Accountability in an Urban Neighborhood School

As teachers enter the building before students arrive, you notice that they are inundated by test slogans and bulletin boards with posted test standards and objectives. A school newsletter in the teachers' mailboxes has reminders about posting test objectives, reading only approved reading texts, and how many days there are until the test, as well as reminders about the no field trip and video policy, and the policy about no recess or specials for students who failed the practice test. A special reminder is given about the no specials policy next year since the district has decided to spend the money on test preparation materials and test tutors instead of on art, music, and PE programs. The teachers post the days' mandatory test objectives and make sure that every activity in their lesson plan book is tied to a test objective. When the first bell rings they head to the library for a quick staff meeting. They enter the room and look up at the overhead screen and find that their names are listed with their students' test scores from last year. They are chastised about getting the scores higher and threatened with the loss of their jobs if the scores are not raised. Teachers whose students have very low scores are asked to meet with the principal after school on Thursdays.

The parents and students begin to arrive and are met with a sign out front that tells them how many days remain until the test. The bell rings and the teachers gather up their students from the playground. They find that half of their students are not in attendance because lice checks were held on the previous day and the students cannot return until their heads are treated. Some students are sent to the office because they came to school sick, probably because their parents had to work or do not have health insurance. Some teachers are confronted by irate parents complaining about some perceived problem at school, but these are often the same parents who are never seen at scheduled conferences and never seem to answer their phone, or do not have a phone.

As the day begins, the principal and reading teacher make the rounds, entering classrooms with their checklists to make sure that the teachers are on the correct time and day of the mandated reading program. They also check to make sure the teachers are not using forbidden novels. In many classrooms, when the teacher announces reading time you hear the students groan.

In one classroom, students who are bored and misbehaving are reminded to pay attention or they will be repeating the grade. As you pass other classrooms you wonder who those students are who are playing on the computer and sitting at desks on the periphery of the room, and you find out later that they are the special education inclusion students. When you ask about them, you are told that "those" students' scores will not count so the teachers cannot be bothered with them.

Overheard in the lunchroom is a discussion about a student who was suspended for assaulting a teacher but is being allowed to return to take the test because his test scores are typically high.

When you enter the kindergarten room where students are resting after recess, the teacher points out the roaches crawling over the students' mats. The teacher tells you the students do not seem to mind; they just seem used to it. The kindergarten teacher sends a student with a note to the office because the intercom system has not worked in years. For the fiftieth time, she gets a note back saying that the district has been called about the problem and will send someone out to treat the roaches soon.

It is raining today, so buckets and tubs are put out to catch the water. Unfortunately, in many classrooms the teacher has forgotten to move students' work and books from near the windows, so they are ruined.

You overhear a conversation between the principal and a teacher. She is being criticized for having her students sing a song as they are getting ready for lunch, because the song has nothing to do with the test. As the principal passes you in the hallway he says, "thirteen more days"; at first you wonder what that is about, and then realize he is talking about the upcoming test.

You follow a teacher to an after-school training session, but one parent stops her and lets her know how upset she is about all the increased homework her son is having to do. The teacher attempts to explain that this increased homework is preparation for the upcoming test and is very important because her son can be retained if he does not pass the test. Just as another teacher is closing her door a parent approaches crying because her boyfriend is in jail and that is why her daughter has been acting up at school.

After school the teachers assemble for training on the controlled curriculum and district-pacing document. Today a reading specialist is supposed to be presenting material on how to improve students' reading ability, and you quickly realize that she has just been hired to continue instruction on more test preparation.

Those in power in urban schools continue to ignore research on the harmful effects of retention on students, and in this high-stakes accountability era they advocate pacing documents and controlled curriculum and the cancellation of what are perceived to be nonacademic subjects such as art, music, and physical education. The teachers and principals have no voice in these schools. Today they receive no training except for test preparation training. If this continues, what urban schools will get in return is the loss of outstanding teachers and administrators, burnt-out teachers who stay, and higher dropout rates among their students.

Inequity even among Different Schools in an Urban District

School A is a magnet school in a large midwestern urban school district. Parents stand in line for hours to get their children admitted after they have passed an entrance exam. Parents also must sign a participation agreement to attend all parent conferences and donate forty hours of volunteer time to the school. School B is a neighborhood school in the same large midwestern school district. The school must take in attendance anyone who lives in the quadrant, including all special education students and any students kicked out of the magnet schools. Parent participation at conferences and school functions is only 10 percent. Compared to School A, School B receives $2,000 less funding per student for the year—a total of $1,000,000 in this school's case.

If you visited the magnet school you would find two parent volunteers and a teacher assistant in every classroom as well as a teacher-student ratio of 20 to 1. In the neighborhood school you would find one teacher assistant for every five teachers and only one parent volunteer in the whole school. Students in the magnet school participate in weekly field trips and have art, music, and PE classes twice a week. Those in the neighborhood school have physical education once a week and no music, art, or field trips because of insufficient funding.

At the magnet school only 30 percent of students qualify for free or reduced lunches. At the neighborhood school the figure is 99 percent. The attendance rate at the magnet school is 98 percent, compared to 87 percent at the neighborhood school.

Near the end of the year the teachers at the magnet school are lauded in the newspaper for their high test scores, while the neighborhood school teachers read about the loss of their jobs and about what terrible teachers they were. Teachers at the magnet school each received a $1,400 incentive check this year for their students' test scores. At the neighborhood school teachers were handed a pink slip because their students' test scores were so low. At the magnet school next year the teachers will be encouraged to be creative in their curriculum; at the neighborhood school the new teachers will have to follow a day-to-day, minute-to-minute, controlled curriculum in which teachers and students are expected to make the correct responses and not deviate from the basic-skills worksheets. The teachers will also have to attend daily one-hour training sessions in the program and be observed weekly to make sure they are complying with the curriculum. In this district, both schools are held to the same standards.

Conclusion

The future of urban schools is not all bleak. Some positive things have come from this accountability. Attention and sometimes increased funding and support have been given to urban schools, and in at least one district the funding for neighborhood schools is surpassing magnet schools for the first time. One teacher commented that these accountability changes have forced teachers in her elementary building to finally work together in order to share best practices, ideas, and activities. In some instances, teachers are also receiving good-quality training that goes beyond teaching to the test. In addition, NAEP (2002) announced that with the assistance of funds from the Reauthorization of the Elementary and Secondary Education Act, sampling of students and comparisons in urban-to-urban districts would take place for the first time. This will allow the large urban districts to benchmark against each other and decide which reforms are working and which are not. Maybe with this sampling the belief that these schools do not want to be held accountable will end, as will the harmful attention to test preparation in the schools.

Comparisons of urban districts and schools can be seen as unfair when important issues are not addressed—issues such as malnutrition, limited access to medical care, lead exposure, decrepit building facilities, and lack of books, materials, and computers. Under this accountability, thousands of students are getting no true reading assistance or true learning, only just what is perceived to be on a test, and they are definitely not receiving culturally responsive teaching. What will become of urban students when art, music, PE, and field trip experiences are taken out of the school or when they are given tutoring on anticipated test items instead of on actual skills such as reading?

Even as the urban schools were trying to involve stakeholders, trying to reform themselves with programs such as site-based management, teaming, new teacher evaluations, lead teacher certifications, and beginning to utilize the change process, authentic assessment, and true staff development, they were hit with high-stakes accountability and unfunded mandates and began to receive decreased resources. Those in power say they want what is best for urban schools and students with this accountability, but the hard quantitative data they actually get, in the form of test scores and attendance rates, do not tell the whole story. Until urban schools have equitable funding and materials, and until their social problems are addressed, there will be no true urban school reform.

STANDARDS

In the twenty-first century, assessment, accountability, and standards appear to be linked together, but in fact they are individual issues. This linkage has led to a great deal of confusion and controversy about standards in particular. There are pros and cons to standards when they can be separated from controversy, accountability, and high-stakes testing. The confusion and controversy concerning standards are probably related to the fact that they came into prominence at a time when high-stakes accountability and assessment also became the push. One reason for this outcome is that as part of *America 2000* the idea of national standards was born. This idea angered most Republicans and Democrats alike: It upset those who thought that local control would be overruled by federal regulation and that if we had national standards we could not be too far from a national curriculum. Furthermore, some charge that the standards are a way for conservatives to have control and power over education and what is taught. Another reason for the controversy is that, for many people, standards signal excellence. Some believe that standards can be scientifically measured. Others, however, feel they can be value based and arbitrary, perhaps because the push for standards was so swift that many were written and regulated by a handful of people instead of involving all stakeholders including teachers, parents, students, and the community.

According to Tanner (1997), the connection between standards and accountability has led to increased dropouts and harm among minority students who make up most urban schools. One issue involves the confusion over separation of content from performance standards. Content standards are basically concerned with what knowledge should be taught, while performance standards ask to what level or to what degree the performance met the standard.

Support for Standards

Supporters of standards believe that standards will lead to true equality of education by providing clear definitions of what is taught and what kind of performance is expected. They also believe that standards can give a clear message for accountability purposes, because if the standards and performance are equal, then comparisons between classrooms, schools, districts, and states will be clearer. An example of this is the confusion that arises in comparisons from state to state or sometimes from school to school within the same district. Some teachers complain that they never know what they are supposed to teach at each grade level. In some instances, they are never even given a textbook or curriculum guide. But when asked about what was positive about standards, teachers stated that they felt relief because they finally knew what was to be taught and enjoyed having the opportunity to finally collaborate with other teachers across and within grade levels.

Urban schools are known for having high staff- and student-mobility rates. If local standards were written on the basis of stakeholders' input, at least within a district, these could possibly be helpful. For example, in many urban schools, students transfer in from another school in the same district with an "A" in reading but are not able to read. Also, some students are retained with no information of what knowledge or skills need to be addressed to assist the student. But with well-written, reliable content and performance standards and some authentic assessment documentation, there is a possibility that much more information would be available to the receiving school and teacher, thereby greatly assisting urban students.

Opposition to Standards

Those who oppose standards believe that standards can actually harm educational opportunities, especially for poor, urban, and minority students, because they further the gap between those from privileged backgrounds and may reflect only the privileged values and content. For example, not many standards address skills that may be needed in the day-to-day lives of the poor, such as how to use bus routes or how to survive homelessness. Some critics also believe that the use of standards could increase the role of the federal government in education and possibly lead to a national curriculum. Others argue that standards are just another form of control of education by a conservative agenda, which would then control schools, teachers, students, and, ultimately, the future. Still others say that standards interfere with true educational reform because they are vague and developmentally inappropriate.

McNeil (2000) described the harm that standardization brought to high-performing minority magnet schools in Texas after the implementation of the Texas Assessment of Academic Skills (TAAS). On the other hand, Adams (2001) found, while looking at fourth-grade classrooms in Ohio, that she could not discern whether standardization was harmful because high-stakes tests and accountability were so interwoven with the standards. She made three observations in particular. First, during the presidential election of 2000 and the controversy in Florida over voting irregularities, even though there was a clear standard about federal and state government issues, the teachers continued to follow the curriculum pacing standards document they were given to practice for the test. They had an opportunity to create a great timely civics lesson but chose not to mention or discuss the election issues. Second, the teachers spent weeks on the goods and services standard even though it was clearly not developmentally appropriate. Third, the textbooks that were supposed to address the standards were test preparation fill-in-the-blank skills worksheets. When the researcher questioned the teachers about the election, the goods and services standard, and the use of the test preparation materials, the teachers replied that a question about the election would not be on the test, that goods and services questions would be on the test, and that they were allowed to use only the textbook and materials that were supplied.

Many researchers question the control and knowledge used by standards. They ask who actually controls the standards and thus the knowledge that is passed on to students, because the control of knowledge and curriculum gives more control and power to those already in power. For instance, the plight for urban schools in particular is that standards do not give credence to minority views and values. They may also not account for diverse needs such as learning styles and multiple intelligences. Even if everyone could agree on the standards to be taught, it is still difficult in urban schools to get true equality of education when basic supplies like toilet paper, writing paper, or pencils are not available. Until the teachers and students have all of the textbooks, resources, and materials needed to address the standards, true equality will remain an unrealistic prospect.

The controversy continues as of this writing in 2002. For instance, in the state of Ohio, there is an ongoing debate about the science standards committees' recommendations and requirements for including or excluding the topics of evolution and intelligent design. Some argue that evolution has a scientific basis, while intelligent design (the idea that life was designed by a higher intelligence) is being used to appease some special interest groups.

Conclusion

Supporters believe that standards are the path to true equality for urban and poor students and can give true comparisons of schools and districts for accountability purposes. Critics claim that standards are biased in favor of those from advantaged backgrounds, may lead to a national curriculum and federal control of education, are vague, and have not been examined by all stakeholders.

Further questions need to be asked. Are standards helpful or harmful? What should students know for the future? How should standards be used? Are the standards developmentally appropriate? (In this connection we should note that some of the best urban teachers we ever observed were enthusiastic about what they taught; whether the subject was dinosaurs or Shakespeare, these teachers gave their students the gift of the quest for knowledge.) As standards are developed and implemented, great care must be taken not to infringe on academic freedom. Only after the current generation of urban students grows up and enters the adult and working world will the helpfulness or harmfulness of standards become apparent.

THE FUTURE

There are many questions left unanswered, but most of us know that rushing from program to program and not allowing enough time for programs to work is not the answer. Educationally we know it is not good practice to give up teachable moments or to place too much emphasis on only two subjects, reading and math; but these things have happened as a result of high-stakes assessment and accountability. National organizations and even pediatricians have called for the end of high-stakes assessment and accountability because they do harm to children. Yet there is some hope. The state of Iowa is allowing the local development of standards, and the state of Nebraska refuses to mandate high-stakes tests.

Maybe the time has come to actually define what is an effective urban school and, along with all stakeholders, proceed to build it. U.S. schools are frequently compared to Japanese schools in terms of test scores, but as Kohn (1999) reminds us, the Japanese schools do not have student comparing, tracking, retention, and elementary standardized tests, but they do have student-centered, progressive, free-play, discussion, and active learning as well as student-directed problem solving. Maybe we need more of such things for urban schools in the United States.

Will assessment, accountability, or standards lead to true equality? Many do not believe that high-stakes accountability will, but some have hope for authentic assessments and well-written, locally controlled, nonbiased standards. These standards and assessments may level the playing field for all children, even the urban poor. The future holds the answer.

REFERENCES

Adams, Kathy. "The Making of Robots: Control and De-skilling of Fourth Grade Teachers in an Urban Appalachian School after the Implementation of the Ohio Proficiency Test." Dissertation, University of Cincinnati, 2001.

Amrein, Audrey, and Berliner, David. "High-Stakes Testing, Uncertainty, and Student Learning." Available online at http://ericcass.uncg.edu/virtuallib/assess/1004.html.

Delandshere, Ginette, and Jones, John. "Elementary Teachers' Beliefs about Assessment in Mathematics: A Case of Assessment Paralysis." *Journal of Curriculum and Supervision* 14, no. 3 (Spring 1999): 216–240.

Elkind, David. "Developmentally Appropriate Practice: Philosophical and Practical Implications." *Phi Delta Kappan* 71, no. 2 (October 1989): 113–117.

Hoover, Randy. "Forces and Factors Affecting Ohio Proficiency Test Performance: A Study of 593 Ohio School Districts." Available online at http://cc.ysu.edu/~rlhoover/OPTIS/index.html.

Kohn, Alfie. *What to Look For in a Classroom . . . and Other Essays.* San Francisco: Jossey-Bass Publishers, 1998.

_____. *Beyond Traditional Classrooms and Tougher Standards.* New York: Houghton Mifflin, 1999.

McNeil, Linda. *Contradictions of School Reform: Educational Costs of Standardized Testing.* New York: Routledge, 2000.

NAEP. 2002. Available online at http://edweek.org/ew/newstory.cfm?slug=3d20distnaep.h21.

Rodriguez, Eleanor, and Bellanca, James. "What Is It about Me You Can't Teach? An Instructional Guide for the Urban Educator" (Eric Reproduction Service No. ED 404 407). 1996.

Tanner, Daniel. "Standards, Standards: High and Low." *Educational Horizons* 73, no. 3 (Spring 1997): 115–120.

Chapter Five

✎ Teaching in Urban Schools

INTRODUCTION

As discussed in Chapter 1, it is hard being a teacher and it is even harder being an urban teacher. There are no typical days but lots of unpredictable ones. The daily dealing with differences, making immediate decisions, taking care of many tasks at once, and doing a very thankless and very public job can be overwhelmingly stressful. Having few resources, having little control over curriculum and pedagogical decisions, and having to work in dilapidated buildings with mold, water leaking, and no air conditioning or heat, can take a toll. The day-to-day bureaucracy of urban schools, and the teachers' concern for the daily lives of their students, leads to many problems. It is never-ending. The teacher bashing that takes place, even from suburban counterparts, makes it an almost impossible job.

Each year urban school districts must hire on average 300 to 400 new teachers. Just a few years ago, excellent teachers were staying on for at least five years, but now many are deciding at the end of the second year not to come back (Cain, 2001). Indeed, Recruiting New Teachers, Inc. (1999), estimates that 9.3 percent of new teachers quit before finishing their first year and more than 20 percent of them leave their positions within three years. Sadly, those students who need the best teachers often get the inexperienced and, sometimes, uncertified ones.

Even after urban teachers are hired, they may have to face poor pay; the uncertainty of moving positions from year to year, grade to grade, or school to school; exposure to lice, impetigo, or other health diseases that can plague the poor; and teaching students with high mobility, high dropout rates, and overwhelming physical, emotional, and mental disabilities. If they get past these difficulties, they find that the overpowering, controlling bureaucracy limits what they can do for students. And, finally, as if this was not enough, they must put up with the recent bashing of urban teachers due to high-stakes assessment.

There are initiatives by universities and groups to assist future urban teachers and to mentor and assist present teachers, but these attempts have fallen short. This chapter will cover the retention and recruitment of urban teachers and some concerns and help for future and practicing urban teachers. In addition, interview information is provided from an urban high school principal and four teachers with different experiences in urban schools. The chapter ends with a section on what it takes to be a great urban teacher.

RECRUITMENT

All schools need highly qualified and certified teachers in all areas, but the most acute shortages of teachers are in math, science, and special education. The problem is worse in urban schools. It is estimated that within some districts over 50 percent of the teachers are teaching out of their field and the retention rate of new teachers is falling below three years. In addition, there is an estimated annual turnover of 300 to 400 teachers in most large urban districts. It is widely believed that urban schools need many more minority teachers but, unfortunately, the Council of Great City Schools, in 1996, found that nine out of ten urban districts have a severe shortage of minority teachers. Attempts to increase the number of teachers, especially urban and minority teachers, include preparatory programs, internships, teacher induction programs, a military Troops to Teachers program, and legislation.

Higher-Education Institutions

Many college-level teacher preparation programs have begun to require aspiring teachers to spend time in urban, suburban, and rural schools so that they have a wide range of experience in these settings. The hope has been that this would increase the teachers' realization of the rewards of urban teaching and encourage them to decide to seek employment there. The reality, however, is that most teachers do not want to move away from their hometowns and are still mostly white, middle-class females around twenty-one years of age who want to teach where they were taught. Sadly, even if we get these teachers to student teach in urban schools, the schools' problems hit them in the face and reconfirm for them why they truly do not want to teach in an urban environment.

Some school administrators and colleges feel that being a student teacher is not enough experience to prepare teachers for teaching, especially in an urban setting, so some institutions are creating urban internships. These internships are training programs that take five years rather than the traditional four years. In these new systems students spend the fifth year as an intern and work on attaining a master's degree while they teach half-time. For example, the interns teach on a half-day schedule and get paid half the salary of a full-time teacher. While in an intern position they are mentored by an experienced teacher and, in some instances, are guaranteed employment the following year with their district. In some cases colleges are still having difficulty keeping interns or recruiting interns for this fifth-year experience because many student teachers want to graduate in four years and receive full pay in their fifth year.

Pre-Service Teacher Academies and Programs

Some urban districts are trying to "grow their own" by having magnet teacher programs or teacher academies. In some instances the magnet program is housed within a high school along with other programs. These programs offer a teaching focus woven throughout the entire curriculum, and practicing teachers in the programs emphasize teaching methods.

In order to enroll in these programs the students are expected to want a career in education. In some instances, the students enter in ninth grade; in others, they are admitted in their junior year. They then spend time in cohort groups, taking some or all of their classes together. This program involves the opportunity to observe teachers in job-shadowing situations, to tutor other students, and to spend a senior internship in an actual teaching situation.

Some known programs include the High School for Teaching and Technology in Cincinnati, Ohio; the Walton-Lehman Pre-Teaching Academy in Bronx, New York; the Mount Pleasant Teacher Academy in Providence, Rhode island; and the Miami Norland Senior High School Center for the Teaching Profession and the Miami Senior High School Professional Education Magnet in Miami, Florida.

Troops to Teachers Program

Troops to Teachers (TTT) was established in 1994 as a Department of Defense program, but responsibility for the program's oversight and funding was turned over to the U.S. Department of Education in 2000. The primary focus of this program is to help recruit quality teachers for schools that serve low-income families. The hope is that TTT will help relieve teacher shortages, especially in math, science, and special education. In addition, the program assists military personnel in making successful transitions to second careers in teaching. This assistance includes funding, counseling, referral, and placement. Yet to be seen is what impact this program will have in urban schools.

Teach for America

Teach for America was the idea of Princeton graduate Wendy Kopp, who in 1989 envisioned a program founded on two beliefs: that low-income children needed high-quality teachers and that many in her generation would be willing to teach these children for two years. The college graduates in this program agree to teach for a minimum of two years and to attend summer training institutes. They are paid full salaries and benefits in their employing districts and receive support during their teaching time. Some may also receive money from AmeriCorps education awards to pay back student loans. The program began in 1990 and since its inception has placed 9,000 individuals in teaching assignments in rural and urban schools. At present, Teach for America teachers are employed in eighteen areas in the United States.

The summer institute consists of professional development and basic-skills lessons for teaching low-income students; the participants also teach for five weeks in a summer school program. Ongoing support during their teaching time is provided by other corps members and alumni, others in their employing district, schools of education, and professional associations.

The research so far has consisted of an independent evaluation in 2001 performed by CREDO, a research group based at the Hoover Institute. Utilizing data from the Houston Independent School District, the researchers found that the Teach for America teachers were more likely to hold bachelor's degrees, more likely to take on more difficult assignments, and less likely to leave after one year. In fact, many of these teachers stayed on beyond their two-year commitment.

No Child Left Behind

The legislation known as the No Child Left Behind Act was created in an effort to equalize the experiences of at-risk students and increase the academic achievement of U.S. schools. This act attempts to address some of the quality and certification issues and teacher shortages facing urban schools by allowing states to permit alternative certification, which lets nonteaching professionals gain a teaching certificate in a shorter period of time than would be possible in a traditional teaching college. Both new and practicing teachers must demonstrate subject-matter knowledge and expertise. The act also provides for merit pay to retain good teachers and bonuses for those who are willing to teach subjects that are experiencing the highest level of shortages, such as science, math, and special education. Nevertheless, many truly believe that if the unique needs of urban schools are not addressed and mandates are not funded, this legislation will be for naught.

Suggestions

Many middle and high schools offer career awareness activities. These activities can range from take-your-child-to-work days to career fairs and career days where professionals from various fields provide talks about their professions and are available to answer questions. Yet sometimes those planning such activities forget to include the teaching profession, perhaps because they are dealing with students who are already in a school with teachers, but the passion of a practicing teacher could go a long way toward encouraging and recruiting the best students into urban teaching.

In order to increase the retention of urban teachers, more needs to be done to recruit teachers earlier, and in different and unique places. The offering of mentoring and financial incentives, including increased salaries, may help. This would include the hiring of teachers earlier by urban districts, assisting aspiring teachers to have early successful experiences in urban schools, and possibly providing paid internships and financial incentives to stay in urban schools. This assistance should continue once teachers are teaching in urban schools with good, quality mentoring. Thinking outside the box to recruit from community colleges and from former teachers, retired persons, and paraprofessionals could also go far in assisting with recruitment.

RETENTION

Retaining teachers appears to be a bigger problem than recruiting them. As Dr. Tom Carroll reports, "It's not that too few teachers are entering our schools, it's that too many are leaving. It is as if we are pouring teachers into a bucket with a fist-sized hole in the bottom" (National Commission on Teaching and America's Future, 2003). When Henke and colleagues (1997) asked public school teachers whether they would choose to become teachers again, nearly one-fifth of the respondents said no. Furthermore, a study completed by the National Commission on Teaching and America's Future (2003) found that one-third of new teachers are leaving in the first three years while 50 percent are gone by five years. Unfortunately, in high-poverty schools the loss is one-third higher. And as noted earlier, there is an estimated turnover of 300 to 400 teachers per year in most large urban districts. Job dissatisfaction and the pursuit of better jobs or careers appear to be the reasons given most often for quitting.

Many believe that urban schools need more minority teachers, but the problems of urban schools hiring late, minority teachers not passing new teacher exams, and the loss to other careers for more money and better working conditions do not appear to be letting up.

Once teachers are employed in an urban school, they are faced with daily challenges such as being moved from school to school and grade to grade; shortages of funding, resources, and support; a powerful bureaucracy over which they have no control; and public ridicule that has become worse since the emergence of high-stakes tests. Promises are made to these teachers—for example, they may be promised support from a team of teachers through their teaching years or all the resources they need—but many of these promises are not kept. And, unfortunately, the newest and most inexperienced teachers are often placed in the most challenging positions.

The answer is probably not mandates for certified teachers or mandates for smaller class sizes. For example, New York mandated certified teachers only to be placed in the neediest schools, but when non-certified teachers got more choices of where to teach, certified teachers left New York City schools and went to the suburbs and parochial schools. Another example is provided by Hasci (2002), who wrote about the problems that occurred in California following legislation that mandated small class sizes in the early grades. California found that finding space and quality certified teachers became a problem. As class sizes were reduced, positions opened up for urban teachers to apply to the suburbs and they fled. This left urban schools with even more uncertified and inexperienced teachers. Finally, in a large midwestern urban school system, after lowered class sizes were mandated, more experienced urban teachers fled to magnet schools. This, too, left inexperienced, new, and less than stellar teachers in neighborhood schools.

Two possibilities for assistance with urban school retention may be mentoring and job sharing. Mentoring or induction programs are available in some districts. They provide training sessions to new teachers, including experienced teachers who are new to urban districts, and at times they assign a teacher an experienced teacher mentor. The problem is that the programs are only as good as the support from the mentor, the quality of the induction program, and the relationship built between the new teacher and the mentor. Also, unfortunately, in some districts the mentor has taken on an evaluator role that may interfere with the true mentor relationship. In addition, some mentors have not received quality mentor training and support themselves.

One innovative program, available in Cincinnati Public Schools in Ohio and in cooperation with the Cincinnati Federation of Teachers union, involves job sharing, whereby two teachers decide to share one teaching position. They work either half-days or on and off days. The district pays them each a 50 percent salary and covers their medical benefits in full. Reports on this program from teachers and principals have been positive. The teachers feel less overworked and stressed but still give 110 percent. The principals say that they feel as though they've gotten two fresh teachers for the price of one. This is one program that has been successful at retaining teachers who have young families or are nearing retirement.

Another suggestion is to work on the content of teacher preparation programs to better prepare graduates for a successful experience in urban schools (Claycomb and Hawley, 2000; Haberman, 1995). Also, help may be available through financial incentives, better salaries, good-quality mentoring and induction programs, and urban districts' support for "growing their own" teachers. Mobility, dealing with the bureaucracy effectively, less stress, more support, continued professional development, and quality leadership (a factor often overlooked, even though a school is only as good as its building administrator) may go far to support the retention of high-quality urban teachers.

Retention is a serious problem in urban schools. Until it is addressed successfully, academic achievement will suffer and the best teachers will not remain where they are needed the most—with urban children.

Teacher Induction, Mentoring, and Teacher Academies

In urban schools induction, mentoring, and teacher academies are becoming more prevalent. The induction programs can include meeting monthly with other new teachers for training, professional development workshops, and mentoring, and, in some instances, actual teacher academies are in place.

The structure of teacher induction programs and their underlying beliefs about teacher development can range from effective teaching criteria, to a broad base of knowledge for true reform in schools, to constructivist approaches that work with teachers' own reflective practice and collaboration to impact student achievement (Weiss and Weiss,

1998; Sclan and Darling-Hammond, 1992). So far the reports on the retention rates from induction are impressive. Urban districts are reporting a 93 percent retention rate for teachers who go through induction (Recruiting New Teachers, Inc., 1999). If the induction programs include mentoring, usually the new teachers are assigned to veteran teachers who assist the beginning teachers to learn about the expected behaviors, philosophy, and cultural values of their school (Little, 1990; Recruiting New Teachers, Inc., 1999). Some new teachers receive regular mentoring and opportunities for collaboration, including observing each other teaching; others see their mentors only occasionally. The quality of the mentoring and the frequency with which mentors and mentees meet are extremely important because this mentoring can have a strong impact on student achievement. Indeed, it has been found that mentored beginning teachers focus on student learning sooner, rather than relying on trial and error. In addition, mentored teachers leave teaching at a lower rate (National Commission on Teaching and America's Future, 1996).

Teacher academies have professional development opportunities not only for new teachers but also for veteran teachers. Often these academies employ high-quality professionals for instruction, utilize frameworks that emphasize teaching skills, have partnerships with higher-education institutions, help to actually redesign teacher education programs, and sometimes offer Masters of Arts in Teaching right on site.

In some instances, school systems, in cooperation with higher-education institutions, are implementing Professional Development Schools. These designated public schools are the feeder schools for novice teachers. The career teacher in the professional development school will often work with the student teacher in a collaborative and reflective way. For example, a career teacher and a novice teacher may observe each other teaching. This symbiotic relationship benefits both teachers. The career teacher, while offering assistance to the novice teacher, also benefits from learning from the novice teacher. In fact, career teachers report that their partnership with novice teachers creates enthusiasm for their own teaching. Weiss (1999) has also found that novice teachers who spend their first year in these professional development schools tend to have higher morale, are more committed to teaching, and plan to remain in the profession longer.

Urban Teacher Quality

Once urban schools have become able to retain teachers, it is especially important that they keep only the best. In an effort to fill positions, an urban district may end up hiring at the last minute. This means that they may have had to lower standards, which, in turn, means that urban schools can become rife with uncertified teachers and those with emergency licenses. This problem is especially critical where high-quality teachers are needed the most: in math, science, and special education classrooms. Ingersoll (1999) reported that only 50 percent of urban schools have a teacher certified in math and science. Furthermore, even when districts get certified, many teachers end up teaching out of their certification area, especially in the core academic subject areas. Even worse, some teachers do not even have a minor in the subject.

The retention and certification of teachers are related to the academic achievement of students in urban poverty schools. For example, years of teacher experience were important for the passage rate of tests for students in Texas. The SBEC Panel (1998) found a significant difference in test scores between students whose teacher had less than five years of experience and those whose teacher had more than five. In addition, the Louisiana Education Department found a correlation between the number of highly certified teachers in a school district and the level of academic achievement in that district. This means that urban schools cannot constantly have young, inexperienced, and noncertified teachers if they are going to truly impact academic achievement.

CAREER LADDER

An innovative teacher career ladder has been in place in Cincinnati Public Schools in Ohio for more than fifteen years. This career ladder not only assists the best teachers to advance but also provides assistance to struggling teachers and, ultimately, contributes to the process of firing incompetent teachers.

The career ladder has five levels: apprentice, novice, career, advanced, and accomplished. Placement on a level is conditional on the results of a comprehensive evaluation. Teachers who apply to become lead teachers must have received an advanced or accomplished level rating.

The application for lead teachers must demonstrate the following:

- Leadership in their profession
- Effective communication skills
- Involvement with parents and the school community
- Teaching techniques and curriculum development that meet all students needs
- Consistent pattern of professional growth

- Articulation of their convictions about teaching
- Cooperation and collaboration with others
- Commitment to teaching as a career
- Has demonstrated his/her philosophy about education in an effective and meaningful instructional program (CFT, 2000)

A teacher who receives National Board Certification is automatically credentialed as a lead teacher under the career ladder.

The application process involves the application itself, interviews with peers, and a review of the personnel file. Lead teachers are reevaluated every five years. They work an additional five days a year and receive additional salaries of $4,500 to $5,500 depending upon their duties.

These duties may include the following:

- Subject area leader
- Team leader
- Schoolwide lead teacher
- Consulting teacher
- Curriculum specialist
- Curriculum council chair
- Program facilitator

In some positions, lead teachers may be out of the classroom for two to four years.

ACADEMIC FREEDOM AND TENURE

When reform came to urban public schools, instead of schools and teachers being given more support and freedom to pursue true academic equality for at-risk students, they got what Linda Darling-Hammond calls "teacher-proofed" curriculum. "Educational reform," she writes, "was 'teacher proofed' with hundreds of pieces of legislation and thousands of discrete regulations prescribing what educators should do" (1996, p. 5).

The recently passed No Child Left Behind Act stipulates that the federal government can help to fund only those educational practices that work. This means that there will be more educational systems that are "prepackaged." In other words, districts will be forced to choose an educational system that dictates what to teach and how it is to be taught. Most of these curriculum systems and programs do not allow much in the way of academic freedom.

In 2003 a teacher in Stillwater, Arkansas, filed an academic freedom suit. She is suing her district administrators for the freedom to choose how she teaches. The teacher, with more than thirty years of experience, finds the science curriculum unacceptable. The curriculum not only doesn't meet her guidelines, but it also takes her out of the classroom for days of training and does not have enough connections to other subjects. In addition, she says that the district's Comprehensive Local Education Plan does not provide for any objective measurement of second-grade students' academic progress in science. She may have a very good point because the scores on the Oklahoma core curriculum tests have gone down in every subject except for science since teachers started using the modules in 1999–2000. A spokesperson from the Arkansas State Department of Education supports her position, saying that the department sets curriculum standards but does not tell teachers how to teach. As of this writing, the courts have not ruled on the case.

One of the past practices utilized to protect academic freedom for teachers has been tenure. Tenure "was created to protect competent teachers from the whims of administrators and pressure groups" (Henson, 2001, p. 417). In 1986, however, the state of New Mexico eliminated teacher tenure but raised salaries for teacher compensation and also increased state expenditures and state mandates to districts and teacher preparation institutions. Some educators worry that other states will follow suit or use some other means to control the academic freedom of teachers.

These issues are extremely important in urban schools for two reasons:

1. No one has clear methods on how to get true equality in schools, but urban teachers may be in a position to know this —especially if given the chance to try new things and, basically, to exercise their right to academic freedom.
2. The retention of outstanding urban teachers is critical. If their academic freedom is not protected, they may choose to leave—especially considering the overwhelming control and bureaucracy they experience in urban schools but not in other schools.

TEACHER BASHING AND BUREAUCRATIC CONTROL

How soon this is forgotten by those who denigrate teachers: "In each classroom in this country there is a highly educated adult with the potential for creating meaningful learning environments that address the needs of every student" (Nelson, 1999, p. 392). Even Secretary of Education Rod Paige (2003) bashed teachers while speaking at a luncheon in Palo Alto, California, promoting the No Child Left Behind Act: "Four out of five students are being taught by a teacher who doesn't believe" in their students' abilities. Furthermore, an Ohio legislator, while discussing the Ohio Proficiency Test, was overheard saying: "We can legislate to teachers, but we cannot legislate to parents."

Haberman (1995, p. 61) defines urban school bureaucracies as "organized for the convenience and maintenance of everyone who works in them—except classroom teachers and students." He (1995) also describes the bureaucracy in urban schools as characterized by high centralization with a top-down chain of command, academic decisions made by committee, facilitators far away from the teachers and students in classrooms, and compulsive rule following. These bureaucracies are able to continue to function by the pressure and operation of a culture of fear, and by implementation of policies, mandates, evaluations, controlled curriculum and standards, and lesson plans that contribute to this control. Above all, bureaucratic control and teacher bashing, whether by those inside or outside of urban schools, are damaging for urban schools because they do not let best practices flourish.

TEACHER EVALUATION SYSTEM

One way to exert control is by tying a teacher's evaluation to the policies and curriculum wanted by those in control. Since the circulation of *A Nation at Risk* report some members of the public have called for a system to rate teachers. In years past, teachers just had to earn a bachelor's degree, which would then be the only education they needed until retirement since teachers were not required to gain additional skills or advanced training. This trend has changed. Today, in order to teach, you must pass a standardized test. Often this includes a general knowledge test that all teachers must pass, as well as a test that measures content-specific knowledge. Teachers who fail either of these tests are not allowed to become certified classroom teachers. Also, a recent change in the state of Ohio has mandated that all new teachers will have to undergo recurring classroom observations and attain a master's degree by their tenth year of teaching.

Districts themselves have started to take steps to ensure that all classroom teachers are highly qualified. Cincinnati Public Schools in Ohio, along with union and district officials, have created a Teacher

Evaluation System (TES) whereby teachers are required to undergo an annual evaluation as well as a comprehensive evaluation every five years. Under TES, teachers who qualify in the highest category are to receive a pay bonus. Teachers who are not doing well may experience a reduction in pay. Also, teachers who cannot meet the minimum requirements are given an additional year of evaluation to improve. If after that second year they do not improve, they are dismissed from the district.

Despite the fact that the Cincinnati Federation of Teachers (CFT) helped to create this system, the rank-and-file members of the union voted not to tie the evaluation to the pay scale. Most members felt that the system was not adequately prepared. Other concerns included the fact that after the pilot program was instituted the majority of the teachers qualified for bonuses, yet the district had insufficient money to pay the increases for all qualified district teachers.

Resistance to the TES system had an effect on the leadership of CFT: The former president who pushed for the implementation of TES was voted out of office while the newly elected president campaigned and won on the platform to reform TES.

TEACHERS' UNIONS

There has been more attention paid to the quality of teachers in urban public schools over the last few decades. The majority of suburban public school teachers belong to the National Education Association (NEA) while the majority of urban schoolteachers belong to the American Federation of Teachers (AFT). NEA is an association and is less like a labor union than the AFT. The AFT is part of the AFL-CIO. AFT local unions are much more likely to use a labor strike as a tool when negotiating new contracts. Labor unions in general have been attacked by conservative politicians. Teachers' unions have therefore been blamed for the perceived failure of public schools. Teachers' unions are often accused of having a "monopoly" on public education due to the fact that they are opposed to educational vouchers and charter schools. As some schools are identified as failing, some critics of public education blame the teachers and the teachers' unions. Secretary of Education Rod Paige, while speaking in 2003 at the aforementioned luncheon promoting the No Child Left Behind Act, blasted teachers' unions and the National Education Association specifically: "I view unions as barriers to what we're trying to get accomplished." In reaction to these charges, though they continue to seek professionalism for teachers and to be teacher advocates, these unions sometimes hinder true urban education reform. For example, unions have supported standards, charter schools, and merit pay (and some still do so today). Also, AFT advocated and pushed for standards while not asking its members' views or thinking about what might come from the implementation of these standards. In another instance, it was actually AFT President Shanker who in 1988, while making an address at the AFT convention, supported the charter school idea and actually coined the term *charter schools*. He described charter schools as schools where teachers could create new and innovative programs. He may not have envisioned that these charter schools would later be utilized for profit making and attacks on urban public schools.

Teachers' unions may also do harm by working to better professionalize the profession. For instance, some teachers' unions have supported merit pay for teachers, despite the fact that neither research nor history supports this pay system. Consider the following passage, which Gerald Bracy submitted to the ARN-L @listsrva.CUA.EDU, on February 6, 2002:

> The effect of [payment for test results] was to narrow all school effort to cramming of content most likely to be tested in the subjects prescribed for the education. The system also caused teachers to concentrate on the average and slightly below average pupils with whom their efforts would pay dividends through a large percentage of passes, and to neglect other students—the bright because they would pass anyway, the dull because they were hopeless or at best a poor risk in terms of expenditure of time.
>
> (A description of an experiment in test-driven instruction in Ontario, 1876-1882)

As noted, research does not support the use of merit pay for teachers. Although there are some short-term benefits, such as increased attendance and, initially, an engagement in innovative and constructive activities, studies suggest that the system hurts teacher morale, hurts true evaluation since the system encourages looking at items that are easily measurable, reduces collegiality, and is costly and time consuming. In addition, the quotas and money available sometimes do not allow all to receive the rewards. Most important, there has been no improvement in performance or impact on student achievement. There is, however, research supporting pay for increased experience and continuing education. Research indicates that teachers improve continuously until their fifth year of teaching, but even though they do not develop as much thereafter, there are reasons, such as retention, that they should be rewarded with salary increases. Furthermore, although continuing education is supported by new licensing requirements by states, it is also important to encourage teachers to keep abreast of current research, experience collegiality with other teachers, and continue modeling life-long learning for their students.

This is one teachers' experience with a union and merit pay in a large midwestern urban district:

> It was an amazing and a quite powerful scene to see almost every teacher in the school district filling the hall for a strike vote. I had chills thinking about the power of the teachers in the room to make good changes for the urban children in the district. I was so proud that the strike was not over money, but the surplusing, possible dismissal of teachers, and loss of job security from a new school evaluation system that was guaranteed to hit neighborhood students and teachers the hardest. What was truly sad was that the district, after years of "win-win" negotiations, had brought in a superintendent to break the union and hired a new law firm known for their antagonistic tactics.
>
> Most of us were quite shocked because it seemed like the next thing we knew, after the strike vote, was being asked to vote for a new evaluation system that would be tied to a personal rating for each teacher and eventually to merit pay based on the rating. The actual merit pay vote to tie the evaluation to pay would come later but was no less shocking. Some of us voiced concern over the subjective criteria of the evaluation system but were not heard. I mostly feared the loss of teaching as an art because the checkboxes contain prescriptive criteria making it appear as if teaching can be done by anyone including a robot. I also worried about the possible loss of great teachers who may not fit in a rating box but could truly reach children in poverty.
>
> This evaluation system received a great deal of media attention even though we have had an enviable and fair teacher career ladder program for years. Our union "leaders" visited the schools and threatened teachers with "You better vote for this or you will get something you don't like!" Immediately after the vote there were rumblings that some schools' votes did not get counted because they were late or the votes were done incorrectly. I spoke to many teachers who said they did not vote for the new evaluation system and did not know anyone who did. Of the few who told me they had voted for it, they told me that they only voted for it because they felt intimidated by the union representatives. Finally, after trying to figure out how this was voted in I spoke to an anonymous high source who informed me that the vote was going to be positive whether we voted for it or not because of the upcoming

school levy. I have heard from many teachers since the implementation of the new evaluation system. They express shock and anger over the time they have to put into the portfolio part of the evaluation. The portfolio requires them to make documentation of everything they do and requires hours of preparation. I was told by one teacher that "It [the portfolio] is just for show. I feel that I am neglecting my students because I don't have time for anything else." They also have expressed concern about the subjectivity of the evaluation and some of the raters. The outcry and anger was quite obvious when the past union president was ousted and someone was put in place from outside the inner circle. The new union president did manage to extend the time for the evaluation and for training of the teachers but many teachers are still not happy. I write now because the merit pay vote is looming. Other teachers in other districts are watching this city district with concern and disbelief. Other teachers, outside the district, have told me that they cannot believe that the city teachers would even consider having merit pay. Many teachers have expressed fear that they will no longer feel supportive of each other because they will wonder how much more money the other teacher is making or that the other teacher may harm them so that they can get a higher rating. One teacher also told me, "I don't believe everyone will get a 4 and get the highest pay because the district can't afford it so they are just going to tell the raters to keep a cap on the ratings." Another teacher told me that "The evaluation system was just another way to put the blame for the failing schools on teachers." It is a great loss that this powerful union, which could be fighting for urban children, is contributing to fear and the loss and control of great teachers who are the very teachers we need in urban schools. I know of at least ten exceptional teachers, including myself, who have left the district. Most of us left because this was the last straw in an endless stupid administrative policy that demonstrated over and over that there is no real caring or support for urban children and teachers. I have finally realized that we are just political and economic pawns because children and teachers are powerless. Sadly, my coalminer grandfather and great-grandfather, who put their lives on the line to have unions, must be rolling in their graves knowing that their granddaughter was betrayed by her own union.

In the two weeks prior to the merit pay vote the union made statements in essence that said they would not support the merit pay due to the administration not keeping good faith bargaining. I was proud that the union finally made a stand but still do not understand the underlying issues of teaching as an art, that teachers do not want an evaluation system that is subjective, and are basically tired of being blamed for all of the problems in urban schools. Arrogantly the superintendent issued a statement that he was confident he had the teachers vote. He was wrong. The votes were only 73 teachers for and 1892 against.

Unfortunately, in this large midwestern urban district, unfair school accountability is in place, with the union supporting payments to schools for test score increases. These group payments consist of an annual check for everyone in the school. It is quite obvious to outsiders, though, that the schools that receive the checks are for the most part high-performing or magnet schools that already contain high-performing students.

Finally, it should be noted that in another urban area—namely New York City—the teachers' union did supply curriculum to match the students' standardized test since no one else seemed likely to do so. Two million dollars were spent on this effort.

TESTING AND TEACHING

The control of urban teachers has worsened since the implementation of accountability and high-stakes tests. The control comes from keeping potentially outstanding teachers out of the profession by utilizing teacher tests and high standards. This also includes controlling curriculum and lesson plans once such teachers are in the profession.

Watras (2002) reported that the first testing of teachers was intended to keep black teachers out of Virginia schools. Today there are still problems with minority and poor teachers passing national teachers' exams and the increased standards, such as higher grade point averages, needed to get into education departments. These assessments may not even be related to teaching abilities (Claycomb and Hawley, 2000). Yet, sadly, these teachers may have the answer to true equality for urban students or may become outstanding urban teachers themselves.

Teachers go along with controlled lesson plans and mandated postings of objectives and standards and administrative observations because they are fearful for their jobs and truly do not want their students to be left behind or to miss something. The testing in schools has also put good teachers in jeopardy of becoming poor teachers. Urban teachers will utilize boring worksheets and test preparation material and blame the boredom and behavioral problems on students. They will at times support retention of students even though they know the research clearly indicates that it leads to dropouts and behavioral problems among students. They will also support the loss of equalizing experiences like library, art, music, physical education classes, and field trips—even though there are clear benefits of these for urban students.

The difference in test preparation by urban versus suburban teachers is well expressed by this suburban teacher: "We have excellent ratings, students do well, our average income of parents is $50,000. We really don't discuss the test, until two weeks before and then do some practice and format of the test; no one comes and observes or checks my lesson plans."

A LEARNING CLASSROOM AND AN URBAN NEIGHBORHOOD CLASSROOM COMPOSITE

A learning classroom is characterized mostly by a happy teacher and happy children. Here, the teacher's passion for teaching is evident. The use of teachable moments and students' interests refines the curriculum. Students work by themselves, with others, and with the teacher to get what they need academically and socially to be successful adults. Parents' input into students' interests and support of the teacher are also evident. Parent contacts start the year on a positive note and include phone calls home and newsletters. The classroom is filled with books and other resources, such as art supplies. It is print rich, the bulletin boards are filled with students' work that has been individually and creatively expressed. Resources outside of the school, such as guest speakers and field trips, are utilized. Teachers continue their professional development by taking courses, attending conferences, and meeting with other teachers to refine their practice. Finally, there truly are only twenty-three students in the classroom.

On the other hand, an urban classroom is plagued by control—control over what the teacher says, decides to teach, and how he or she teaches. Rule following is explicit. For example, most words out of a teacher's mouth involve some correction to the rules, and rules must be posted in the classroom for the teacher to get a good evaluation. Teachers must turn in their lesson plans, and they must match the objectives and standards. Teachable moments are no longer allowed because of the controlled curriculum. There are constant interruptions from the intercom during the day. The classroom walls and bulletin boards are lined with mandated students' work and postings that all look alike. The classroom contains very few books, and these are outdated, and other resources—sometimes even basics like chalk, paper, and pencils—are not available. The teacher and students try to teach and learn in buildings that leak and have mold and crumbling ceilings. The students are not safe on the playground; they may have to come back in from recess if the police clear it for safety or shots have been fired. There is no playground equipment anyway, so the children do not miss recess too much. Parent contact usually involves some negative incident that happened at school or has something to do with the child not returning homework. The teacher is told that her students' test scores are not good enough and as a teacher she is not good enough so she has to continue to go to mandated training that may not even have anything to do with what she teaches. The teacher constantly worries about her students, her students' test scores, possibly moving to another school, or teaching another grade next year. There are forty-two children in the classroom, but the district will report a ratio of 20 to 1—a ratio that includes support staff and administrators who are not directly in the classroom with students.

These composites have been provided as an example of the best and worst that school can be. This is not to say that there are no learning classrooms in urban schools, because there are; rather, the point is that there are *many* of these urban classrooms in urban schools.

INTERVIEWS WITH URBAN EDUCATORS

A Principal

This urban high school principal has twenty-eight years in the same urban district, ten as a teacher and eighteen as an administrator. When asked about the positives and negatives of being an urban principal, he said:

> Positives: . . . Oh, challenging. Some people may see that as a negative, I see it as a positive. Ah, because it is rewarding as well and I don't think that you get the rewards if you don't have the challenges. I feel that what I do, what we all do in urban education is important, it is meaningful and it gives us a real sense of accomplishment. The negatives are some of the obvious ones: lack of resources, lack of parental involvement and by that I recognize that we have a number of parents that are actively involved, but I don't think you see the same level of involvement as you do in the suburban or the private or parochial schools. And most urban districts tend to be very large and when you have that you tend to run into bureaucracies and sometimes those bureaucracies and the politics and the unions and the civil service regulations and all those types of things sometimes make it difficult to make the changes that are necessary.

The principal also felt that recruitment was more of a problem than retention of urban teachers and that teacher education programs are not doing a good job of preparing urban teachers. He expressed support of the lead teacher program but believed that the district was not doing enough to utilize the potential of many teachers in the district. In addition, although he thought the evaluation criteria were good, he found the new teacher evaluation system to be time consuming. As for the bureaucracy and the politics, his response was mixed. He commented that politics can be worse in the suburbs and that bureaucracy can at times be helpful by causing an administrator to get lost in the system.

When asked about high-stakes tests, he commented:

> You know, it's interesting that you ask that question right after we've talked about the teacher evaluation system because if anyone in this district looked at the teacher evaluation system and those standards and that teacher determined whether or not the student passed his or her course on a single paper-and-pencil objective test that was given at the end of the school year we would say that teacher is terrible and ought to be fired. And yet the politicians across the country at the federal level and the state level have decided that that is the best way to assess whether or not school districts are doing a good job; schools are doing a good job, teachers are doing a good job, and we are just not that smart to come up with a single test that we can administer one time a year that is going to tell us all that. It just is bad education and what is troubling is that we in education haven't stood up to the media, to the politicians, to all these people, and said this is nonsense. Should we have standardized tests? Sure, let's have standardized tests and let's look at the results as one measure of how students are performing, how teachers are performing, how principals and schools and districts are performing, but let's look at all the other stuff that we need to be looking at to make a final assessment as well.

His thoughts on urban public education:

> All I can say is that I think in order for our country to remain strong and prosper we need a strong public education system. And I think we need strong urban centers. So we need those two things and it only follows that we need strong urban public school systems. So I think the cities and the country need strong urban public education. Have we as a country really supported urban education? I would say no we haven't. I think we have not done a very good job. Are some of these political de-

cisions going to help urban education? From what I know and from my experience I would guess not. I don't know if they are necessarily going to damage it. I think regardless of those types of things it will survive and it won't be fatally harmed, but I guess the real negative is that people will be spending all this time and energy and limited resources on things that won't necessarily help us to become what we need to become. And so many of those political solutions I think are misguided and detract us from making the necessary repairs and improvements that need to occur.

His thoughts on the solutions for urban public education:

Students, good parents, good teachers. The reason I say that is that over time what has happened, for a number of reasons, is that good students and good parents have left urban school districts and good teachers have not necessarily been attracted to the urban districts. And so we have to bring all those people back so that the problems become manageable. If 10 percent of your students are special education and 20 percent of your students are below the poverty level and 30 percent of your students have academic deficiencies, then the problems in the school become manageable. When the good students and the good parents move away and now those percentages become 40, 50, 60, 70, 80 percent, now the problems become so large it becomes very difficult for an individual school to deal with those problems. Or an individual teacher in the classroom to deal with those problems.

(The complete transcript of this interview can be found in Appendix C.)

A Practicing Teacher

This practicing teacher has taught for seven years in urban schools—five in a magnet school, and two in a neighborhood school.
His thoughts on teaching in urban schools:

Well, there are a lot of internal rewards. You are certainly doing a service and you should be proud of it. Number one for being a teacher because that is challenging enough, then being a teacher in an urban setting; it takes quite a bit, and those who can stay more than a couple of years really should be proud. It feels good when you take a student who obviously needs you and needs your skills and bring them to the point that that student can succeed. Negative is the typical ones that most people see, such as the parental support; sometimes it seems that the society that the student comes from doesn't value education. And it is also the lack of stuff you need. The basic stuff like copy paper and money to buy films and computers that work and so forth, and that the students themselves can be a challenge. The place where the students come from is different than what people know, and when you have them in your classroom it takes different strategies to teach them. Not only teach them to do classroom management and all the kind of things like that. So now there is quite a bit, but again I think that the rewards, if you can take it, outweigh the negatives—provided you can deal with the stress.

His comments on the teacher evaluation system:

I'm against it. I think that teachers should be evaluated; they should be observed by practically anyone who wants to come in. I have no problem with anybody coming into my classroom to observe, from my building administrator to the superintendent to a parent. But the problem I have is that they try to apply these standards and they do a strict interpretation of them. I think that it is very unfair; for example, there is something in my evaluation system that says, "Do you provide a warm and caring classroom?" Well what the heck is that? If you go into a kindergarten classroom you would expect to see one thing. If you go into a twelfth-grade calculus classroom you would expect to see something else. And a lot of these things are subjective. And teaching is a challenge anyway. I know a lot of colleagues of mine who are spending so much time on their portfolio stuff that they have to turn in and they are making sure that everything is cleaned up and tidy and I think that they are spending less time on creativity as far as designing lessons and implementing lessons for their students. So I believe that teachers should be evaluated, but the current system that we have—when you are rubriced against this, that, and the other—is too much of a waste of time for the teacher and I think that the administrators are really catching it too. They have enough to do to begin with and you are talking about annual observations for every single teacher in the building plus comprehensive evaluations, which is six visits I believe between them, and somebody from the district, so I think it is too much and I think that they are trying to measure the wrong thing.

This teacher's views on the teachers' union were mixed. He sees a need for the union but also said that it may draw more negative attention to the teachers.

His final thoughts:

I just find it sad that the people who want to jump on the bandwagon and criticize urban schools and slam the teachers, slam the students, slam the system and stuff like that are the same guys who never spend any time in these schools. Politicians do this and most of your politicians come from a different area of the state or the city and they have no real understanding of what is going on and they really need to spend some time to talk to the principals, the teachers, and above all else the students. And a group that I blame even more than politicians is the media. In my opinion, and I am ranting here, the media has lost its investigative edge. The media takes whatever is said by politicians and others at face value without doing any investigation. It would be wonderful if we had a camera crew follow around those students for a period of time and do some exposé kind of stuff on it. But that doesn't happen. They show up and have their cameras in front of the school and interview somebody and say "Back to you, Johnny." And they don't really delve deep to find out what is going on. Our urban schools are hurting. They are hurting from funding to direction, and to be honest with you there are some teachers who need to leave, there are some administrators who need to leave. I think that there is enough blame to go around, but it is not hopeless. The students who go to our schools deserve the best that we can give them. I try to do that; it is hard to do that on a daily basis, but I try to give them a decent education. As a society we know that it is a heck of a lot easier to pay for education than it is to pay for their prison cells. As far as money goes they are hurting. To be honest with you as an urban teacher I am paid pretty well compared to a suburban district. That doesn't hold true everywhere, but I feel that a lot of other teachers are paid a little bit more and I feel that their job is more challenging. But there are other needs in the urban schools. I hear a lot of especially conservative politicians attack urban schools because they spend more per child than a lot of affluent suburban schools; but they don't look at the big picture. You don't have the security concerns, you don't have the run-down buildings, you don't have the need for a higher population of special education students. There is a lot more to it. And a lot more can be done. I don't want to feel complacent and I don't think that urban teachers should hurt their arms patting themselves on the back, because I think that we can do more. But for a country to be what it should be, it should take care of the students who need the education services the most.

(The complete transcript of this interview can be found in Appendix D.)

A First-Year Teacher

A discussion was held with an urban teacher at the end of her first year of teaching. She sought out the authors after she decided she was thinking about leaving. We asked her about this decision as well as about her first year.

When asked why she was thinking about leaving, she said, "I love the kids, but you know it was so hard leaving the problems at school. My principal and 'supposed' mentor just added to my stress. They would bother me about silly things instead of trying to support what I was doing."

She discussed not having basic supplies such as paper, pencils, and enough copies and books. She said that sometimes half her class was out with lice for three days at a time and it was difficult to continue lessons. She could not get parents in to discuss their children, or their phone numbers were disconnected. She had students who came to school for two months, disappeared for a few months, and returned near the end of the year. She found that of the thirty-two children she started the year with, only ten were still in her classroom by May. She said even though the students were in and out, she was still held accountable for their test scores and attendance. And she was extremely frustrated to be informed that the following year she would be teaching a new grade.

At the end of the interview, when we asked her whether she'd come back as an urban teacher for another year, she said, "I love the kids and I really believe they need me . . . but I don't know if I can continue to do this. . . . I thought I could just teach."

An Urban Teacher with Ten Years' Experience Who Decided to Leave Teaching

I chose to go to urban schools because I always felt that these were the students that needed me. I passed the national teachers' exam in the 99th percentile and had a 3.9 grade point average. I could have been or done anything. I had all outstanding teaching appraisals. After ten years I just couldn't take it. It was not the kids, really . . . though I never could leave their problems at school and I guess I probably cried once a week . . . but it was the other things. The worst was having roaches crawling on my kindergartners while they were on the floor, and the moving from year to year from first to seventh to third grade and in different schools because of budget cuts. Like being put down in the paper because of where I was teaching and the changes in curriculum

and observations of me while I was teaching . . . always feeling like I
had to prove things.

When we asked this teacher why she didn't go to a suburban or
private school and continue teaching, she commented, "An opportunity
came to still work with children but not in schools so I took it. If not, I
guess I would have gone back to being a waitress."

A Teacher Who Retired after Thirty Years

I stayed for thirty years for the kids; but don't get me wrong, there was a
lot of BS. About the fifteenth year I realized I made too much to go to
the suburbs, . . . [and the] last ten years I was not directly in the classroom but was working with teachers. I think it also always came down
to, these were the students that needed me.

A Teacher's Comments about Teaching
in an Urban Neighborhood School

Neighborhood schools have very different priorities than when I grew
up. Children have to deal with where they are going to live or what is
going to happen at their house or in their neighborhood at night; they
don't care what happened during the Boston Tea Party and why. I can't
say that I blame them for their lack of wanting to learn. They don't have
good role models to show them that an education will help them in
their future. They only see what their parents show them and that is
nothing. No one in my class wants to be anything professional when
they grow up. They want to be a gate monitor and work making only
$7.00 an hour. I struggle every day to see the importance in teaching
what a noun is when they have dreams of being on welfare when they
get older. It really makes teaching a hard profession to do sometimes.

LEARNING ORGANIZATIONS

Factors that would give rise to at least some hope for true reform in
urban schools include the involvement of all stakeholders (including
parents and others from site-based management), administrators who
view their positions as instructional leaders, and true professional development.

Site-based management is defined as an attempt to create learning organizations involving all stakeholders in a school. There are differ-

ent forms of site-based management; these range all the way from one school steering committee to teacher-led schools.

In one school this may mean a group of teachers who are elected and make recommendations on curriculum, budget, programs, field trips, professional development, and the day-to-day operations of the building. Sometimes groups of parents and other interested community members serve on committees in the schools. And in teacher-led schools, the teachers may run the school with or without an administrator.

Site-based management allows the search for true answers for academic achievement because parents and other stakeholders are listened to while making decisions for what is best for their local school. In some cases, site-based management has allowed principals to become instructional leaders instead of the only person in charge of everything. As collaborative leadership partners in the educational process, administrators can spend their time looking at curriculum, students, and teachers while emphasizing student learning. They are able to do this because major responsibilities and decisions about budgets and running the facilities are shared. These administrators are able to look at students' work and improve classroom observations for true teaching effectiveness. They also participate in their own professional growth through personal enrichment and training, reading, and utilizing research.

Principals in these schools are moving away from holding staff meetings for reminders and announcements to discussing student achievement and utilizing the time spent on increasing individual teachers' knowledge and addressing their needs. The time for staff meetings is now spent on teacher-led meetings on student achievement, research findings, and disaggregating data on students.

In 2002, the Chicago Teachers Union established a graduate school for teacher leadership. The members of this union envision the school as being one way to prepare teachers to share school leadership. A graduate program for teacher leaders has been in operation at Wright State University in Dayton, Ohio, for over twenty-five years. (More information on this program can be found in Appendix B.)

Historically, external forces have dictated staff development. With the realization that true teacher staff development should have something directly to do with an individual teacher's career, staff development has begun to involve more than just taking a workshop. The state of Ohio has moved its certification to licensure and, in this way, has opened doors to opportunities other than college-credit or workshop classes for renewing licenses. The approval for continuing development has been turned over to local districts. The districts form committees that meet and decide whether an activity is acceptable and what a teacher needs to do. Some of these activities may now include writing an article, self-study, attending a conference, or leading professional development activities for others.

GREAT URBAN TEACHERS

Haberman's (1995, p. 1) point is clear when he writes, "For the children and youth in poverty from diverse cultural backgrounds who attend urban schools, having effective teachers is a matter of life and death." But what does it take to be a great urban teacher?

According to Haberman (1995), "star teachers" of urban children display certain teaching pedagogy, methodology, and beliefs. These are as follows:

- ➤ Star teachers realize that if they have a classroom that is interesting and pertinent to their students' lives, they will rarely have discipline problems. If they do have a discipline problem, they know there is some reason behind it and will just redirect children and punish rarely.
- ➤ They realize that homework is meaningful and that students must be able to complete it independently because they may not have someone at home to help with it. This also means that, in the classroom, students share the homework rather than just checking it.
- ➤ They start the year with a positive rapport with parents. This includes making calls, making home visits, and making sure parents know they are part of the learning process. Star teachers also never blame parents.
- ➤ They do not place much emphasis on standardized tests but are more concerned with students' effort and take personal responsibility for this effort.
- ➤ Star teachers understand the collaborative aspect of the curriculum. They make it very apparent that students' interests are considered, and they are involved in the day-to-day activities of the classroom.
- ➤ They model being life-long learners themselves and incorporate the events in students' own lives into their teaching in order to capture students' love of learning.
- ➤ They share of themselves, including what they are interested in. They model reading, writing, and drawing. They listen to

students' stories about their activities and seek information from parents about students' interests. They also confer with other teachers about the students.

➡ They reflect on their own experiences and grow.
➡ They utilize words like *caring, trust,* and *respect* when discussing children.

Haberman (1995) further writes that star teachers in urban schools do not burn out because they learn early how to deal with bureaucracies. For example, they learn early what to read, work around, ignore, and make do with. In addition, they find a support system for themselves consisting of people who, like themselves, truly want to help, such as secretaries, janitors, and other teachers. Finally, they always continue their own enthusiasm for learning and teaching.

Being a great urban teacher is not easy. Doing what it takes to be "great" can also put one's job at risk. The bureaucracy is overpowering, and teachers must sometimes fight for equalizing experiences like field trips, ignore state mandates on subjects and minutes per day to teach, and teach outside the curriculum or the required test preparation materials. They succeed by finding ways around these problems and by picking and choosing their battles carefully. Mostly, they work tirelessly for what is best for children.

CONCLUSION

Palmer (1998, p. 3) reminds us that "[i]n our rush to reform education, we have forgotten a simple truth: reform will never be achieved by renewing appropriations, restructuring schools, rewriting curricula, and revising texts if we continue to demean and dishearten the human resource called the teacher on whom so much depends. Teachers must be better compensated, freed from bureaucratic harassment, given a role in academic governance, and provided with the best possible methods and materials. But none of that will transform education if we fail to cherish—and challenge—the human heart that is the source of good teaching." Nelson (1999) also clearly asserts that we must have highly educated teachers.

Retention and recruitment of high-quality urban teachers are critical for the academic achievement of urban students, but unless changes are made in urban schools these efforts will be for naught. Students must have learning classrooms free from bureaucratic control so that teachers can utilize culturally nonbiased teaching and high-quality curriculum. Parents and other community members and stakeholders must play significant roles in the education of children. True professional development utilizing quality best practices and research must be encouraged. Resources including high-quality new textbooks and equalizing experiences must be available. And, finally, teachers and administrators must be trusted to do their jobs to the best of their ability free from judgment and control.

The future of urban schools and urban teachers is in flux. Hopefully, the next generation of teachers can truly make a difference in these children's lives.

REFERENCES

Cain, Michael S. "Ten Qualities of the Renewed Teacher." *Phi Delta Kappan* 82, no. 9 (May 2001): 702–705.

CFT. *Collective Bargaining Agreement.* Cincinnati, OH, 2000.

Claycomb, Carla, and Hawley, Willis D. "Recruiting and Retaining Effective Teachers for Urban Schools: Developing a Strategic Plan for Action" (Eric Reproduction Service No. ED 451 147). 2000.

Council of Great City Schools. 1996. Available online at http://www.cgcs.org/urbaneducator/.

Darling-Hammond, Linda. "The Quiet Revolution: Rethinking Teacher Development." *Educational Leadership* 53, no. 6 (March 1996): 4–10.

Haberman, Martin. *Star Teachers of Children in Poverty.* Lafayette, IN: Kappa Delta PI, 1995.

Hasci, Timothy A. *Children as Pawns: The Politics of Educational Reform.* Cambridge, MA: Harvard University Press, 2002.

Henke, Robin R., et al. "America's Teachers: Profile of a Profession, 1993–94" (Eric Reproduction Service No. ED 410 225). 1997.

Henson, Kenneth T. *Curriculum Planning: Integrating Multiculturalism, Constructivism, and Education Reform,* 2nd ed. Boston: McGraw-Hill, 2001.

Ingersoll, Richard M. "The Problem of Underqualified Teachers in American Secondary Schools." *Educational Researcher* 28, no. 2 (March 1999): 26–37.

Little, J. W. "The Mentor Phenomenon and the Social Organization of Teaching." In C. B. Courtney (Ed.), *Review of Research in Education.* Washington, DC: American Educational Research Association, 1990.

National Commission on Teaching and America's Future. "No Dream Denied: A Pledge to America's Children." 2003. Available online at http://www.nctaf.org.

Nelson, Wade W. "The Emperor Redux: Extending the Minnesota Metaphor." *Phi Delta Kappan* 80, no. 4 (January 1999): 387–392.

Paige, Rod. 2003. Speech at luncheon promoting No Child Left Behind. Available online at http://www.baycitynews.com/.

Palmer, Parker. *The Courage to Teach: Exploring the Inner Landscape of a Teacher's Life.* San Francisco: Jossey-Bass Publishers, 1998.

Recruiting New Teachers, Inc. *Learning the Ropes: Urban Teacher Induction Programs and Practices in the United States.* Belmont, MA, 1999.

SBEC Panel on Novice Teacher Induction Support System Data Request. *An Analysis of the Effects of Teacher Experience on Achievement from the Texas Assessment of Academic Skills.* Austin, TX, 1998.

Sclan, Eileen, and Darling-Hammond, Linda. (1992). "Beginning Teacher Performance Evaluation: An Overview of State Policies." *Trends and Issues Paper* No. 7. Washington, DC: ERIC Clearinghouse on Teacher Education, American Association of Colleges for Teacher Education (Eric Reproduction Service No. ED 341 689).

Watras, Joseph. *The Foundations of Educational Curriculum and Diversity.* Boston: Allyn and Bacon, 2002.

Weiss, E. M. "Perceived Workplace Conditions and First-Year Teachers' Morale, Commitment, and Planned Retention: A Secondary Analysis." *Journal of Teaching and Teacher Education* 15, no. 8 (November 1999): 861–879.

Weiss, E. M., and Weiss, S. G. "New Directions in Teacher Evaluation." Washington, DC: ERIC DIGEST, ERIC Clearinghouse on Teaching and Teacher Education, AACTE (Eric Reproduction Service No. ED 429 052).

Chapter Six

❧ Politics and Funding in Urban Schools

POLITICS

The issue of public education registers at the top of the list of concerns of most citizens. Political candidates consistently list education among their top priorities when running for political office. A large percentage of Americans perceive an educational crisis in the United States, but some of these perceptions are not clearly supported with survey evidence. For example, over the past twenty-five years the majority of the parents of school-age children have graded their district as good or excellent (Doherty, 1998). In 1997, 46 percent of Americans gave the district in which they lived a grade of either "A" or "B." But only about 23 percent of those surveyed gave the same high marks to the condition of public education throughout the country (Doherty, 1998).

The percentage of support for urban districts is much lower—and this finding is especially troubling given the fact that forty-seven urban school districts educate 75 percent of all minority children in the United States (Doherty, 1998). In suburban districts there is a great deal of support from parents and the community, but this is not the case in the city centers. It seems that most of the stakeholders in urban public education see a broken system.

The fix for urban public education remains elusive. Many politicians honestly believe that school funding is an issue, yet many also believe that a raise in funding levels alone will not solve the problem. Some of the more conservative portions of U.S. society are unwilling to support increased funding levels without evidence of significant educational gains as measured by standardized tests.

Urban public school educators have cited lack of parental support, malnutrition, and the many problems associated with low socioeconomic status as the main barriers to school achievement. Conservative forces have accused the same educators of hiding behind these difficulties instead of taking drastic educational steps to correct them. They have also demanded that urban schools be treated the same way as suburban schools in the areas of achievement, retention, and discipline. In short, they argue that urban schools should be held to the same standard.

The difficulty involved in drumming up support for urban public schools as they currently stand may dominate the images that most Americans have about such schools. The problems associated with urban public schools include high dropout rates, crime, graffiti, violence, and poor performance. These images seem to be branded into the minds of public and elected officials. They are further compounded by the failure of so many attempts at reform.

In 1966, a study called "The Equality of Educational Opportunity" was released. This study, which came to be known as the Coleman Report, stated that student achievement is not necessarily linked to the quality of the school that the student attends. In other words, no matter how good the school is with regard to teachers, facilities, and curriculum, it does not have a major influence on achievement. This report identified families and peer groups as having much more of an influence on students than the schools themselves.

Different forces used the findings of the Coleman Report to support their own positions. Educators claimed that until urban families and economic factors improve, urban schools will never achieve at the same level as suburban schools—and, therefore, it is unfair to compare them. Conservative forces used the report to try to make a case for family values in society. They also argued against the implementation of large and expensive reform efforts.

When one pictures an urban school district, scenes from the movies *Dangerous Minds* or *The Blackboard Jungle* come to mind. Urban districts have an overly large minority population, many of whom come from poverty-stricken backgrounds. The fact is that prior to *Brown v. Board of Education,* the majority of students enrolled in urban districts were white and middle class.

African Americans in general were happy when the U.S. Supreme Court struck down segregation as unconstitutional. The lead attorney in the case, Thurgood Marshall, argued that the standard of "separate but equal" was not realistic because schools attended by African American students were consistently of lower quality than those attended by white students. Both the facilities and the faculty at black schools were questionable. The cost of raising the quality of black schools to match that of white schools would have run into the billions of dollars. Instead of forcing this cost on the states, the Supreme Court outlawed segregation in public schools.

As African American students started to attend the better white schools, the white population decided to leave both the cities and the schools. This phenomenon is often referred to as "white flight." Even though desegregation allowed black students to attend inner-city white schools, the population of these schools changed. In Baltimore, for example, 70–80 percent of the city population was white in 1955. By 1970, that figure had dropped to 50–60 percent; by 1990, it had dropped even further to 40 percent (Orr, 1998).

The ratio of public school students also changed, but on a much more slanted scale. In 1950, the student population of Baltimore's public schools was between 60 and 70 percent white. By 1990, that figure had dropped to less than 10 percent. It seemed that white citizens who could not move to the suburbs were taking measures to ensure that their children did not have to stay in the public system. One such measure was the enrollment of their children into parochial and other private schools. A stark visual reminder of this can be found in the yearbooks of Cincinnati Public Schools. In most of the high schools during the early part of the twentieth century, the yearbook pictures were almost exclusively those of white students. After 1954, there was only a smattering of African American students. And today the population is overwhelmingly African American with a smattering of white students.

After the white residents started leaving the cities the urban schools were once again segregated. This new segregation was caused not by law but, rather, by location and socioeconomic status. Because of this new segregation, efforts were made to desegregate the schools. One of the most controversial methods to desegregate public schools was forced busing.

The idea behind busing was that a portion of students from predominantly black schools would be bused to districts and schools that had a predominantly white population. Then a portion of white students would then be bused to the black schools. The goal of busing was that both the predominately white and black schools would have a more favorable ethnic mix of students. Some of the busing was ordered by the courts; some was set up by district policies. Overall the idea of busing was unpopular.

Busing is one of the most unpopular attempts at school reform in the history of mandatory public education. Most of the white parents, along with some black parents, were outraged that their children had to spend several hours a day riding a bus to a school that many perceived to be inferior. There were also some white parents who did not want their students to go to school with a large African American student population. Demonstrations were held in several cities, one of the first of which was Boston.

Organizations such as the NAACP sued several districts and government agencies on the basis of desegregation. In lieu of forced busing, compromises were made in several districts. For example, in the Cincinnati Public School District, in Ohio, magnet schools were created. As noted, magnet schools are public schools that have a particular focus or style of curriculum such as Montessori. Parents can sign up their children for the school that they want even if that school is out of their neighborhood. By allowing some school choice, the demands of desegregation were in some cases somewhat satisfied.

The perceived performance of urban schools has declined dramatically over the last several years. Despite efforts such as Head Start, Title I, and desegregation, most urban students do not achieve at the same level as their affluent suburban counterparts.

Attempts to narrow the divide start at the local level. The mayor or local legislature sometimes appoints local school boards. More commonly, the school board members are elected to office. Unfortunately, the election of school board members, both at the local and state levels, gets little attention during the political season. Other issues such as the election of a president or governor receive much more of the public's attention. Yet the election of school board officials is one of the most important decisions that a community can make because of the power that the board holds. For example, the school board has the final say on hiring and firing, curriculum, school spending, and if and when a levy is placed on a ballot. It can also overrule decisions made by other administrators such as the superintendent and individual building-level principals. One such example of this power over curriculum was seen in Kansas when religious conservative forces were able to place several members on the state board of education. These forces were then able to change the state science standards to eliminate evolution as the main theory on creation in favor of creationism. During the next election these same conservative board members were voted out of state office. Once citizens realized how much power state school board members had, they began to pay more attention to the issue of who held these positions.

In today's political environment, money is needed for any elected office, thus allowing money and power to influence what happens in urban schools. Organizations have recently been created to ensure that school board members who reflect the views of these organizations are elected. For example, in Ohio, members of the Cincinnati Business Community (CBC) donate large sums of money to the candidates they favor who are running for the Cincinnati Public Schools Board of Education. Through campaign donations from its members, the CBC has successfully controlled some of the membership of this school board and is thus able to affect policy without the legal standing of direct control. In addition, organizations with ties to the Cincinnati Federation of Teachers (CFT) have been created to both promote and raise money for candidates and issues that are favored by this organization.

FUNDING

Probably the hottest issue connected to public education is that of funding. The cost of running a school is expensive by anyone's definition. Districts have to pay the salaries and benefits of teachers, administrators, secretaries, custodians, nurses, tutors, accountants, contractors, security personnel, and consultants. Districts have to pay for the buildings themselves as well as for books, teaching supplies, computers, software, transportation, security, insurance, electricity and water, and general maintenance. The costs for all of these things have risen dramatically during the last few decades. Due to the fact that most public schools receive the majority of their operating funds from taxes, the debate over funding runs hot in all fifty states.

In most states the lion's share of public education funding comes from local and state-level agencies, primarily in the form of tax revenues. In most cases, the state is responsible for 48 percent of funding whereas local taxes make up about 45 percent. Of the needed funding the federal government kicks in only about 7 percent, down from 10 percent just twenty years ago. In Ohio, for example, part of the money goes to the schools through the state government. This state money comes from the general budget, which was created by income taxes, property taxes, sales taxes, and the state lottery. Some states place taxes on items such as cigarettes or gasoline in order to help raise needed revenue. Taxes on individual items such as cigarettes are called *excise taxes*.

About 85 percent of a district's budget goes to salaries and benefits for individuals who work in the district. These benefits include health and dental insurance as well as sick days and professional development. Teachers' unions typically negotiate a contract with the district that includes salary, benefits, and standards for professional training. The unions make the legitimate claim that fair salaries and benefits are necessary in order to attract qualified teachers. This is especially true in urban districts where the challenges of educating students are more substantial than in the suburbs.

Most states delegate money to districts based on the number of students and the characteristics of the district. Urban districts typically receive more money than suburban districts because of the challenges faced by urban districts. The number of students with special needs, the number of students seeking vocational education, and the costs of maintaining older buildings are higher in urban environments. Funding is often based on assigned weights for each student. For example, a regular education student is given a value of 1, a student with special needs may be given a value of 2.1, and a student who qualifies for free or reduced lunches may be given a value of 1.2. The numbers based on this formula are calculated annually. Critics of the system contend that it is flawed because some districts identify students as having special needs when the students may not meet those criteria.

Individual states have different systems for how public education is funded. For example, Hawaii pays over 80 percent of the cost of public education whereas other states pay less than 10 percent. This system often suffices during good economic times but problems arise during recessions and economic slow downs. The funding needs of the public schools do not diminish during bad economic times but the amount of funding that a state can provide may change. Funding needs for public education often have to compete with the needs of other services provided by state government.

On the local level the amount of funding that a district may receive is mostly based on property taxes. Residents vote on operational levies. An operational levy is a percentage of the value of property that is paid in taxes that go directly toward school funding. The percentage is measured in mils. For example, one mil equals 1/1000 of the value of a house. Property taxes are based on the value of the property itself. If a district asks for a six-mil operational levy, then it is asking property owners to increase the percentage of tax they pay on their property each year. The amount of money depends upon the value of the property in that district. The percentage of higher-value property will raise more money than the same mil amount in lower property value.

The more valuable the property, the more money the individual will have to pay in property taxes. The value of a property is based on a property assessment. If a homeowner decides to have his or her property assessed in order to qualify for a loan, then that person runs the risk of paying more property taxes. The need to place operational levies on the voter ballet is based on inflation and on changes in the number of students in a district.

One of the problems with operational levies is that they expire after a number of years in most states. This requires the district to ask the voters to renew the levy in order to maintain its current level of funding. Districts will also ask taxpayers to increase the amount for an operational levy in order to adjust for inflation. In addition, most states do not allow the amount of money to increase in order to keep pace with inflation. Districts often play a guessing game as to how much money they will need in the future.

If a district needs to build additional buildings due to an increase in student enrollment or to replace worn-out and obsolete buildings, then it must pass a bond issue. A bond issue is different from an operational levy in that the additional money will go for a specific purpose such as constructing a new building, updating electric and phone lines, or creating computer hookups.

One problem with operational levies and bond issues is voter backlash. It is sometimes difficult to convince a retired individual, living on a fixed income, to voluntarily pay more in taxes to a district when all of his or her children have already graduated. It is also difficult to raise additional funding in districts where the general population lives right at or below the poverty line.

Due to the high cost of running an urban district, conservative organizations and individuals often attack these districts, claiming that the districts waste money through bureaucracies and inefficiency. However, contrary to the perceptions of some people, there is little fat to trim in most urban districts. Often hard choices have to be made and some positions have to be cut. Many urban schools have fewer custodians than is optimal due to the scarcity of funds; many also operate without librarians, counselors, nurses, security, and specialists such as art and music teachers.

Some districts are fortunate in that they may have a business located within the district that picks up a large portion of the needed money in property taxes. There is definitely a case of "haves and have nots" in public school districts. In some districts the population is relatively affluent, allowing for more funding due to the higher overall value of the homes in those districts compared to others.

The problem with reliance on industry as a school tax base is that the company might move or go out of business. Since the district is used to a certain level of funding from the business, it may suddenly find a need to seek additional money to cover the losses. For example, if a district is accustomed to receiving funds from an assembly plant located within the district, the effects can be devastating when that plant moves or shuts down. Sometimes leadership officials will take measures to try and attract other businesses to fill the funding void caused by the movement of the former business.

State and local governments can also inadvertently affect funding for public schools. Often a government will offer tax abatements for businesses that are willing to move to a local area. Tax abatements are used to entice businesses to locate in the area by reducing or eliminating the amount of taxes for a period of time. The purpose of the abatement is to bring jobs to the local area. The harm comes when, because of reduced property taxes, local districts have to educate more children with less tax revenue.

The performance of a district may also affect whether or not operational levies and bond issues are passed. Standardized testing has become more and more popular in the fifty states. With standardized testing, districts are often ranked and the test results are published on each district in the local newspaper. It is a hard task to convince the voting public to support higher taxes for a district that has scored low or has shown little or no progress in testing results.

This is particularly hard on urban districts given the unique problems faced by urban educators. In general, urban schools receive more money per pupil when compared to their suburban counterparts, so critics perceive that the urban schools are wasting tax dollars and the chance of raising additional money becomes harder. The voting public is often unaware of the additional challenges of educating the urban child. The demographics of the district influence how much money is needed to run the district. If an urban district identifies students with special needs or has run-down buildings, for example, the needed amount of money to run that district goes up. Critics often do not take these facts into account and simply look at the dollar amount spent per pupil.

Some states are trying to fix the funding differences between wealthier and poorer school districts. For example, the Texas courts have ruled that funds will be distributed from property-wealthy districts to poorer districts. Some districts and private individuals in other states have also taken the states to court in order to create a fairer school funding policy. Suggestions for funding equity include a foundation approach or a guaranteed tax base (GTB) as possible solutions for additional money. The foundation approach would seek additional funds for less wealthy areas to meet minimal standards, but the belief is that not enough funds would be raised. With the GTB, the idea is to pool all of the taxable money in a state and divide the money based on student enrollment.

The amount of money that comes from the federal government has historically been minimal compared to that of state and local governments, but for the most part this amount has risen over the past century. The exception to this trend occurred during the Reagan administration, when the federal contribution declined (Hacsi, 2002). In 2002 the amount of federal dollars increased with the No Child Left Behind bill signed into law by President George W. Bush.

For some states, funding from state governments has dropped over the last twenty years. In 1977, the Pennsylvania state government funded 50 percent of the needed operational funds for public school systems. That percentage has steadily gone down. During the 1996–1997 school year the state provided only 35.6 percent of public school funds; due to this reduction, local tax revenue must make up the difference. States, such as Oregon, have been affected by economic downturns that have affected the budgeting for school districts. The state of Oregon provides about 70 percent of the funding for local school districts' budgets. During the last few years, however, the state has experienced a budget crunch due to its declining tax revenue. In fact, Oregon is facing a $178 million education-funding deficit for the 2003 school year. The state legislature considered a temporary income tax increase to offset the deficit, but opinion polls indicate that it has little chance of passing. So Oregon is considering shortening the school year by fifteen days in order to offset costs. But rather than shorten the school year by eliminating the last fifteen days in the year, it is considering eliminating certain Friday school days. This would save the state from having to pay some unemployment benefits since the state law stipulates that unemployment is based on a five-day workweek. Without the five-day workweek, unemployed teachers would not be paid unemployment benefits. Obviously the state teachers' unions are up in arms over the suggestion.

The American Federation of Teachers union has created a Budget Crisis Tax Force for 2003 shortfalls and has submitted the following recommendations to states:

- ⟶ Uncouple the state's tax structure from the federal tax code
- ⟶ Develop progressive, equitable strategies that fairly tax individuals and businesses
- ⟶ Change the tax structure to reflect an economic climate where services play a more important role but contribute nothing to the tax base
- ⟶ Close tax loopholes that allow large corporations to avoid paying any tax in states in which they operate
- ⟶ Encourage efficient government procurement and operations (American Federation of Teachers, 2003, p. 9)

Given an overreliance on property taxes there are funding disparities. For example, in Ohio, the Beachwood Public School District spends about $16,449 per student while the Bethal-Tate School District spends only $5,307 per student. The disparity between rich and poor districts has sparked political and legal action.

Politics and Courts Funding

Districts are affected by economic downturns on the state level as well. Some states may not be able to provide the amount of funding that they traditionally give to a district due to tighter budgets, so some districts have decided to fight back.

Attempts have been made to change the funding levels and the funding systems themselves in several states. In California, the funding was mostly done at the local level. It was found that the wealthier districts spent more money per pupil than did poorer districts. Several school districts banded together and sued the state. In the case of *Serrano v. Priest*, the plaintiffs tried to show that there was a funding discrepancy in a system that overly relied upon local property taxes to fund public education. This case continued for almost a decade and went through several levels of the state and federal court systems. Finally, the California supreme court found the system to be unconstitutional and the state legislature was given several years to find a better system (Hacsi, 2002).

In Ohio, a group of public school districts successfully sued the state. In this case, *DeRolph v. The State of Ohio*, some school districts in Ohio contended that the current system of public school funding is unconstitutional based on the fact that there is an overreliance on property taxes. The Ohio supreme court narrowly agreed and has found the state in contempt for not changing the funding formula. It should be noted that the state legislature did increase the dollar amount distributed per pupil throughout the state, but the Ohio supreme court continually found that the efforts had fallen short.

Attempts were made by conservative forces in Ohio to change the Ohio supreme court's makeup rather than changing the funding system in Ohio. The Ohio Chamber of Commerce spent huge sums of money targeting one Ohio supreme court justice during the 2000 election. The chamber's efforts to oust one of the justices who had ruled against the state of Ohio failed in 2000. In 2002, however, one of the justices who voted with the majority announced his retirement from the Ohio supreme court. Conservative forces then spent large sums of money for the candidate of their choice and this time they were successful in placing a member on the court who was perceived to be more likely to make decisions that favored conservative issues on business, labor, and education.

As of December 2002, the Ohio supreme court found the funding system still inadequate, but it has not mandated any changes. Given the changing demographics of the Ohio supreme court, most educators are pessimistic about adequate changes to the system.

In the landmark case of *San Antonio School District v. Rodriguez,* a lower court found that the state of Texas funding system was unfair based on the equal protection clause of the Fourteenth Amendment. The U.S. Supreme Court struck down the lower court's decision. Justice Potter Stewart voted with the majority. He found the system to be unfair, but he also found that the system did not violate the Constitution. This case kept the property tax system in play and also kept the federal government out of state control over public school funding.

Florida recently passed an amendment to the state constitution over the objections of the state governor. This amendment sets class-size limits for public schools throughout the state. However, although it mandates smaller class sizes, it has not guaranteed additional funding for the schools. This situation sets up a potential showdown between a conservative legislature and governor against a mostly democratic-affiliated state supreme court.

The federal government had traditionally stayed out of school funding, and there is no mention of education in the body of the Constitution. Education is largely thought to be a reserved power of the states. The first effort by the federal government to provide public education for U.S. citizens was the Northwest Territory Act. Created by the government under the Articles of Confederation, it provided land in each township that could be sold to create and maintain schools for the township's education. Because this act preceded the creation of the Constitution, it did not have to pass constitutional muster.

After the Northwest Territory Act, the federal government tended to stay away from the issue of public education until the twentieth century. During the Depression it saw that the individual states needed help and thus started programs under the New Deal. One program was the free lunch program for poor students.

One of the largest steps taken by the federal government in regard to school funding was the Elementary and Secondary Education Act (ESEA), created during the 1960s as part of President Johnson's war on poverty. The purpose of this act was to help close the achievement gap between wealthy and poor students.

One federal program designed to help urban schools was, and is, Head Start, created to help prepare underprivileged children for school by providing help with academic and social skills. Head Start is run by the states, although they are required to meet federal guidelines. Since

Head Start is operated at the state and local levels there is a large variation of quality from one center or state to another. Critics of the system assert that it is too expensive and does not provide the results needed by students to prepare them for their academic careers. Conservative lawmakers want to either eliminate the program or change it so that the academic portion of the program is stressed over all others.

Studies have found that the students who are enrolled in Head Start show a short-term positive effect: Specifically, they are less likely to be retained in a grade and also less likely to be identified as having special needs. Other studies show that, in the absence of other interventions, the benefits of Head Start fade out by about the third grade.

Other critics like the program but are dismayed to find that only about 35 percent of eligible children are enrolled in it. Since Head Start is not an entitlement, it is funded through annual appropriations, thus putting the funding at the mercy of politics and available federal dollars. This means that if the funds run out, children who wish to enter the program are turned away.

Title I represents one attempt by the federal government at helping fund special programs for schools. Created as part of President Johnson's "Great Society" program, Title I was also part of the Elementary and Secondary Education Act (ESEA) of 1965. It was designed to try and help narrow the achievement gap between rich and poor students. Title I funding is based on the percentage of students who receive free or reduced lunches and, as such, gives additional federal funds to individual schools that have a large percentage of these poor students. Unfortunately, Title I serves only about one-third of all eligible children.

A recent twist to the entitlement of these funds came about under the 2001 reauthorization of ESEA. Specifically, the federal contribution to education further increased with the recently passed No Child Left Behind Act. For example, the state of Ohio received $850 million from the federal government during the 2001 school year and $971 million during 2002. This increased money comes with a price, however. States are required to implement standards and to assess students on these standards in order to receive federal funding from ESEA. Schools that fail to make progress on the standards have to implement interventions such as technical assistance, school choice, and staff turnover. Districts must also set aside Title I funds for supplemental education services for low-performing students. The parents of these students can seek the services at the place of their choice. Title I funds can even be used to pay for transportation of these students to the schools of their choice.

Schools with populations of underprivileged students totaling over 40 percent can use their Title I funds on school-wide programs.

Districts are also encouraged to involve parents within the school. Schools that receive Title I funds are required to create a parental involvement plan and to make efforts to increase parental involvement within the school. Organizations such as the National PTA support the changes in ESEA and believe that school accountability is important.

Proponents of Title I praise the system. They proclaim that, without Title I revenue, the job of educating children would be nearly impossible. Critics argue that the original purpose of the program has not been met and that the achievement gap has widened since its inception.

Funding Controversies

One of the largest public school controversies is that of school choice. With the increased use of standardized tests, a movement in favor of school choice has arisen; but there is a debate as to the best system for providing school choice to parents of public school students, especially in the urban areas.

Charter schools were created as a means to increase school choice. These schools are typically set up by groups of citizens to provide an alternative to the public school. If parents choose to place their children into a charter school, they take the funding directed to the public school with them. For example, if a district spends $4,000 per pupil, then that $4,000 is taken from the neighborhood school and given to the charter school.

Charter schools have grown in popularity over the last decade. Some are created to serve a select group of students. For example, the "Life Skills Center," located in Cincinnati, Ohio, concentrates on at-risk students. Most of these students have experienced problems while attending public schools and are trying to receive their high school diploma.

Charter schools have affected public schools due to lost funding, inasmuch as most funding formulas are based on student enrollment: The greater the number of students who enroll in charter schools, the less money is available for public schools. For example, even if a student has enrolled in a charter school, the public school is responsible for providing the student's transportation to that charter school as well as other services such as testing for exceptionalities. Some had thought, and still believe, that charter schools are a "magic pill" that will force public schools to perform better or lose funding. So far, however, research on charters schools has not supported this position. As noted earlier in this book, the performance and organization of some charter schools have fallen short of the expectations of charter school proponents.

Given some public dissatisfaction with public school performance, and in response to sectors of the public who wanted religion placed back in schools, some lawmakers have successfully crafted legislation that has created an educational voucher system. Privately funded voucher systems have been in place for years. For example, they have been supported by Walton Family Foundation, Inc., which is associated with the Wal-Mart Corporation. Wealthy individuals and private companies have donated money to provide the means for lower socioeconomic students to attend private schools. These private voucher systems allow urban students to attend a school that their parents may not have been able to afford. Private vouchers do not affect public schools, however, since the funding is provided by the organization rather then coming from public school coffers.

Educational vouchers can take other forms as well. For example, the state of Pennsylvania has started a program that allows businesses to donate to a private voucher system the taxes that would otherwise have gone toward the public system. This program affects public schools in the same manner as charter school systems inasmuch as available dollars are taken away from the district budgets and sent to private schools and programs.

Voucher programs have been started in Cleveland, Ohio, in Milwaukee, Wisconsin, and in a statewide system in Florida. In the Cleveland system, students are given about $2,500 each to apply toward the tuition of any school that they wish to attend, including religious schools.

Critics contend that vouchers drain off money from the public school system—a system that already lacks not only funding but also motivated students with supportive parents. They also maintain that the majority of these tax-supported dollars go to parochial and other religious-affiliated schools. They may very well be right, given that the parochial school system is the largest recipient of voucher dollars due to the scarcity of nonreligious-affiliated private schools.

The argument that educational vouchers violate the separation of church and state, based on the First Amendment and the establishment clause of the Constitution, has recently been laid to rest by the U.S. Supreme Court. In a divided decision (5–4), the Court ruled that the Cleveland educational voucher system did not violate the Constitution. This ruling reversed decisions made by lower federal courts and gave a lift to educational voucher proponents. It is too early to gauge the consequences of this decision, but it has the potential to have a dramatic effect on urban public school districts.

Funded and Unfunded Mandates

A mandate is a policy change that is required by law. Mandates usually come down from an elected legislature in the form of policy. For example, there were many policy changes indicated in the Individuals with Disabilities Education Act (IDEA) that required significant changes in the way public schools place students with special needs.

According to IDEA, a special needs student must be placed in the least restrictive environment. This means that, among other things, the public school must make physical changes to the building that allow students in wheelchairs access to the school. Some schools have had to add elevators to the existing structures in order to accommodate these students. IDEA also affects students without physical challenges. Students with other special needs, such as behavior or learning challenges, must also be placed in the least restrictive environment. In some cases these students are placed in classrooms with a tutor or other assistant who accompanies them throughout the school day. Often the funds needed to make the mandated changes are not included in the original legislation and the tab must be funded through the regular funding of the school district.

IDEA is funded through annual appropriations. This means that if the government were to shut down due to a failure to pass a budget, then the funding for special education would stop. Educators are also worried because the funding for IDEA can be increased or decreased at the whim of Congress and the president who signs the budget; but the support for these students must continue.

Currently there is a fight to fully fund IDEA, which would make the funding mandatory. Given the current recession and the possibility of more bad economic news in the future, educators want the full funding to ensure that they have the tools to educate students with special needs.

Politics has entered the fray on this issue. Several recent presidents have successfully influenced Congress to create federal tax cuts. However, after these cuts are enacted there is often less money left over for domestic programs such as IDEA. Traditionally, Democrats push for full funding while Republicans have fought against such programs.

Republicans argue that instead of new funding, IDEA needs reform. Republican lawmakers contend that, with the reading initiatives of the No Child Left Behind Act, there will be fewer special education students. They also argue that there are too many students identified as having learning disabilities and that this is one of the main problems with the needed funding levels. In other words, if there were fewer students who met the qualifications of the provisions of IDEA, then fewer dollars would be needed.

There is a higher cost facing urban schools due to the larger numbers of students identified as learning disabled in these schools. Urban districts have a disproportionately larger percentage of the student population identified as students with special needs who qualify for the benefits of IDEA. Educators contend that the huge cost of providing intensive medical and education services to students with severe disabilities is a huge problem that takes up a large percentage of available education dollars.

As noted, one of the main aspects of IDEA concerns the district's provision of the least restrictive environment for students. This has led to reforms such as inclusion, whereby special needs students are placed in a regular education classroom with or without a tutor to help those students adapt. In the past, special needs students were sometimes shelved away in institutions or kept all day in the same class away from regular education students.

The number of self-contained special education classrooms has decreased. Inclusion is more widespread than ever before, but this reform comes with a price. The salary of tutors to stay with students all day long is considerable, and the cost of providing educational services to students with medical conditions such as spina bifida and cerebral palsy is prohibitive. All of these changes are funded by the local school district. In many cases, the legislative body that created these changes did not increase the funding to the district to pay for them.

Another mandate example in Ohio is the implementation of the Ohio Proficiency Test (OPT), a statewide standardized test that is used as a gateway for graduation. A student who does not pass all five parts of the OPT in high school does not get to graduate. In addition, the OPT is one of the largest factors in rating school districts. Districts that do poorly on the OPT are placed in certain categories such as Academic Emergency. In such cases, if the districts do not show satisfactory improvement they run the risk of being taken over by the state.

When the OPT was first mandated, there was no extra funding for tutors, study materials, or additional staff training; yet the individual districts were forced to implement the system by law. All changes to meet the requirements of the OPT were funded at the district level. Urban schools were hit especially hard since the school population needed additional help and more resources to pass the tests.

Indeed, urban districts are hit harder by unfunded mandates than their suburban counterparts. Typically the buildings in such districts are older and, in any case, were not built with the needs of exceptional children in mind. In the Cincinnati Public School District in Ohio, for example, many of the high schools are close to 100 years old. These buildings did not initially have ramps, elevators, or even adequate electrical wiring for computers. And, obviously, the funding for these improvements takes money away from academic materials and resources in the classrooms.

CONCLUSIONS

The challenges of providing adequate educational funding are many and the answers to these challenges are in dispute. Many feel that simply throwing money into urban districts will not solve the problems associated with declines in achievement, attendance, and graduation levels—and that solutions can be attained, instead, through implementation of free market reforms that allow for more school choice and competition.

It may be too early to draw conclusions about school choice and its effect on funding and school politics. Different groups interpret preliminary results in different ways. The Government Accounting Office concluded in 2002 that educational vouchers do not have a large impact on student achievement, but conservative groups are quick to point out the support of vouchers in the African American community.

Charter schools were once thought to be a way to provide choice and force lower-achieving school districts to make needed reforms. However, research and achievement statistics provide little evidence to support this assertion.

Others in the educational establishment contend that additional funding is needed, especially in the urban centers. It is often cheaper to completely replace an older school building than to update that building to meet the needs of physically challenged students, to upgrade its electrical systems, and to make other physical changes such as adding air conditioning and removing asbestos.

The environment from which urban students come has a dramatic effect on their achievement. For example, in the case of *Abbot v. Burke*, the New Jersey supreme court made it clear that disadvantaged students in urban schools need more than just equity in funding and program quality. They also require supplemental and compensatory assistance. Indeed, this ruling should help all to realize that true equality of education will never be realized without additional assistance.

Both sides have valid points, and both agree on the premise that changes need to be made. Throwing money at the problems in urban public education will not by itself fix these problems; yet it is naive to think that they can be solved without additional funding. Those who dispute either conclusion should heed the words of Horace Mann, who in 1848 wrote the following in his Twelfth Report to the Massachusetts Board of Education:

> That Political Economy, therefore, which busies itself about capital and labor, supply and demand, interest and rents, favorable and unfavorable balances of trade, but leaves out of account the element of a widespread mental development, is nought but stupendous folly. The greatest of all the arts in political economy is to change a consumer into a producer; and the next greatest is to increase the producing power—an end to be directly attained, by increasing his intelligence. (quoted in Alexander and Alexander, 1992, p. 27)

Changes need to be made as well in the politics of urban education. It would be nice to think that all who are engaged in the debate over urban public education have the best interests of the students in mind, but this is simply not the case. Many are involved in protecting the financial interests of their constituents rather than the educational interests of the students who attend these schools. There is a need for additional high-quality comprehensive research in public schools. Elected officials need to read the research that has already been studied to get a better picture as to the source of these problems and, ultimately, to improve on the suggested solutions.

As for the case being made for school choice and educational vouchers, we would like to see some experimental research that fairly compares parochial schools with regular urban public schools. A study could be set up that identifies several urban public schools and several parochial schools in the same geographic area. Students would be randomly assigned, and both types of schools would receive the same amount of funding. Each individual school in the study would be responsible for providing all of the services associated with public education, including transportation, special education services, free and reduced meals, and testing; each school would have to accept all of the students assigned to that school; and each school would not be allowed to remove any student from the school. Over a three-year period the students would be tracked on achievement as measured by required statewide-standardized tests as well as attendance, discipline, and student attitude surveys. Indeed, only through comprehensive research that meets the parameters of fair competition can the issue of school choice be properly assessed and judged on its own merits.

REFERENCES

Alexander, Kern, and Alexander, M. David. *American Public School Law*, 3rd ed. St. Paul, MN: West Publishing Company, 1992.

American Federation of Teachers. "Once and for All." Washington, DC: 2003.

Doherty, Kathryn M. "Changing Urban Education: Defining the Issues." In C. Stone (Ed.), *Changing Urban Education*, pp. 225–249. Lawrence: University Press of Kansas, 1998.

Hasci, Timothy A. *Children as Pawns: The Politics of Educational Reform*. Cambridge, MA: Harvard University Press, 2002.

Orr, Marion. "The Challenge of School Reform in Baltimore: Race, Jobs, and Politics." In C. Stone (Ed.), *Changing Urban Education*, pp. 93–117. Lawrence: University Press of Kansas, 1998.

Chapter Seven

✎ Current Trends and Issues in Urban Schools

A NATION AT RISK

How did our nation's urban schools become associated with such negative images of minority children attending schools in dilapidated buildings taught by incompetent teachers who belong to greedy unions? Some believe that these beliefs and images were compounded by the *Nation at Risk* report.

Under the Reagan administration public schools in general, and urban public schools specifically, came under attack. The secretary of education at the time, Terrell Bell, created a commission to study the perceived decline of the U.S. public education system. The commission came to be known as the National Commission on Excellence in Education. The commission spent two years gathering data and published a report called *A Nation at Risk*. The report was sensationalized by the media and accepted without question by the general public.

The authors of the report cited examples of how our international allies were outdoing our children on standardized tests, especially in the areas of math and science. They also contended that the U.S. educational system was experiencing negative events such as low graduation rates, the "dumbing down" of curriculum and textbooks, and poor-quality teachers.

The education establishment considered the report to be another attack on public education by the Reagan administration. The educational establishment was wary of the Reagan administration because it had harshly criticized the public school system as well as pressed for changes such as school prayer and tax credits (vouchers) for parents. (Both were intended to promote school choice.) Educators maintained that the problems of public schools were a result of a larger phenomenon—the socioeconomic status of the students and their parents—and argued that until the overwhelming problems of poverty were solved there would continue to be a disparity between rich and poor students and districts.

A Nation at Risk has had an immense influence on public school systems. Different states took different approaches in their attempts to address the concerns cited in the report. Efforts to improve the quality of teachers, site-based management, and additional standardized tests were implemented after the report.

President George H. W. Bush continued the effort to reform the U.S. educational system with his *America 2000* program. Included in the program's broad goals for education were the following:

➥ All children in America will start school ready to learn.
➥ The high school graduation rate will increase to at least 90 percent.
➥ American students will leave grades four, eight, and twelve having demonstrated competency in challenging subject matter including English, mathematics, science, history and geography.
➥ Every school in America will ensure that students use their minds well, so that they may be prepared for responsible citizenship, further learning, and productive employment in our modern economy.
➥ U.S. students will be the first in the world in science and mathematics achievement.
➥ Every adult American will be literate and will possess the knowledge and skills necessary to compete in a global economy and exercise the rights and responsibilities of citizenship.
➥ Every school in America will be free of drugs and violence and will offer a disciplined environment conducive to learning. (*America 2000*, 1991)

President Clinton adopted many of the same goals and changed the name of the program to *Goals 2000*. Although teachers' unions held much more clout during the Clinton administration, they were unable to change some of the aims of *America 2000* or *Goals 2000*. These programs identified problems, but they made no effort to help states to solve them. School districts were expected to deal with these challenges without additional financial support and guidance from the federal government.

It seemed that some expected the urban public schools to improve and meet standards without any movement toward solving huge problems such as poverty. The perceived lack of importance of education in the household, poor nutrition, lead poisoning, and other problems of poverty not faced by more affluent districts were not, and still are not, taken into account when comparisons about academic achievement are being made.

NO CHILD LEFT BEHIND ACT

During the 2000 presidential election, George W. Bush proposed new education standards to improve the perceived mediocre education system. Bush won the presidency and was able to broker a bipartisan deal that increased the amount of federal funding for public schools, along with several new layers of standardized testing.

President Bush signed the No Child Left Behind Act in January 2002. As noted in Chapter 6, this act is actually the reauthorization of the Elementary and Secondary Education Act (ESEA). A large number of the changes to ESEA deal with assessment. States are required to test children during several different stages of their academic careers. The tests are state-created and must assess reading and math proficiency. The requirements for testing will begin in 2007, but many states have already created tests to track achievement.

School districts are required to show adequate progress. In particular, they must issue annual report cards to the public. These report cards must contain information on student achievement, race, and disability, as well as comparison data with other schools in the district and state. Any school that receives Title I funds but has not made adequate progress in student achievement for two years in a row is identified as a school in need of improvement. The district in which it is located is then required to develop an improvement plan. The new plan must be implemented in the district during the school year immediately following identification of the school in question. If a district continues to struggle for four years, then radical steps can be taken. These include replacing the entire school staff, forcing the implementation of a new curriculum, decreasing the management authority at the school level, appointing an outsider to advise the school, extending the school year or day, or restructuring the school. In addition, the parents of students in the school must be notified. The students will then be allowed to transfer to a better-performing school and the failing school must provide transportation to the other school. Two problems with this provision is that there may be a shortage of performing schools to transfer into and the more affluent suburban schools may not allow the transfer of students to their districts.

Another component of the No Child Left Behind Act affects the qualification of teachers and assistants. By the year 2005, a qualified teacher must teach every child. This means that all teachers must be certified by the state to teach in their subject area. This requirement also applies to long-term substitutes. Districts are required to notify parents in cases where a teacher who is not qualified has been teaching their child for a period of over four months. In addition, as of the 2002–2003 school year, instructor assistants must have at least a high school diploma to teach, and after this year they must hold an associate's degree or must have completed two years of college. Exceptions can be made if the state creates a test that ensures that instructor assistants are competent to assist in the classroom. Current instructional assistants have several years to attain the needed credentials before they are forced from their current positions.

Critics of the No Child Left Behind Act contend that there is too much emphasis on testing and not enough on alternative assessment, and that the huge body of research on how alternate assessments are conducive for minority and poor students and its connections to true academic achievement has been ignored. In addition, experts complain that the year-to-year deviations that typically occur in standardized test results can unfairly identify a school as failing for statistical reasons rather than educational reasons (Fletcher, 2003). But the problem with this act that most critics cite is the requirement to track achievement levels in five racial and ethnic subgroups, low-income students, and students with limited knowledge of English. Any drop in the scores of students in any of these categories over two consecutive years can identify a school as failing, even if scores in other categories go up (Fletcher, 2003). If, for example, a school experiences a drop in academic performance among its African American population one year and a drop among its Hispanic population the next year, then that school will be identified as low-performing even if the scores for its African American population improve after the first year. The problem is even more pronounced in larger districts. Even in a suburban school, if a small population of students is tracked under the No Child Left Behind Act, judgment will be passed on the school based solely on the academic progress of those students—even if the majority of the school demonstrates large gains in achievement in every category.

Given the problems of students in urban schools, this act could have serious consequences. Schools will be punished if they do not show steady across-the-board achievement; yet they may be unable to meet these requirements because they do not have the resources they need to improve. There is a great potential for a vicious cycle of low achievement and reduced funding for schools that need additional funding to meet the requirements.

Some individual states are concerned over the requirements and implementation of this act. For example, North Carolina has a highly re-garded school-accountability system that is credited with improving student achievement and closing racial and economic achievement. State officials are worried that, when the state is fully under the scrutiny of the No Child Left Behind Act, 60 percent of its schools will not meet the federal standard. Kentucky has some of the same concerns. Al-though it has a critically acclaimed accountability system, it will have to make significant changes to meet the new federal guidelines.

Some states are actually refusing to change their education sys-tem. Louisiana is one example. Under the No Child Left Behind Act, up to 85 percent of Louisiana schools would be considered low-performing schools within three years (Fletcher, 2003). The governor of Louisiana has threatened to fight the law so that it does not wreck the state's cur-rent system.

Other states are concerned that they will not be able to continue with their own reforms. For example, Mississippi, which has consis-tently been ranked toward the bottom of the fifty states with respect to the quality of public education, recently ensured that every one of its public school classrooms has a computer that is connected to the Inter-net; yet state officials fear that a large percentage of Mississippi's schools will be identified as low performing despite recent gains in students' achievement.

Another criticism of the No Child Left Behind Act concerns fund-ing. The law boosted federal funds for education by $4 billion, but the 2.8 percent increase that the president is seeking for the current budget will do little to help schools meet the requirements of the law given the challenges of finding and paying for teachers and assistants who meet the standards outlined in the act as well as other requirements.

STANDARDIZED TESTING

Public education has changed dramatically over the last fifty years, and it continues to do so. Changes in funding, teacher accountability, school accountability, dress codes, and security issues, as well as the changing demographics of student populations, have challenged educators to keep up.

One of the most important changes in public education concerns the importance of, and attention on, standardized testing. Of course, standardized testing is nothing new. It has long been used as a tool to gauge student progress and aptitude. Recently, though, standardized tests have become high stakes.

A standardized test is a test that is taken by several different populations of students at the same time. For example, the Ohio Proficiency Test (OPT) is given during a certain week in the school year. All public school students in the state of Ohio must take the test at that time.

Scores on standardized tests can be either normed on a preset score or compared to those of the other students who took the same test. For example, an Ohio student must score at least 200 to pass the citizenship portion of the OPT.

The U.S. army originally used standardized testing during World War I. Having experienced a large influx of men, the army needed a tool to sort soldiers into the jobs for which they were best suited. For example, if a potential soldier had a high aptitude for math, as determined by a standardized test, that individual could become a member of the artillery rather than the infantry.

Today the U.S. Armed Forces still use a standardized test called the Armed Services Vocational Aptitude Battery (ASVAB). This test is used to determine the occupations for which potential soldiers are qualified. For example, if a potential soldier scores low on the test, he may qualify only for infantry; but if he scores high, he can choose from several different occupations or even attend officer candidate school.

Standardized tests have influenced American education since the middle part of the twentieth century. U.S. officials, dismayed when the Soviet Union launched Sputnik and when they learned that our students did not perform as well in science and math as the Japanese on standardized tests, insisted that an increased emphasis be placed on science and math in schools.

Such cross-nation comparisons are not valid, however. It is unfair to compare Japanese and American students because the Japanese tend to place a higher value on education than we do. For example, Japanese students attend school six days a week compared to our five days a week, and Japanese students often hire tutors to better prepare themselves for the standardized test that will determine whether they are allowed to enter the state-run universities. Japan also has a less diverse student population than the United States. Finally, standardized test scores cannot be compared across nations because the United States uses the entire student population to compare scores whereas other countries use a select student population.

Currently, standardized testing is characterized by a high-stakes approach, especially in education. Rather than being used as tools to determine areas that need attention, the tests have become thresholds that affect individual students as well as school systems. In Ohio, for example, it was proposed that if students did not pass the fourth-grade section of the OPT, they could not proceed to the fifth grade. This policy was changed when it was discovered that close to half of the fourth-grade population would be retained. (High school students must still pass the Ninth-Grade Proficiency Test by the end of their senior year or they do not receive a diploma.)

Ohio also rates school districts annually on twenty-two different criteria. The OPT is the leading indicator of a perceived good or bad district. There are five ratings for public school districts: Effective, Excellent, Continuous Improvement, Academic Watch, and Academic Emergency. If the district reaches the Effective level, it receives additional funding from the state; but if it is rated as Academic Emergency, the district is in danger of being taken over by the state.

The effects of standardized tests on urban school districts have been dramatic. It is no surprise to those who understand the relationship between the results of these tests and socioeconomic and minority status that the large urban districts always rate at the bottom. The other two comparisons, attendance and graduation rates, also put these districts at a disadvantage.

Many states are using tests to rank and evaluate individual schools and school districts. Funding is sometimes pulled from a district that is doing poorly. In fact, in some cases involving low test scores, the state has come in and taken over the district. And in at least one instance, voucher programs have been based on test scores. Under the terms of Florida's educational voucher system, when a school does poorly on standardized tests, the parents of the students have the right to use vouchers to send their children to other schools, including religious-affiliated schools.

Proponents of high-stakes standardized testing contend that it identifies poorly performing schools. They believe that, in the past, schools used social promotion to graduate students who did not have the basic skills needed to perform after high school; but by relying on a test that measures basic skills, citizens are assured that every student who graduates has the needed tools to perform in society.

Critics contend that most standardized tests use a white, upper-middle-class style of language that discriminates against minority students and that, because these tests are biased, they are not a true measure of students' achievements. They also believe that standardized tests may be useful tools but should not stand as a barrier to attainment of a diploma or be utilized to make retention decisions.

Educators, too, are concerned about the narrowing of curriculum that occurs with high-stakes standardized testing. Typically, certain standards are measured by these tests and, owing to the importance of high scores, districts have shifted the emphasis to these standards and only these standards. Some educators also fear that students receive a very narrow curriculum that does not allow for the exploration of multiple intelligences, critical thinking, and problem solving.

Science teachers, for example, like to rely upon inquiry-based processes, whereby students learn from doing rather than by watching the teacher perform an experiment. But a highly structured curriculum does not allow for such processes—and due to the importance of test scores, teachers are sometimes forced to resort to other methods, such as repeated drills and worksheets, to ensure that their students are prepared for the tests. As a result, students have insufficient time to explore their scientific interests and, even worse, do not look forward to science class (Jorgenson and Vanosdall, 2002).

STATE TAKEOVER OF SCHOOLS

Due to the amount of criticism experienced by urban public schools after the release of critical reports such as *A Nation at Risk,* efforts have been made by various branches of government to take over districts that are perceived to be failing. Virtually all of the districts taken over by government agencies are urban with large minority populations.

Some of the more high-profile takeovers have occurred in Chicago and Cleveland. In these instances, the state government has decided that the school districts have too many problems to solve on their own. These problems include financial issues as well as high dropout rates, low graduation rates, and low standardized test scores. In one case, that of West Virginia, an entire state school system was taken over: For more than fifteen years this school system has been overseen by a district judge. Complaints had been brought in front of this judge about inequity in funding as well as poor academic performance throughout the state.

TEACHER ISSUES

A teacher shortage is expected to hit the nation within the next few years. The problem of finding qualified teachers has already affected many school districts. There is a severe shortage of math, science, and special education teachers, and it is estimated that one out of every four middle and high school teachers are not trained in the subject they are teaching.

The newly passed No Child Left Behind Act gives states some flexibility in finding and retaining teachers. First, it allows states to permit alternative certification that will let nonteaching professionals gain a teaching certificate in a shorter period of time than if they attended a traditional teaching college. Second, it provides for merit pay to retain good teachers and bonuses for those who are willing to teach subjects that are experiencing the highest level of shortages such as science, math, and special education.

The problem is worst in urban schools. It is estimated that, in some districts, over 50 percent of the teachers are teaching out of their field. In addition, the retention rate of new teachers is falling below three years, and annual turnover in most large urban districts now totals 300–400 teachers.

More attention has been paid to the quality of teachers in urban public schools over the last few decades. As some schools are identified as failing, some critics of public education blame the teachers themselves for the shortcomings. These negative feelings toward teachers are sometimes based on the fact that most teachers belong to a union. The majority of suburban public school teachers belong to the National Education Association (NEA) while the majority of urban school teachers belong to the American Federation of Teachers (AFT). NEA is an association and is less like a labor union than the AFT. The AFT is part of the AFL-CIO. AFT local unions are much more likely to use a labor strike as a tool when negotiating new contracts. Labor unions in general have been attacked by conservative politicians. Teachers' unions have therefore been blamed for the perceived failure of public schools. In addition, because these unions are opposed to educational vouchers and charter schools, they are often accused of having a "monopoly" on public education.

Since the circulation of *A Nation at Risk*, some members of the public have called for a system to rate teachers. In years past, teachers had to earn just a bachelor's degree, which would then serve them until retirement; they were not required to gain additional skills or advanced training. Today, however, teachers must pass the National Teacher Examination (NTE)in order to teach. The NTE is a standardized test that pre-service teachers are required to take. It consists of a general test that all teachers must pass as well as a test that measures content-specific knowledge. Teachers who fail either of these tests are not allowed to become certified classroom teachers. In Ohio specifically, all new teachers also have to undergo classroom observations and attain a master's degree by their tenth year of teaching.

Some school administrators and college officials feel that being a student teacher is not enough experience to prepare teachers for teaching, especially in an urban setting. Some colleges have decided to create five-year training programs in place of the traditional four years for pre-service teachers. In these new systems, students spend the fifth year as an intern and work on attaining a master's degree while they teach half-time. They also get paid half the salary of a full-time teacher.

Some colleges have also found that new teachers have trouble adjusting to an urban setting. At Miami University in Ohio, pre-service teachers are required to spend half of their student teacher experience in a suburban setting and half of their experience in an urban school.

As noted in Chapter 5, districts themselves have started to take steps to ensure that all classroom teachers are highly qualified. Cincinnati Public Schools in Ohio have created a Teacher Evaluation System (TES) requiring teachers to undergo an annual evaluation as well as a comprehensive evaluation every five years. Under TES, teachers who qualify under the highest category receive a pay bonus, whereas those who are not doing well may experience a reduction in pay and are given an additional year of comprehensive evaluation to improve. If they do not improve after that second year, they are dismissed from the district.

Even though the Cincinnati Federation of Teachers (CFT) helped to create this system, the rank and file members of the union voted not to tie the evaluation to the pay scale. Most members felt that the system was not adequately prepared. They also expressed concern over the fact that after the pilot program was instituted the majority of the teachers qualified for bonuses, yet the district had insufficient money to pay the increases for all qualified district teachers.

SCHOOL AND CURRICULUM ISSUES

Because the No Child Left Behind Act stipulates that the federal government will help fund only those educational practices that work, more educational systems will be "prepackaged." In short, districts will be forced to choose an educational system that dictates what to teach and how it is to be taught. Most curriculum systems do not allow much in the way of academic freedom.

The public backlash against perceived failing schools has initiated changes in several states. As noted earlier, the Cleveland Public School District was taken over by the state of Ohio based on poor performance. And in New York, new legislation placed control over the New York City Public Schools in the hands of the mayor of New York City. The mayor, in turn, chose the schools' chancellor as well as seven other members of the new thirteen-member school board.

As discussed in Chapter 6, the rise in power of conservative and religious organizations has also had an impact on urban public schools. In Kansas, for example, people opposed to teaching evolution were elected to the state board of education and succeeded in eliminating evolution from state standards. Kansas reversed itself after a few years when new members were elected to the state board of education. Similar efforts to reduce the influence of evolution have affected Ohio, where board members tried, with partial success, to change the science curriculum to include intelligent design. (Intelligent design supports the concept that the events that created life on earth are too complex to have happened randomly, so a higher power must have directed it.) Proponents of intelligent design wanted it to be taught in addition to evolution. The Ohio Department of Education compromised by allowing science teachers to talk about alternatives to evolution and to teach that evolution is a much-debated theory.

SCHOOL CHOICE

Critics of urban public education believe that school choice is the most important tool for forcing schools to change for the better. The school-choice option most commonly chosen is charter schools—publicly funded schools that are formed by groups of citizens, organizations, or even public schools themselves. Students who attend a charter school essentially use the funding that would otherwise have gone to a public school. Charter schools and public schools compete for students in order to get needed funding. Some charter schools are created to deal with a specific population of students. For example, the Life Skills Center, located in Cincinnati, Ohio, was set up to deal with students who are unable to perform in the public school system.

Critics point out that, on average, charter schools do not perform as well as public schools on standardized tests, and that some charter schools have problems attracting qualified teachers due to the fact that they cannot match the public school pay scale for teachers. Charter schools have also come under attack for being underfinanced and failing to meet state policy requirements. For example, in Ohio, the percentage of students who pass the fourth-grade proficiency test is about 16 percent in charter schools, compared to the state average of about 45 percent. In addition, all but one of the Ohio urban school districts had a better passage rate than the statewide charter school average.

Charter school proponents defend the academic record of these schools. They claim that the students who enter their doors are already one or two years behind the average and that the schools are not set up to deal specifically with these students. Urban public school educators counter by arguing that urban public districts draw from the same populations as the charter schools.

Charter schools face a great many challenges. In some cases the school officials are not prepared for the funding challenges associated with a school. For example, the Ohio Attorney General's office requested that the court freeze the assets of a Cincinnati charter school, the Greater Cincinnati Community Academy, as of November 2002, after the school refused to allow the state to inspect the school and its records. A state audit had shown that the school officials misappropriated $229,007 and that the school operated at a $1.6 million loss during the 2000–2001 school year (Ludlow, 2002).

For-Profit Education

One trend affecting school choice has to do with for-profit schools and organizations. Several attempts have been made to create a for-profit school system and remove the bureaucracy from the public school system. For example, Education Alternatives Inc. tried to run the Hartford, Connecticut School system, but it failed. White Hat Management Company currently runs twenty-five charter schools in Ohio and Arizona, but the teachers' unions in Ohio have sued the state claiming that it is illegal to allow a for-profit company to run a charter school in Ohio.

The largest for-profit education company is Edison Schools Inc., which controlled 133 public schools in the United States at one time. There was speculation that one out of every ten public schools would be run by the Edison Company by the year 2020, but expectations for this outcome have faded due to setbacks recently experienced by the company.

Edison officials argue that they can run a school more effectively and for less money than the public school districts can. The Edison Company extends the school day as well as the school year. It also uses a standardized curriculum and a rigid class schedule.

The Edison Company has run schools in San Francisco, Dallas, and Boston (among other cities) and recently signed a contract with the state of Pennsylvania to run twenty of the Philadelphia public schools after they were taken over because of poor test scores. As noted above, however, the schools under the Edison system have not always performed well. For example, the San Francisco school district removed the charter from the Edison Company in June 2001, citing the fact that the school had a huge teacher turnover. Teachers were not happy with the extended school day and year, the emphasis on standardized test preparation, and the regimented curriculum. The district also found evidence that Edison officials had worked to remove disruptive or poor-performing students from the school. Apparently their belief was that these students would not do well on standardized tests and thus would drag down the school average. Unfortunately, the California Board of Education renewed the charter for this school and the Edison Company continued to run the school. It was recently ranked 75th out of 75 schools in the San Francisco Public School System.

The Edison Company is also in financial trouble. Its stock once sold for $38 but now is barely high enough to keep it listed on the New York Stock Exchange. In addition, the company has been accused of improper bookkeeping and ten class action lawsuits have been filed against it (Woodward, 2002).

Vouchers

With the recent favorable ruling on educational vouchers by the Supreme Court, the number of publicly funded educational voucher systems is expected to increase substantially—especially given the support that vouchers have with President George W. Bush. The No Child Left Behind Act gives parents the option of removing their children from failing schools. The problem, however, is that there are not enough high-achieving private, public, and charter schools to accommodate these students.

Despite the favorable ruling, voucher advocates do not see a huge increase in voucher systems. They cite the fact that thirty states have had voucher initiatives on the ballot over the last few years but none of these were voted in by the public.

Some of the most ardent supporters of educational vouchers include the Republican Party, conservative organizations such as the Heritage Foundation, and various religious organizations such as the Christian Coalition. Supporters feel that educational vouchers allow the parents of underprivileged students the same opportunities as the parents of well-to-do students. They also claim that vouchers are considered "saviors" by the parents of minority students, who make up the majority of the urban public school population.

There is evidence that the African American community also supports educational vouchers. Organizations such as the Black Alliance for Educational Options (BAEO) claim that the majority of African Americans endorse vouchers on the grounds that they help to desegregate the public schools by allowing mostly minority students to experience a private school education. These organizations also argue that black parents should have the same opportunity as white parents when it comes to school choice.

Indeed, proponents of educational vouchers believe that parents should have choices for their children. If the district is not adequately educating their children, they should be able to send the children to the school of their choice. Proponents also claim that the increased competition will force public schools to improve. They seem to perceive a public school monopoly that needs an incentive to improve. In other words, if public schools cannot attract more students, they will receive less funding and be forced to make cuts in staffing.

Voucher opponents dispute the claim that groups such as the BAEO are mainstream. First, they argue that such groups do not represent the views of most African Americans but, rather, are simply conservative organizations that represent an anti–public school stance.

Second, opponents claim that educational vouchers have created a segregated Catholic school system. With the movement of white students from the urban parochial schools to the suburbs, minorities now comprise the overwhelming majority of urban Catholic school students, whereas the majority of suburban Catholic school children are white.

Third, opponents assert that the dollar amount of vouchers will never allow poor students to attend affluent private schools, which can charge over $10,000 a year in tuition. The same schools use entrance exams, record reviews, and interviews to ensure that incoming students will be high achieving. Given such entrance restrictions, as well as the transportation problems facing urban students, the possibility that voucher recipients will attend the better-rated private schools is remote.

Fourth, opponents argue that vouchers are unconstitutional, based on the premise that they violate the separation of church and state. They insist that public funds should not be spent to provide religious instruction, but this argument has been rendered impotent given the recent U.S. Supreme Court ruling.

Finally, opponents contend that vouchers drain off some of the highest-achieving students. This lowers the potential for public schools to do as well on proficiency tests, furthering the loss of revenue and the flight of motivated students.

Here is an example in support of this position:

> In a large urban city area there is a high achieving parochial high
> school that I will call St. Y. In this same area there is also an urban pub-
> lic school that I will call Public P.
> In order to be accepted to St. Y a student must meet tuition require-

ments that are in excess of $10,000 a year. In order to attend St. Y potential students must pass an admissions examination. In order to attend Public P they must show up.

The majority of the parents of St. Y students are college graduates. The majority of Public P parents are not. The majority of St. Y parents are upper middle class or higher. The majority of the students who attend public P qualify for free or reduced lunches.

Students who demonstrate attendance, achievement, or discipline problems are expelled from St. Y, and Public P must accept these students. Public P can take administrative action for students who demonstrate disciplinary problems, but the stats of these students count on the statewide ranking criteria.

St. Y does not provide special education services. Public P must provide special education services to all qualifying students, including those attending St. Y. The students who attend St. Y must provide their own transportation. The district pays for transportation services for Public P students.

The overwhelming majority of students who attend St. Y are Caucasian. The majority of students who attend Public P are African American. St. Y students are expected to purchase a laptop computer that meets the school criteria. The students who attend Public P are not.

Both of these high schools are held to the same federal and state standards.

THE CHANGING FACE OF HIGH SCHOOL

Given the challenges faced by urban schools, major changes in the way they do business have begun. One such change is the shift toward smaller schools. Studies have shown that large schools seem to "lose" students, who end up dropping out. Smaller schools, on the other hand, are designed to have a focus that will interest students.

The city of Chicago has created 130 new small public elementary and high schools since the mid-1990s. Some districts have created smaller schools from scratch while others have divided larger schools into smaller schools within the same building.

Due to the challenges of meeting proficiency requirements, neighborhood schools in the Cincinnati Public School District in Ohio have divided their student population into two parts: Preparatory Academy and Senior Institute. The Preparatory Academy includes students who have not passed the proficiency tests. These students receive intense preparation to pass the required tests. Once they have passed these tests, they move on to the Senior Institute. The Senior Institute, in turn, may offer either traditional college preparatory classes or a focus such as technology or business.

Although efforts at desegregation have been made following *Brown v. Board of Education,* the majority of the student population in urban schools consists of minorities, and attempts to combine urban districts with suburban districts have met with stiff political resistance.

One way of satisfying desegregation criteria is to create magnet schools, which, as noted earlier, are schools within a district that have a special concentration or theme. Some magnet schools are college preparatory in nature and require that potential students pass an entrance exam in order to be enrolled. Other magnet schools offer a different curriculum such as the Montessori and Paideia styles of learning. Still others have concentrations in certain subjects such as math and science.

Yet, unfortunately, segregation continues within urban schools and districts. The Civil Rights Project, which has been following trends in desegregation for three decades, has found that as of 2003 desegregation rates are the highest in history, with Latino students becoming the most segregated minority group. These rates reflect the fact that students are assigned to courses and schools based on gender and minority status. For example, there is still an inordinate number of white males in college preparatory, math, and science classes and programs, and, conversely, an inordinate number of minorities and males in special education classes and among those students most likely to be suspended from school. Clearly, both forms of segregation must be addressed in urban schools.

CONCLUSIONS

The challenges faced by urban districts are enormous and will not be solved through any one effort. For example, although an increase in funding is needed, it will not solve the deeper problems of poverty that interfere with the aims of increased achievement, attendance, and graduation numbers.

Indeed, truly effective school reform must address the issue of social equality before improvements can be realized. All of the players—students, teachers, administrators, and politicians—need to come together in the common cause of creating an education system that serves as a true equalizer for all. Unfortunately, not all of the stakeholders have joined this cause. Some lack the motivation or the political courage to conduct true reform.

There is a concern in the educational community that many of the decisions affecting urban public schools are being made by groups and individuals who do not live in urban areas and thus are unlikely to spend much time in an urban school. From time to time, in newspapers or on television, we see photos of politicians at urban schools. But it seems to some that these individuals are more concerned with having their picture taken than with making the courageous political and budget decisions required to make a real difference for at-risk students.

Recent efforts such as educational vouchers, charter schools, and increased standardized testing will not solve the problems facing urban public education. There is some validity to the argument that increased competition will force urban districts to improve. Educators must also look inward to ensure that all efforts are being made to improve achievement. But even with maximum efforts from the educational community, urban districts will still not see the gains that are needed to satisfy educational policies and standards mandated by elected legislatures.

The issues of poverty, social inequality, and poor motivation must be overcome before any other reforms are to bear fruit. All stakeholders must place the needs of the students above their own and be willing to consider other options and strategies that will ensure not only academic progress but also better ways to measure that progress.

REFERENCES

America 2000: An Education Strategy Sourcebook. U.S. Department of Education, Washington, D.C., 1991.

Civil Rights Project. "A Multiracial Society with Segregated Schools: Are We Losing the Dream?" Available online at www.civilrightsproject.harvard.edu.

Fletcher, Michael. "States Worry New Law Sets Schools Up to Fail." *Washington Post* (January 2, 2003). Available online at http://washingtonpost.com.

Jorgenson, Olaf, and Vanosdall, Rick. "The Death of Science? What We Risk in Our Rush Toward Standardized Testing and the Three R's." *Phi Delta Kappan* 83, no. 8 (April 2002): 601–605.

Ludlow, Randy. "Audit: School Finances a Mess." *Cincinnati Post* (April 15, 2002). Available online at http://www.cincypost.com/2002/apr/15/audit041502.htm.

Woodward, Tali. "Edison's Failing Grade" (June 2002). Available online at http://www.corpwatch.org/issues/PID.jsp?articleid=2688.

Chapter Eight

•❖ Selected Print and Nonprint Resources

This chapter provides a listing of articles, books, reports, and nonprint resources related to the topics covered in the book. Although the listing is by no means exhaustive, it contains information that should be useful for future research.

PRINT RESOURCES

Books and Articles

Assessment, Accountability, and Evaluation

Ascher, Carol. **"Testing Students in Urban Schools: Current Problems and New Directions."** Urban Diversity Series No. 100, 1990 (Eric Reproduction Service No. ED 322 283).

The author warns that standardized tests do not accurately measure poor minority students' achievement and thus recommends the use of performance-based assessments. She also postulates that portfolios and other types of assessment may actually improve urban education.

Ascher, Carol. **"Can Performance-Based Assessments Improve Urban Schooling?"** ERIC Digest Number 56. 1990 (Eric Reproduction Service No. ED 327 612).

The author offers suggestions as to how performance-based assessments can be used in place of standardized tests to more accurately evaluate poor minority students' academic achievement. Such assessments allow students to show mastery of skills, to use multiple ways of expression, and to demonstrate learning similar to that in real life. The author also includes examples of performance-based assessments.

Elford, George W. *Beyond Standardized Testing: Better Information for School Accountability and Management.* Lanham, MD: Scarecrow Education, 2002.

The author presents a model for utilizing standards and teacher judgment in place of standardized testing. This model utilizes computer-based scoring rubrics at the district level to make better decisions about students' achievement.

Falk, Beverly. *The Heart of the Matter: Using Standards and Assessment to Learn.* Portsmouth, NH: Heinemann, 2000.

The author discusses clear strategies for utilizing meaningful standards and assessment for student learning. Specifically, she provides ideas for the creation of performance assessments, information on how to utilize standards for effective and appropriate instruction, and guidelines for how to organize the curriculum and the standards.

Goodwin, A. Lin. (Ed.). *Assessment for Equity and Inclusion Embracing All Our Children.* New York: Routledge, 1997.

This book contributes to the debate between alternative and standardized assessment.

Graves, Donald. *Testing Is Not Teaching: What Should Count in Education.* Portsmouth, NH: Heinemann, 2002.

The author presents information on current high-stakes testing and its impact on teacher freedom and achievement. He also offers coping strategies for teachers.

Hasci, Timothy A. *Children as Pawns: The Politics of Educational Reform.* Cambridge, MA: Harvard University Press, 2002.

This book provides a concise historical review of the evaluation research and policy regarding five main topics: Head Start, bilingual education, class size, social promotion, and school funding. In particular, the author suggests that Head Start should be funded for all eligible children, that program and teacher quality is important, that small class sizes should be provided for disadvantaged children, and that there is no simple solution to social promotion.

Hillocks, Jr., George. *The Testing Trap: How State Writing Assessments Control Learning.* New York: Teachers College Press, 2002.

The author analyzes writing assessments in Illinois, Kentucky, Oregon, New York, and Texas and explains why they do not encourage quality writing. He also provides examples of how to evaluate writing assessments.

Johnson, Ruth S. *Using Data to Close the Achievement Gap: How to Measure Equity in Our Schools.* Thousand Oaks, CA: Corwin Press, 2002.

The author addresses five stages of equity reform and describes research findings in relation to the data collected on this subject.

Kohn, Alfie. *The Schools Our Children Deserve: Moving Beyond Traditional Classrooms and Tougher Standards.* Boston: Houghton Mifflin, 2000.

The author criticizes testing and the standards movement, backs up his criticisms with research and stories from classrooms, and gives suggestions for creating authentic learning.

McNeil, Linda. *Contradictions of School Reform: Educational Costs of Standardized Testing.* New York: Routledge, 2000.

The author critically examines standardized testing, describes how students and teachers are evaluated for effectiveness, and explains how this endangers effective teaching pedagogy.

McNeil, Linda, and Valenzuela, Angela. **"The Harmful Impact of the TAAS system of Testing in Texas: Beneath the Accountability Rhetoric"** (ERIC Reproduction Service No. ED 443 872).

The authors criticize the high-stakes Texas test known as TAAS and discuss its negative impact on urban minority and poor students.

National Education Association. **"Data-Driven Decision Making and School Report Cards."** January 2001. Available online at http://www.nea.org/accountability/reportcards.html.

This article provides a link to an example of a school report card. States use this format to disseminate information to the public on test scores, attendance, and dropout and graduation rates.

Ohanian, Susan. *What Happened to Recess and Why Are Our Children Struggling in Kindergarten?* New York: McGraw-Hill Trade, 2002.

The author discusses the issues involved in testing school children and describes what parents are doing to address this situation.

Paris, Scott, and Ayres, Linda. **"Becoming Reflective Students and Teachers with Portfolios and Authentic Assessment."** Washington, DC:

American Psychological Association, 1994 (ERIC Reproduction Service No. ED 378 166).

The authors demonstrate how students and teachers utilize portfolios and authentic assessment. A section on the characteristics of a reflective teacher is included.

Popham, W. James. *The Truth about Testing: An Educator's Call to Action.* Alexandria, VA: Association for Supervision and Curriculum Development, 2001.

This book is clear about the damage caused by high-stakes standardized tests. The author appeals to educators to prohibit these tests and provides guidelines for developing more appropriate means of testing and evidence gathering in the classroom.

Sacks, Peter. *Standardized Minds: The High Price of America's Testing Culture and What We Can Do to Change It.* Cambridge, MA: Perseus, 1999.

The author gives a good description of the history of testing and explains how standardized tests impact peoples' lives from birth to adulthood. He also demonstrates support for authentic assessment.

Schank, Roger. *Scrooge Meets Dick and Jane.* Mahwah, NJ: Lawrence Erlbaum Associates Inc., 2001.

The author writes a story in the fashion of Charles Dickens's *A Christmas Carol* in an attempt to inform readers about the future of education if the emphasis on standardized testing continues.

Swope, Kathy, and Miner, Barbara. *Failing Our Kids: Why the Testing Craze Won't Fix Our Schools.* Milwaukee: Rethinking Schools LTD, 2000.

This publication contains more than fifty articles about the effects of standardized tests and offers alternative ways to assess learning.

Curriculum

Banks, James, and Banks, Cherry (Eds.). *Handbook of Research on Multicultural Education.* New York: MacMillan Publishing Company, 1995.

These editors have compiled a reference book on the major theories and research on multicultural education. Each of the forty-seven chapters discusses a specific topic in multicultural education. Of specific note with respect to urban education is the information on ethnic groups, immigration policy, education of immigrants and ethnic groups, academic achievement, and school reform.

Barton-Calabrese, Angela, and Osborne, Margery. *Teaching Science in Diverse Settings: Marginalized Discourses and Classroom Practice.* New York: Peter Lang Publishing, 2001.

This book contains a collection of essays on the issue of liberating pedagogies to address the needs of diverse learners. Included are cases where instructors have applied theory to practical classroom experiences.

Compton-Lily, Catherine. *Reading Families: The Literate Lives of Urban Children.* New York: Teachers College Press, 2003.

The author examines society and racism in terms of their impact on the literacy of urban children and gives recommendations for supporting the literacy that urban children come to school with. She also suggests that reading needs to be examined in a higher societal context.

Delpit, Lisa. *Other People's Children: Cultural Conflict in the Classroom.* New York: The New Press. 1996.

This book consists of three main parts: Part One contains essays about literature and literacy, Part Two explains the impact of culture on education today, and Part Three discusses ways that society can make the changes that are needed to teach children from diverse cultures. The author stresses that all students should be encouraged to reach their fullest potential and that educators must make sure that skills and knowledge are available to all children, especially those from diverse cultures.

Devries, Rheta; Zan, Betty; Hildebrandt, Carolyn; Edmiaston, Rebecca; and Sales, Christina. *Developing Constructivist Early Childhood Principles and Activities: Practical Principles and Activities.* New York: Teachers College Press, 2002.

This book contains descriptive vignettes along with practical and theoretical information on constructivism. It is an extremely useful book for someone trying to better understand constructivist teaching and how it differs from other types.

Eisner, Elliot W. *The Kind of Schools We Need: Personal Essays.* Wesport, CT: Heinemann, 1998.

The author makes a case for the use of the arts to assist students with academic achievement and discusses how the arts can bring about improvements in educational practice.

Gardner, Howard. *Multiple Intelligences: The Theory in Practice.* New York: Basic Books, 1993.

The author explains his theory of multiple intelligences and gives a description and examples of each of the seven intelligences.

Helm, Judy, and Beneke, Sallee. (Eds.). *The Power of Projects: Meeting Contemporary Challenges in Early Childhood Classrooms. Strategies and Solutions.* New York: Teachers College Press, 2003.

The authors featured in this book provide information on curriculum project activities designed to assist students in poverty. The display of children's work samples and the section on frequently asked questions and advice are especially helpful.

Kliebard, Herbert. *Changing Course: American Curriculum Reform in the 20th Century.* New York: Teachers College Press, 2002.

This book contains essays on the history of efforts to reform American curriculum. These essays include information on the effects of grading on curriculum and teaching, the changes in social studies, the Cardinal Principles and the Committee of Ten, the changes in high school curriculum, and cultural literacy. Of special note are Chapters 6 and 9, where the author discusses why many curriculum reforms fail.

Kohn, Alfie. *What to Look For in a Classroom . . . and Other Essays.* Indianapolis, IN: Jossey-Bass, 2000.

In essay format, the author discusses various educational issues including behavior modification, school choice, student uniforms, grade inflation, character education, and tracking.

Ohanian, Susan. *Caught in the Middle: Nonstandard Kids and a Killing Curriculum.* Portsmouth, NH: Heinemann, 2001.

The author provides stories about real-life children and discusses the effects of a standardized curriculum. She also advocates that teachers teach what their students need, not what outside bureaucrats and politicians want.

Nieto, Sonia. *Affirming Diversity: The Sociopolitical Context of Multicultural Education.* New York: Longman, 1992.

The author uses case studies to highlight the use of multicultural curriculum for student learning.

Perry, Theresa, and Delpit, Lisa. (Eds.). *The Real Ebonics Debate: Power, Language, and the Education of African-American Children.* Boston: Beacon Press, 1998.

This is a collection of essays on the teaching of Black English or, as some call it, Ebonics. Although all of the featured authors agree that respect should be shown for the language spoken by African American children, they argue that the children must also be taught Standard American English. A resources section gives suggestions for further information.

Queen, Allen J. *The Block Scheduling Handbook.* Thousand Oaks, CA: Corwin Press, 2002.

This manual serves as a reference on strategies to implement block scheduling.

Shannon, Patrick. *Reading Poverty.* Westport, CT: Heinemann, 1998.

The author examines the ways in which poverty is portrayed and discusses how these portrayals affect textbook content and standards.

Slavin, Robert, and Madden, Nancy. *One Million Children,* 2nd ed. San Francisco: Jossey-Bass, 2001.

This book documents the Success For All program. It includes research on the program that addresses the reading, writing, and family support components.

Wiggins, Grant, and McTighe, Jay. *Understanding by Design.* Upper Saddle River, NJ: Prentice-Hall, 2000.

The authors write about designing curriculum that emphasizes enduring knowledge and learning that deepens into understanding.

Zucker, Andrew; Kozma, Robert; Yarnall, Louise; and Marder, Camille.

The Virtual High School: Teaching Generation V. New York: Teachers College Press, 2003.

This book outlines a study done on virtual courses in high school. It provides information on the strengths and weaknesses of online learning and the implications for the future of education.

Funding, History, and Politics

Avis, James; Bloomer, Martin; Eland, Geo; Gleeson, Denis; Hodkinson, Phil; and Avid, James. *Knowledge and Nationhood: Education, Politics, and Work.* New York: Continuum, 1996.

This is a collection of works by the featured authors, without an independent editor. The contents focus on the interplay between the new conservative and national education systems in Great Britain. The authors present evidence that the long tenure of conservative rule in England ignored the process of globalization. They also take a look at the professionalism of new educators.

Carr, Wilfred, and Hartnett, Anthony. *Education and the Struggle for Democracy: The Politics of Educational Ideas.* Bristol, England: Open University Press, 1996.

The authors examine the political and educational environment in both England and Wales, provide a short history of education in England, and make connections to the movements of the 1980s and 1990s. They also look at the efforts of the conservative movement to influence the education system and roll back previous efforts.

Goertz, Margaret E., and Mitchell, Douglas E. *Education Politics for the New Century: The Twentieth Anniversary Yearbook of the Politics of Education Association.* New York: Routledge Falmer, 1990.

This book contains a collection of works from various authors on subjects dealing with urban education. These works include such subjects as federal education policy, urban high school, the politics of school restructuring, the politics of technology utilization, business involvement in education during the 1990s, business leaders and their effect on school reform, education politics and funding in Australia, and education issues that affect us as we enter the new century.

Goodenow, Ronald K., and Ravitch, Kiane. (Eds.). *Schools in Cities: Consensus and Conflict in American Educational History.* New York: Holmes & Meier Publishers, Ltd., 1983.

This book is a collection of works that take a chronological look at urban education in various cities, from New York to Atlanta. A variety of subjects are covered, including industrial education, politics, progressive reforms, and community issues. These subjects are considered in the context of both the nineteenth and twentieth centuries.

Grover, Samuel K., and Wirt, Frederick M. (Eds.). *Political Science and School Politics*. Washington, DC: Heath and Company, 1976.

This book is a collection of written works from various authors on subjects dealing with politics and education. Included are works on innovation, school finance, and policymaking systems in the U.S. Congress as well as a philosophical look at change.

Mirel, Jeffery. *The Rise and Fall of an Urban School System*, 2nd ed. Ann Arbor: University of Michigan Press, 1993.

This is a comprehensive work that traces the history of the Detroit public school system from 1907 on, as citizens fought a corrupt system. The author discusses how hard the Detroit area was hit by the Great Depression, efforts by labor and African American leaders to influence school board decisions, and the violence and decline that occurred during the late 1960s and 1970s. In the latter part of the book he describes the efforts at reform made after the first printing.

Rich, Wilber C. *Black Mayors and School Politics: The Failure of Reform in Detroit, Gary and Newark*. New York: Garland Publishing, 1996.

The author describes what happened in the urban school districts of Detroit, Gary, and Newark after African Americans took control of both the school boards and the leadership of these manufacturing cities. (Each city is looked at individually.) He also takes into account the economic problems associated with the decline of industrial output as it affects these cities and considers other issues such as race and politics.

Stone, Clarence N. (Ed.). *Changing Urban Education.* Kansas: University Press of Kansas, 1998.

This book is a collection of written works from various authors on subjects dealing with urban education. The subjects range from desegregation to school reform and business involvement. Most of the contributors are college professors, but several are doctoral candidates.

Tyack, D. B. *The One Best System: A History of American Urban Education.* Cambridge, MA: Harvard University Press, 1974.

The author writes about the history of urban education. He includes narratives from participants and information on conflicts and attempts at reform. The last chapter ends with a discussion of the years 1940 to 1973.

Vega, José E. *Education, Politics and Bilingualism in Texas.* Washington, DC: University Press of America, Inc., 1983.

In this study of the efforts at education reform in the state of Texas, the author traces the efforts to integrate bilingual education so as to serve one of the largest Mexican-American populations in the United States. He also details how various proposed bills to create a bilingual system moved through the Texas state government. Included is a discussion of the interaction between federal and state courts on education and race issues.

Students

Aronson, Rosa. *At-Risk Students Defy the Odds: Overcoming Barriers to Educational Success.* Lanham, MD: Scarecrow Education, 2001.

The author presents the stories of seven resilient students and offers suggestions for schools working with at-risk children.

Bempechat, Janine. *Against the Odds: How "At-Risk" Students Exceed Expectations.* San Francisco: Jossey-Bass, 1998.

In the context of polices and curriculum, the author provides guidelines for assisting all children to reach their potential.

Brown, Thomas J. *Teaching the Poor and Children of Color.* Seattle, WA: Brown and Associates, 1999.

The author writes about the use of strategies that attempt to overcome the inequities experienced by children of color and in poverty. His premise is that resources are available but those in power do not feel an urgent need to truly help these children.

Bullough, Robert V. *Uncertain Lives: Children of Promise, Teachers of Hope.* New York: Teachers College Press, 2001.

The author richly describes the story of thirty-four children in poverty at an urban school. While acknowledging the hardships of their lives, he leaves the reader with hope for them and their teachers.

Dunbar, Jr., Christopher. *Alternate Schooling for African American Youth: Does Anyone Know We're Here?* New York: Peter Lang Publishing, 2001.

The author writes about the experience of students in a middle-school alternate behavioral school.

Gibson-Taylor, Joyce. (Ed.). *Educating the Throw-Away Children: What We Can Do to Help Students at Risk.* San Francisco: Jossey-Bass, 1998.

This book gives examples of successful programs for helping at-risk children. Of special note is the section on how to assist teenagers who have lost interest in school.

Kozol, Jonathan. *Amazing Grace: The Lives of Children and the Conscience of a Nation.* New York: Harper Perennial, 1996.

The author utilizes stories about poverty-stricken children to demonstrate their plight in the United States.

Kozol, Jonathan. *Savage Inequalities: Children in America's Schools.* New York: Crown, 1991.

This book provides rich, vivid descriptions of the plight of children in urban schools. It helps to demonstrate the poor facilities, overcrowding, and shortage of books and supplies that are inherent in urban schools. Although the author's observations were made in the late 1980s, they are still valid today.

Payne, Ruby. *Framework for Understanding Poverty*, rev. ed. Texas: aha! Process Inc., 2001.

The author writes about the hidden rules that govern how people act in society. She postulates that these rules must be understood in order to help students in the classroom. The book contains excellent questionnaires on differences among people from poor, middle-class, and wealthy backgrounds. It is a good resource for educators in poverty-stricken schools who want to better understand students and their families.

Soto-Diaz, Lourdes. (Ed.). *Making Differences in the Lives of Bilingual/Bicultural Children.* New York: Peter Lang Publishing, 2002.

This book critically examines methods by which teachers can meet the needs of linguistically and culturally diverse learners.

Watson, Marilyn, and Ecken, Laura. *Learning to Trust: Transforming Difficult Elementary Classrooms through Developmental Discipline.* San Francisco: Jossey-Bass, 2003.

This case study of one urban schoolteacher's experience highlights the need for trusting and caring relationships with children. The author writes about classroom management in terms of attachment theory techniques.

Wells, Amy, and Crain, Robert. *Stepping over the Color Line: African American Students in White Suburban Schools.* New Haven, CT: Yale University Press, 1997.

This book richly describes integration efforts made in St. Louis, Missouri, while also encouraging the reader to consider the larger issue of racial inequality.

Teachers and Teaching

Bartoli, Jill S. *Celebrating City Teachers: How to Make a Difference in Urban Schools.* Wesport, CT: Heinemann, 2001.

The author highlights two Philadelphia urban schools that are successful with poor and minority students. Included in the book are interviews with parents, teachers, students, administrators, and community members.

Danielson, Charlotte. *Enhancing Professional Practice: A Framework for Teaching.* Alexandria, VA: Association for Supervision & Curriculum Development, 1996.

This book provides a framework based on the Praxis III to address steps that teachers can take to promote student learning.

Foster, Michele. *Black Teachers on Teaching.* New York: The New Press, 1996.

The author utilizes black teachers' stories about teaching to present the pros and cons of segregation.

French, Nancy. *Managing Paraeducators in Your School: How to Hire, Train, and Supervise Non-Certified Staff.* Thousand Oaks, CA: Corwin Press, 2003.

The author offers suggestions for implementing strategies for the best use, management, and recruitment of instructor or teacher assistants.

hooks, bell. *Teaching to Transgress: Education as the Practice of Freedom*. New York: Routledge, 1994.

The author writes in essay format about class, gender, and race in the classroom and postulates that education is failing because the stress is on overfactualized knowledge instead of on students' histories. She criticizes teachers for utilizing power and control in the classroom in ways that stifle student learning.

Goodlad, John. *Educational Renewal: Better Teachers, Better Schools*. San Francisco: Jossey-Bass, 1998.

The author criticizes the methods used to prepare teachers but provides strategies to create better teachers and, ultimately, better schools. His basic premise has to do with quality partnerships between universities and secondary schools.

Khatri, Daryao, and Hughes, Anne. *American Education Apartheid— Again?* Lanham, MD: Scarecrow Education, 2002.

The authors offer a teaching model to assist with poor and minority children.

Ladson-Billings, Gloria. *The Dreamkeepers: Successful Teachers of African-American Children*. San Francisco: Jossey-Bass Publishers, 1997.

In exploring the stories and experiences of eight successful teachers of African-American children, this book provides a good model for culturally relevant teaching.

Lent, ReLeah, and Pipkin, Gloria. (Eds.). *Silent No More: Voices of Courage in American Schools*. Portsmouth, NH: Heinemann, 2003.

This book contains first-person accounts of teachers battling high-stakes tests and mandated curriculum to the detriment of their jobs and, ultimately, fighting policies that are harmful to children.

Long, Delbert, and Riegle, Rodney. *Teacher Education: The Key to Effective School Reform*. Westport, CT: Bergin & Garvey, 2001.

The authors examine teacher education and discuss teacher recruitment and retention and the encouragement of quality teachers as keys to effective school reform. In the second section of the book they make suggestions for improving teacher education, and in the third section they discuss the future of teacher education.

Maniates, Helen; Doerr, Betty; and Golden, Margaret. *Teach Our Children Well: Essential Strategies for the Urban Classroom.* Westport, CT: Heinemann, 2001.

The authors offer strategies for establishing positive urban classrooms, including rapport, tradition, pride, sense of belonging, personal best, and independence.

Nieto, Sonia. *What Keeps Teachers Going?* New York: Teachers College Press, 2003.

The author examines what effective veteran urban teachers do to remain enthusiastic in their teaching.

Peterson, Kenneth. *Teacher Evaluation: A Comprehensive Guide to New Directions and Practices.* Thousand Oaks, CA: Corwin Press, 2000.

This book serves as a reference guide for recently developed methods of using standards and student data for teacher evaluation.

Portner, Hal. *Training Mentors Is Not Enough: Everything Else Schools and Districts Need to Do.* Thousand Oaks, CA: Corwin Press, 2001.

This book provides practical strategies for how to develop or improve a teacher mentoring program.

Prince, Cynthia D. *Higher Pay in Hard-to-Staff Schools: The Case for Financial Incentives.* Lanham, MD: Scarecrow Education, 2003.

The author argues that to attract and retain the most highly qualified and educated teachers in the neediest schools, financial incentives must be provided. The book contains information on the current incentives available in districts.

Richin, Roberta; Banyon, Richard; Stein, Rita; and Banyon, Francine. *Induction: Connecting Teacher Recruitment to Retention.* Thousand Oaks, CA: Corwin Press, 2003.

This book offers resources for the best practices to recruit and retain the best teachers. Specific strategies for the first to third years are given.

Routman, Regie. *Invitations: Changing as Teachers and Learners K–12.* Portsmouth, NH: Heinemann, 1994.

The author provides a resource for teaching at-risk students that utilizes whole language, encourages teachers to reflect on their teaching, and gives strategies for daily management.

Shor, Ira, and Pari, Caroline. (Eds.). *Education Is Politics: Critical Teaching across Differences, K–12.* Westport, CT: Heinemann, 1999.

This book encourages teachers to teach about inequities that are imposed by those in power. It is influenced by Paulo Freire's work.

Weiner, Lois. *Urban Teaching: The Essentials.* New York: Teachers College Record Press, 1999.

The author presents good suggestions for teaching in urban schools. The topics covered include relationships with other teachers, administrators, students, and the union. Also included is a chapter on political and moral obligations.

Wilson, Catherine. *Telling a Different Story: Teaching and Literacy in an Urban Preschool.* New York: Teachers College Press, 2000.

A teacher and her assistant describe teaching practices in their Head Start classroom.

Wiske-Stone, Martha. (Ed.). *Teaching for Understanding: Linking Research with Practice.* San Francisco: Jossey-Bass, 1997.

This book presents the results of a study conducted by the Harvard Graduate School of Education on teaching for understanding. Also included are examples of practical classroom ideas for implementing these practices.

Zachary, Lois J. *The Mentor's Guide: Facilitating Effective Learning Relationships.* San Francisco: Jossey-Bass, 2000.

This book guides the reader through the mentor process from the initial question of whether one is ready to mentor to setting goals, monitoring progress, and determining how to end the relationship. It also contains suggestions for avoiding common pitfalls.

Urban Schools and Education

Anyon, Jean. *Ghetto Schooling: A Political Economy of Urban Educational Reform.* New York: Teacher College Press, 1997.

The author's premise is that urban schools' problems are economic and political issues. She utilizes interviews and media reports to document her position and suggests solutions to the problems of urban education.

Ascher, Carol. **"Changing Schools for Urban Students: The School Development Program, Accelerated Schools, and Success for All."** *Trends and Issues* No. 18, 1993 (Eric Reproduction Service No. ED 355 313).

The author reviews three programs that are utilized in urban schools for restructuring purposes: Comer's School Development Program, Slavins's Success for All, and Levin's Accelerated Schools. Each program is examined in terms of assessment and what type of learning is emphasized. A resource section for the programs is also included.

Berliner, David, and Biddle, Bruce. *The Manufactured Crisis: Myths, Fraud, and the Attack on America's Public Schools.* New York: Addison-Wesley, 1995.

The authors defend American public schools and the achievement level of students. They charge that some groups have attacked the schools and thus, in essence, have attacked public education. They do support the notion that urban schools are underfunded and, as such, substandard.

Bizar, Marilyn, and Barr, Rebecca (Eds.). *School Leadership in Times of Urban Reform.* Mahwah, NJ: Lawrence Erlbaum Associates Inc., 2001.

This book of case studies examines eight urban elementary and high schools as they go through the reform process.

Borman, Geoffrey; Stringfield, Samuel; and Slavin, Robert (Eds.). *Title I: Compensatory Education at the Crossroads.* Mahwah, NJ: Lawrence Erlbaum Associates Inc., 2001.

This book describes the history of Title I and presents research on the evaluation of programs.

Danielson, Charlotte. *Enhancing Student Achievement: A Framework for School Improvement.* Alexandria, VA: Association for Supervision & Curriculum Development, 2002.

The author writes that if student learning is truly to improve, the focus must include what educators want, what they believe, and what they know. She also provides a framework to address these issues through action planning.

Darling-Hammond, Linda. *The Right to Learn: A Blueprint for Creating Schools That Work.* San Francisco: Jossey-Bass, 1997.

The author writes about ways to improve schools. Her most significant premise is that teachers must be allowed to teach and children must be allowed to learn. She supports curriculum that is relevant, challenging, and able to be explored in depth. She also writes about and supports inside-out change and professional development.

Doyon, Juanita. *Not with Our Kids You Don't: 10 Strategies to Save Our Schools.* Portsmouth, NH: Heinemann, 2003.

The author offers a step-by-step guide on how to become an activist for educational change that does not involve the current high-stakes standards and tests.

Dryfoos, Joy, and Maguire, Sue. *Inside Full-Service Community Schools.* Thousand Oaks, CA: Corwin Press, 2002.

This book serves as a research guide for developing full-service schools. Topics include getting started, funding, staffing, and working in rural and urban settings.

Eberts, Randall, and Stone, Joe. *Unions and Public Schools: The Effects of Collective Bargaining on American Education.* Lexington, MA: Lexington Books, 1984.

The authors discuss the costs of collective bargaining and the roles that unions should and should not play in schools.

England, Crystal. *None of Our Business: Why Business Models Don't Work in Schools.* Portsmouth, NH: Heinemann, 2003.

The author makes a case against the business models and reforms currently being implemented in schools. She balances practical suggestions with research to demonstrate why the business model does not support real learning by real teachers.

Farber, Barry, and Ascher, Carol. **"Urban School Restructuring and Teacher Burnout,"** 1991 (Eric Reproduction Service No. ED 340 812).

The authors warn that restructuring can actually decrease performance—specifically, by increasing stress on participants. They also caution against not having appropriate staff development, mentoring, and peer coaching for the changes that are planned, and make the point that only curriculum changes can improve learning and teaching.

Frase, Larry, and Streshly, William. *Top Ten Myths in Education: Fantasies Americans Love to Believe.* Lanham, MD: Scarecrow Education, 2000.

The authors write about the myths accepted by the public about education. They back up their suppositions with research and offer cost-effective solutions for schools.

Glickman, Carl D. *Renewing America's Schools: A Guide for School-Based Action.* San Francisco: Jossey-Bass, 1998

The author presents questions about the purposes of public education and the role of schools as a resource for those involved in school change.

Goldberg, Mark F. *15 School Questions and Discussion: From Class Size, Standards, and School Safety to Leadership and More.* Lanham, MD: Scarecrow Education, 2002.

The author presents background and definitions on current issues. These include class size, vouchers, tests, curriculum, rubrics, school safety, and quality teaching.

Good, Thomas, and Braden, Jennifer. *The Great School Debate: Choice, Vouchers, and Charters.* Mahwah, NJ: Lawrence Erlbaum Associates Inc., 2000.

The authors discuss the strengths and weaknesses of voucher systems and charter schools.

Hammond, Linda Darling. *The Right to Learn: A Blueprint for Creating Schools That Work.* San Francisco: Jossey-Bass, 1997.

The author writes that the emphasis in schools needs to be on learning rather than testing, but the school bureaucracy leaves little time for teachers to actually teach. She suggests that teachers need to have more time to collaborate and to teach for understanding.

Hirsch, Jr., E. D. *The Schools We Need: And Why We Don't Have Them.* New York: Random House, 1999.

The author postulates that American schools need to teach core knowledge to students instead of progressive theory–based learning, since the latter encourages social inequity and economic competitiveness.

Goodlad, John I. *A Place Called School: Promise for the Future.* New York: McGraw-Hill Trade, 1984.

The author utilized trained investigators to visit schools in urban, rural, and suburban areas of the United States. These investigators then interviewed teachers, students, administrators, school board members, parents, and community members to report on school improvement.

Katz, Michael. *Reconstructing American Education.* Cambridge, MA: Harvard University Press, 1987.

This book includes chapters on the origins of public education, alternate models, the bureaucracies of urban systems, the Boston case from 1850 to 1884, history and reform, and the politics of educational history. It concludes with a chapter on the moral crisis of the university.

Kauffman, James M. *Education Reform: Bright People Sometimes Say Stupid Things about Education.* Lanham, MD: Scarecrow Education, 2002.

The author postulates that current reform efforts, which have political agendas, are not working. He suggests utilizing judgment and critical thinking as ways to address true reform.

King, Deborah. **"The Changing Shape of Leadership."** *Educational Leadership* 59, no. 8 (May 2002): 61–63.

This article describes the role changes that occur when administrators become instructional leaders. These changes affect both teaching and learning and involve the use of data to better inform decisions and the use of resources more creatively.

Kohn, A. **"Only for *My* Kid: How Privileged Parents Undermine School Reform."** *Phi Delta Kappan* 79, no. 8 (April 1998): 568–577.

The author writes that powerful parents disrupt school reform by accepting ultraconservative political agendas and, ultimately, hurt their own children's learning.

Kugler, Eileen G. *Debunking the Middle-Class Myth: Why Diverse Schools Are Good for All Kids.* Lanham, MD: Scarecrow Education, 2002.

The author makes the case that diversity in school and, thus, in life is important for children. She includes information from eighty interviews with parents, students, and educators.

McLaren, Peter. *Life in Schools: An Introduction to Critical Pedagogy in the Foundations of Education,* 4th ed. Boston: Allyn & Bacon, 2003.

The author presents critical pedagogy with examples from students in schools. He also takes a critical look at race, gender, and class issues. Throughout the book, issues relating to urban education are apparent.

McLaughlin, Milbrey; Irby, Merita; and Langman, Juliet. *Urban Sanctuaries: Neighborhood Organizations in the Lives and Futures of Inner-City Youth.* San Francisco: Jossey-Bass, 2001.

This book highlights organizations that are assisting and having an impact on urban children.

Meier, Deborah. *The Power of Their Ideas: Lessons for America from a Small School in Harlem.* Boston: Beacon Press, 2002.

The author describes her experience of building a successful inner-city school in Harlem. She writes that the problems facing public education result from economic inequities, school bureaucracies, and unrealistic expectations for academic performance.

Meier, Deborah. *In Schools We Trust: Creating Communities of Learning in an Era of Testing and Standardization.* Boston: Beacon Press, 2002.

The author writes that educational practices could be improved through smaller schools with communities of learners that emphasize parent involvement and teachers' collegiality.

Murphy, Michael. **"Let's Change Staff Development to Professional Learning."** *Principal* 81, no. 4 (March 2002):16–17.

This article supports changes in traditional staff development. The author advocates looking at goals for students and the best design for learning. He also recommends that teachers hold study groups, discuss students' work, and observe and coach each other.

Murrell, Peter. *Like Stone Soup: The Role of the Professional Development School in the Renewal of Urban Schools.* Indianapolis, IN: Jossey-Bass, 1998.

The author expands on the current framework for professional development schools to present ideas about alternative collaborate partnerships for urban schools.

Pankratz, Roger, and Petrosko, Joseph. (Eds.). *All Children Can Learn: Lessons from the Kentucky Reform Experience.* Indianapolis, IN: Jossey-Bass, 2000.

This book highlights the statewide Kentucky reform efforts, includes various program components, and discusses initiatives that worked and did not work.

Schlechty, Phillip C. *Shaking Up the Schoolhouse: How to Support and Sustain Educational Innovation.* Indianapolis, IN: Jossey-Bass, 2000.

The author presents a guide on transformative leadership for successful schools.

Schwebel, Milton. *Remaking America's Three School Systems.* Lanham, MD: Scarecrow Education, 2003.

The author makes the case that the public is given a distorted view of the state of American schools and offers ideas to address social-class differences and involve parents in their children's education.

Shields, Carolyn, and Oberg, Steven. *Year-Round Schooling: Promises and Pitfalls.* Lanham, MD: Scarecrow Education, 2000.

This book discusses year-round school schedules and their effects on teachers, parents, students, and facilities.

Reports

American Federation of Teachers. *Making Standards Matter.* Washington, DC, 2001. Available online at http://www.aft.org/edissues/standards/index.htm, 2001.

This report specifies which states have standards but condemns those that impose consequences without giving clear support to schools. It also recommends provision of high-quality support and intervention with comprehensive and clear standards.

Carnegie Forum on Education and the Economy. *A Nation Prepared: Teachers for the 21st Century.* Hyattsville, MD, 1986.

This report draws attention to the importance of teachers and teaching for school reform. It also suggests changes necessary to make sure that teachers are well prepared.

Civil Rights Project. *A Multiracial Society with Segregated Schools: Are We Losing the Dream?* Available online at www.civilrightsproject. harvard.edu.

This report warns that schools are becoming even more segregated than they were in the past three decades. It also indicates that the Latino student population is becoming the most segregated minority group.

Education Week. **"Quality Counts 2003."** Available online at www. edweek.org, 2003.

This is an annual survey conducted by *Education Week* on standards-based reform by states. The 2003 version focuses on recruitment, preparation, and retaining of qualified teachers.

McDonnel, Lorraine, and Pascal, Anthony. *Teacher Unions and Educational Reforms.* Santa Monica, CA: RAND, April 1988.

This report describes how unions have utilized political action and collective bargaining and discusses their impact on reform.

U.S. Department of Education. *A Nation at Risk: Imperative for Education Reform.* Washington, DC: National Commission on Excellence in Education, 1983.

This report led to many educational reform efforts, which, in turn, especially impacted urban schools.

NONPRINT RESOURCES

Media

Across the River: Saving America's Inner City

Length: 57 minutes
Source: Films for the Humanities and Sciences
PO Box 2053
Princeton, NJ 08543
800-257-5126
www.films.com

This video documents the efforts of people trying to make a difference in urban areas. Filmed in Washington, D.C., it displays a mentor program for students, a public housing project, an economic program, and a program to lure the middle class back to the city.

As American as Public School: 1900–1950

> *Length:* 55 minutes
> *Source:* Films for the Humanities and Sciences
> PO Box 2053
> Princeton, NJ 08543-2053
> 800-257-5126
> www.films.com

This video documents the changes in U.S. education that occurred during the early twentieth century. Subjects include immigration, child labor laws, John Dewey's progressive ideas, and the Cold War.

Awakenings 1954–1956

> *Length:* 60 minutes
> *Source:* PBS video
> Customer Support Center
> 1320 Braddock Place
> Alexandria, VA 22314
> 800-344-3337

This video—part of a series of videos made in 1954–1965 highlighting the Civil Rights Movement—focuses on the murder of a fourteen-year-old African American boy (including the killers' testimony at the trial) as well as on Rosa Parks and the bus boycott in Montgomery, Alabama. It includes interviews with those who worked for civil rights.

Becoming a Star Urban Teacher

> *Length:* 179 minutes
> 7 videocassettes
> *Source:* Association for Supervision and
> Curriculum Development
> University of Dayton
> School of Education
> 300 College Park
> Dayton, OH 45469

This video series was created by two University of Dayton professors to assist urban teachers. It contains video case studies that include commentary and constructive tips from experienced urban teachers.

Blackboard Jungle

> *Length:* 101 minutes
>   MGM Home Entertainment
> *Source:* www.amazon.com

This movie, produced in 1955, focuses on a teacher in an urban all-male high school. Urban-school issues such as delinquency and racism are highlighted.

Boston Public

> http://www.fox.com/bostonpublic/homeroom/index.htm

This television series highlights contemporary urban high school issues as seen through the eyes of teachers and administrators.

The Bottom Line in Education: 1980 to the Present

> *Length:* 55 minutes
> *Source:* Films for the Humanities and Sciences
>   PO Box 2053
>   Princeton, NJ 08543-2053
>   800-257-5126
>   www.films.com

This video explores alternate educational reforms including vouchers, charter schools, privatization, and academic standards.

Children in America's Schools with Bill Moyers

> *Length:* 120 minutes
> *Source:* South Carolina ETV
>   Free copy of video:
>   www.ohiocoalition.org/video.htm

This documentary compares rich and poor schools in Ohio, illustrating the inequities inherent in supporting schools with local property taxes. The plight of urban schools and students is visually very apparent.

The Common School: 1770–1890

> *Length:* 55 minutes

Source: Films for the Humanities and Sciences
PO Box 2053
Princeton, NJ 08543-2053
800-257-5126
www.films.com

This video highlights reformers Thomas Jefferson, Noah Webster, Horace Mann, and others to create tax-supported schools for all children.

Common Threads

Length: 20 minutes
Source: Insight-Media
www.insight-media.com

This video details the history of U.S. education, including information on the impact of technology.

Cultural Bias in Education

Length: 28 minutes
Source: Films for the Humanities and Sciences
PO Box 2053
Princeton, NJ 08543-2053
800-257-5126
www.films.com

This video highlights the bias in standardized testing. It also examines cultural diversity, focusing in particular on the Latino population.

Dangerous Minds

Length: 99 minutes
Hollywood Pictures
Don Simpson and Jerry Bruckheimer production
Source: www.amazon.com

This movie is based on a true story, as told in the book *My Posse Don't Do Homework* by LouAnne Johnson. Focusing on a female ex-marine who becomes an urban teacher, it highlights issues involving urban schools and education.

The Ebonics Controversy

Length: 30 minutes

> *Source:* Insight-Media
> www.insight-media.com

This video discusses Ebonics, the difference between languages and dialects, and the Oakland, California School Board's decision to implement Black English in the curriculum.

Evaluating Preschool Education

> *Length:* 25 minutes
> *Source:* Films for the Humanities and Sciences
> PO Box 2053
> Princeton, NJ 08543
> 800-257-5126
> www.films.com

This video, which highlights a Michigan study on a preschool program that is similar to Head Start, contains research findings in support of preschool education. The study followed 123 African American students for twenty-five years. By third grade, these students had caught up with their peers academically; by the age of fifteen, they demonstrated higher academic achievement and lower arrest and teen pregnancy rates than their peers.

Fighting Back 1957–1962

> *Length:* 60 minutes
> *Source:* PBS Video
> Customer Support Center
> 1320 Braddock Place
> Alexandria, VA 22314
> 800-344-3337

As part of a series highlighting the Civil Rights Movement, this video focuses on the *Brown v. Board of Education* decision and other education laws.

Language Development: Approaches for Urban Educators

> *Length:* 32 minutes
> *Source:* Insight-Media
> www.insight-media.com

This video examines the language-development needs of urban students, including the identification of possible language delays.

The Merrow Reports

> *Source:*   Learning Matters, Inc.
>   www.pbs.org/merrow/

> **The Fifty Million Dollar Gamble**
> *Length:* 120 minutes
>   1994

This documentary highlights the Essential Schools movement and its founder, Theodore Sizer.

> **Teacher Shortage: False Alarm?**
> *Length:* 60 minutes
>   1999

This video highlights alternate certification and professional development schools as alternatives to traditional teacher-training programs.

> **Testing . . . Testing . . . Testing . . .**
> *Length:* 60 minutes
>   1997

This video presents twelve questions on issues concerning the measurement of achievement, learning, and children's intelligence.

> **Toughest Job in America**
> *Length:* 120 minutes
>   1998

This video highlights the problems facing urban schools, including discussion of the belief that poor and minority children cannot achieve.

Nurturing the Love of Learning: The Montessori Method

> *Length:*   9 minutes
> *Source:*   Insight-Media
>   www.insight-media.com

This video demonstrates the Montessori Method. It highlights students from three to six years of age.

Performance Assessment: Moving Beyond the Standardized Test

> *Length:*   28 minutes
> *Source:*   Films for the Humanities and Sciences
>   PO Box 2053

Princeton, NJ 08543-2053
800-257-5126
www.films.com

In this video, Dr. Art Costa, a professor emeritus, discusses the need for the creation of alternate assessments in place of standardized testing.

Rethinking High School: Best Practice in Action

Length: 40 minutes
Source: Heinemann
88 Post Road West
PO Box 5007
Westport, CT 06881
800-225-5800
www.heinemann.com

This video highlights a Best Practices high school where teachers and students worked together to compile a curriculum and a strong school community.

Saviors

Length: 47 minutes
Source: Films for the Humanities and Sciences
PO Box 2053
Princeton, NJ 08543
800-257-5126
www.films.com

This video highlights the federal government's role in civil rights. It includes information on the *Brown v. Board of Education* decision, the role of the Supreme Court, and the Reagan and Bush eras.

A Struggle for Educational Equality: 1950–1980

Length: 55 minutes
Source: Films for the Humanities and Sciences
PO Box 2053
Princeton, NJ 08543-2053
800-257-5126
www.films.com

This video documents both the gains made by some minority students and the inequities experienced by others during the period 1950–1980.

Teaching to Multiple Intelligences

> *Length:* 60 minutes
> 2 volumes
> *Source:* Insight Media
> www.insight-media.com

This video utilizes classroom interactions to demonstrate how to teach using a multiple-intelligences approach.

Testing Our Schools

> *Length:* 60 minutes
> *Source:* Learning Matters Inc.
> www.pbs.org/frontline/

This video highlights President George W. Bush's plan to increase testing and, ultimately, accountability in schools.

Unequal Education

> *Length:* 40 minutes
> *Source:* Films for the Humanities and Sciences
> PO Box 2053
> Princeton, NJ 08543-2053
> 800-257-5126
> www.films.com

This video focuses on the students at two New York City middle schools and demonstrates the funding inequities apparent within the school system.

Zero Tolerance in Schools

> *Length:* 21 minutes
> *Source:* Insight-Media
> www.insight-media.com

This video examines zero-tolerance policies. It includes interviews with parents, educators, students, and police officers.

Websites

From the many websites available for further information and research, we have chosen a few, listed below, that are especially pertinent to the issues covered in this book. (It is imperative to note that, since anyone can create a website, the reader should always be cognizant of who published the information.)

American Association of School Administrators
www.aasa.org

This organization, founded in 1865, holds an annual conference and publishes a monthly journal on education issues pertaining to school leadership. The website contains multiple links on education issues, including recent legislation and reform efforts.

American School Board Journal
www.asbj.com

This journal, founded in 1891, is published online and covers many topics including urban education, school law, governance, and research.

Center on Reinventing Public Education
www.crpe.org

This organization looks at issues pertaining to fairness and equity in education. Its website contains links to such topics as governance and reform of education, teachers, schools, finance, and leadership.

Corporate Watch
www.corpwatch.org

This website contains privately funded information on corporations and their effects on various issues, including education.

ERIC Clearinghouse on Urban Education
http://eric-web.tc.columbia.edu/about.asp

This national information database provides the results of educational research pertaining to urban schools and education. The site is funded by the U.S. Department of Education.

Labor Notes
www.labornotes.org

This organization works with union activists and publishes current labor-movement information, including information on education. On its website are current issues of its publication, book titles, and information about conferences.

Making Standards Matter, 2001
www.aft.org/edissues/standards/msm2001

This website focuses on the American Federation of Teachers union, which has studied state standards, curriculum, and assessment and accountability programs and procedures and has reported information on these areas. Included in this information is a state-to-state chart that provides answers to the following questions: Are existing tests aligned with standards? If yes, are all of those tests based on strong standards? Is there at least a basic curriculum in each of the aligned test areas? If there are promotion/graduation policies, are they based on aligned tests? If there are promotion/graduation policies, do they all include intervention?

National Commission on Teaching and America's Future
www.nctaf.org

This website contains information on a downloadable version of the report "No Dream Denied: A Pledge to America's Children." It also provides links relating to school, district, state, educators', and parents' support. The commission itself supports efforts to retain and recruit quality teachers for every child.

Network of Educators on the Americas: Teaching for Change
www.teachingforchange.org

This nonprofit organization of educators supports economic and social justice through education. Its website contains information on many organizations and resources for educators.

Pioneer Institute for Public Policy Research
www.pioneerinstitute.org

This website provides links on research, urban entrepreneurship, charter schools, publications, and other related issues. The research organization itself promotes challenges to current public policy thinking in Massachusetts and is privately funded and nonpartisan.

Urban Advocate
www.nsba.org/cube/pubs.htm#urban_advocate

The Urban Advocate is published quarterly and issued free in PDF format by the Council of Urban Boards of Education. Recent issues included articles on vouchers, privatization, funding, and safety.

Listed below are selected website resources for the following topics:

Charter Schools

http://edreform.com/charters.htm
http://csr.syr.edu/
http://www.uscharterschools.org

Curriculum

www.rand.org
http://www.ascd.org
http://pzweb.harvard.edu/Research/MISchool.htm
http://www.indiana.edu/~eric_rec/ieo/bibs/multiple.html
www.edexcellence.net/evolution/
http://www.paideia.org
www.aep-arts.org
http://www.Monte

Diversity

http://www.ed.gov/pubs/EdReformStudies/EdReforms/chap1a.html
http://www.ncrel.org/skrs/areas/issues/educatrs/presrve/pe300.htm

Education Law

http://law.touro.edu/patch/CaseSummary.html
http://www.law.cornell.edu:80/topics/education.html
http://supct.law.cornell.edu/supct/topiclist.html

Funding

http://www.wcer.wisc.edu/cpre/
http://epn.org/prospect/36/36/rothf.html
http://www.futureofchildren.org/sch/

History of Education

http://www.greatbook.com/homepage/history.htm
http://www.indiana.edu/~eric_rec/ieo/bibs/histedus.html
http://fcis.oise.utoronto.ca/~daniel_schugurensky/assignment1/index
     .html

Politics of Education

http://www.gseis.ucla.edu/courses/ed191/transparencies/transparencies
/html

Portfolios and Authentic Assessment

http://www2.ncsu.edu/unity/lockers/project/portfolios/portfolio
intro.html
http://www.oise.utoronto.ca/~czmach/second~1.htm
http://transition.alaska.edu/www/portfolios/site98.html
http://www.nwrel.org/eval/ea_bibs/folio.html
http://www.nwrel.org/eval/toolkit98/integratel.html
http://www.business1.com/IRI_SKY/Assess/htaali/htm

Year-Round Schools

www.summermatters.com
www.nayre.org

Chapter Nine

☙ Organizations, Associations, and Government Agencies

The following are organizations, associations, and government agencies that can provide further information on the issues discussed in this book.

The Albert Shanker Institute
555 New Jersey Avenue, NW
Washington, DC 20001
202-879-4401
www.shankerinstitute.org

This organization was founded in 1998 to honor the late AFT president, Albert Shanker. Its mission is to uphold a commitment to democracy, to provide quality public education, to be a voice for working people, and to hold open and free debate about all of these issues. Links to other education resources are available on the website.

American Association of Colleges for Teacher Education (AACTE)
1307 New York Avenue, NW
Washington, DC 20005
202-293-2450
www.aacte.org

This voluntary organization serves universities and colleges that have teacher education programs. It publishes a newsletter titled *AACTE Briefs* and a refereed journal titled *Journal of Teacher Education*, and its website contains information on teacher accreditation, diversity issues, teacher preparation, and educational research.

American Educational Research Association
1230 17th Street, NW
Washington, DC 20036
202-223-9485
www.aera.net

This organization offers the most respected educational research available, has over 20,000 members, and publishes the *American Educational Research Journal,* among other periodicals. Its website contains information on just about every educational topic, including professional development, grants, and current educational issues.

American Federation of Teachers
555 New Jersey Avenue NW
Washington, DC 20001
202-393-8642
www.aft.org

This union was established in 1916. In 2003 it had more than 1 million members. It represents not only teachers but also paraprofessionals, higher-education faculty, nurse associations, and other health-care professionals. In addition, it publishes numerous publications including *American Educator* and an email newsletter called *Inside AFT.* Its website provides numerous references on standards, privatization, funding, and other education issues.

Annenberg Institute for School Reform
Brown University
PO Box 1985
Providence, RI 02912
401-863-7990
www.annenberginstitute.org

This organization's mission is to disseminate and act on knowledge to improve schools, especially those with urban and disadvantaged children; at present it is specifically working on school redesign, leadership, accountability, and community-centered partnerships. Its website contains a downloadable version of the report *Research Perspectives on School Reform: Lessons from the Annenberg Challenge,* which describes research on the programs and achievements of some Annenberg projects and other resources.

Association for Supervision and Curriculum Development
1703 N. Beauregard Street
Alexandria, VA 22311
800-933-2723
www.ascd.org

This association, founded in 1943, has more than 160,000 members in

135 countries. Originally focused just on curriculum and supervision, it has since expanded to cover all education topics and issues. ASCD holds an annual research conference and publishes many award-winning education books, videos, and other materials. Its website is rich with information on many education issues and topics.

Bill and Melinda Gates Foundation
PO Box 23350
Seattle, WA 98102
206-709-3140
www.gatesfoundation.org

This organization is involved in education initiatives, especially in urban areas and with disadvantaged youth. Its website contains information on the foundation's efforts and includes research, grant, and scholarship information.

Center for Education Reform
1001 Connecticut Avenue, NW, Suite 204
Washington, DC 20036
202-822-9000
www.edreform.com

This organization represents the conservative side of the reform debate on school choice, assessment and standards, curriculum, and other reform efforts. Its website provides links to other federal and state educational agencies as well as to educational research.

Center for Reinventing Public Education
University of Washington
PO Box 353060
Seattle, WA 98195
206-685-2214
www.crpe.org

This organization looks at issues pertaining to fairness and equity in education. Its website contains links to such topics as governance and reform of education, teachers, schools, finance, and leadership.

Center for Research on the Education of Students Placed at Risk
CRESPAR
Johns Hopkins University
Baltimore, MD 21218

410-516-8810
www.csos.jhu.edu/crespar/

This organization, centered at Johns Hopkins and Howard Universities, is a federally funded national research center that focuses on the education of students deemed at-risk due to poverty, race, and language issues.

Children's Defense Fund
25 E Street, NW
Washington, DC 20001
202-628-8787
www.childrensdefense.org

This organization, a private nonprofit funded by corporations, foundations, and individual donations, is concerned with being the voice for all children, especially those who live in poverty, have minority status, or are disabled. Its aim is to educate people about the needs of children and to support preventive efforts to keep children healthy and educated, and its website contains information on current events, publications, and advocacy opportunities.

Coalition of Essential Schools
CES National
1814 Franklin St., Suite 700
Oakland, CA 94612
510-433-1451; fax 510-433-1455
www.essentialschools.org

This coalition consists of a network of schools, regional centers, and a national office, and it supports common shared beliefs called common principles. These principles include individualized instruction, small schools and classrooms, multiple assessments with an emphasis on authentic assessment, a democratic approach to practices and policies, and close partnerships with the community.

Consortium for Policy Research in Education
3440 Market Street
Suite 560
Philadelphia, PA 19104
215-573-0700
www.cpre.org

This organization brings together five leading education institutions to disseminate practical research on education issues. The institutions are

Harvard University, Stanford University, the University of Pennsylvania, the University of Michigan, and the University of Wisconsin–Madison. Its website provides information on the organization, research results, and links to other educational resources.

Consortium on Inclusive Schooling Practices
1 Allegheny Center
Suite 510
Pittsburgh, PA 15212
406-243-5467
http://ruralinstitute.umt.edu/Community/cisp.asp

This organization is concerned with systematic reform for all children, not just those with disabilities. In addition, it supports the National Institute for Urban School Improvement, which in turn supports urban schools' inclusion efforts. Its website contains information on current projects and links to disability information.

Council of the Great City Schools
1301 Pennsylvania Avenue NW
Suite 702
Washington, DC 20002
202-393-2747
www.cgcs.org

This council was formed in 1956 and today encompasses a coalition of almost sixty of the nation's largest urban public school systems. It promotes urban education legislation, research, the media, and special projects, and its website contains a list of member districts, annual and research reports, and links to other education sources. An annual conference is held in the fall.

Center for Research on Evaluation, Standards, and Student Testing (CRESST)
PO Box 951522
300 Charles E. Young Drive
North Los Angeles, CA 90095
310-206-1532.
www.cse.ucla.edu

This government organization, which is funded by the U.S. Department of Education and the Office of Educational Research and Improvement, conducts research on issues related to educational testing.

CUBE
1680 Duke Street
Alexandria, VA 22314
703-838-6742
www.nsba.org/cube/

CUBE, an acronym that stands for the Council of Urban Education Boards of Education, is part of the National School Boards Association. This organization encompasses 104 districts, including the ten largest. Established in 1967, it holds an annual conference, provides legislative advocacy, and provides publications and other links of interest. In particular, it publishes the *Urban Advocate* quarterly.

Education Commission of the States
700 Broadway
#1200
Denver, CO 80203
303-299-3600
www.ecs.org

This nonprofit government organization was formed in 1965 to help state officials make informed educational decisions. Formed with grant money from the Carnegie Corporation and the Ford Foundation, it was originally seen as a way to balance the federal role in education that was so prevalent in the mid-1960s. Its website provides information on affirmative action and state takeovers of school districts and schools, has links to other government education agencies, and is an excellent source regarding current education issues and what is happening in individual states. The organization itself prints numerous publications throughout the year.

Educators for Social Responsibility
23 Garden St.
Cambridge, MA 02138
617-492-1764
www.esrnational.org

This nonprofit organization, founded in 1982, seeks to assist educators who want to teach social responsibility and create a classroom and school climate that is conducive to caring, safe, and respectful learning. Its website provides specific links to such topics as early childhood, elementary schools, middle schools, high schools, after-school programs, and special projects.

FairTest
324 Broadway
Cambridge, MA 02139
617-864-4810
www.fairtest.org

FairTest is also known as the National Center for Fair and Open Testing. This advocacy organization promotes an end to the misuse of standardized tests for students and workers, and aims to eliminate racial, gender, class, and cultural barriers to true equal opportunity. It also provides technical assistance and information on testing issues. A quarterly newsletter along with a catalog of materials and fact sheets are available through this organization, and its website provides an Assessment Reform Network listserv. FairTest serves as a discussion forum to support students, parents, teachers, and others in the fight against overuse and misuse of standardized tests; it also promotes authentic assessment.

Ford Foundation
320 East 43rd Street
New York, NY 10017
212-573-5000
www.fordfound.org

The Ford Foundation's mission is to reduce poverty and injustice, promote international cooperation, advance human achievement, and strengthen democratic values. It provides grants and loans that support knowledge building and organization strengthening, and has been a positive force with some programs in urban schools and communities. Its website lists the foundation's policies, grant information, and current projects.

International Reading Association
800 Barksdale Road
PO Box 8139
Newark, DE 19714
302-731-1600
www.reading.org

This international literacy organization promotes literacy through the improvement of reading and holds an annual conference with research presentations from throughout the world. Its website provides exceptional information on just about every literacy-related topic imaginable and includes an online peer-reviewed journal containing further research information.

Knowledge Works Foundation
One West Fourth Street
Suite 200
Cincinnati, OH 45202
513-929-4777
www.kwfdn.org

The main goal of this foundation is to make educational opportunities available to all. Centered in the state of Ohio, it is instrumental in providing funds for Ohio urban schools and school districts, but it also disseminates related information throughout the United States. Its website contains links to a resources library and other educational organizations.

National Alliance of Black School Educators
310 Pennsylvania Ave, SE
Washington, DC 20003
202-608-6310
www.nabse.org

This organization, founded in 1970, has a membership of more than 5,000 African American educators. Its primary aim is to bring together educators to make an impact on all students' education and to promote African American educators into leadership positions. Accordingly, it offers information on professional development, disseminates research, and provides grants for people seeking a career in education. The organization also publishes a journal and holds an annual conference.

National Association for Multicultural Education
733 Fifteenth Street, NW
Suite 430
Washington, DC 20005
www.nameorg.org

This association seeks to further multicultural education in all educational institutions. Its website provides a good definition of multicultural education, along with lesson plans, a reference library, and links to other organizations that support multicultural education.

National Board for Professional Teaching Standards
1525 Wilson Blvd.
Suite 500
Arlington, VA 22209
703-465-2700

www.nbpts.org

This organization seeks to promote the professionalization of teaching and the establishment of a recognizable credential for excellence in teaching. Its website provides information on high-quality teaching and links to other educational resources.

National Center for Education Statistics
1990 K Street, NW
Washington, DC 20006
202-502-7300
http://nces.ed.gov/

This government agency provides statistics on just about every education-related topic there is. Its website provides school and district locators, quick tables and graphs, and excellent search engines for statistics and other data.

National Education Association
1201 16th Street NW
Washington, DC 20036
202-833-4000
www.nea.org

This is one of two main teachers' unions in the United States. Founded in 1857, it has over 2.7 million members as of 2003. Its website provides a link to the code of ethics for the teaching profession as well as links to other educational publications and resources.

New American Schools
675 North Washington Street
Suite 220
Alexandria, VA 22314
703-647-1600
www.naschools.org

This nonprofit organization, formed in 1991, serves as a clearinghouse for nationally recognized comprehensive school reform designs. It provides support, both financial and technical, for education entrepreneurs with proven educational programs; consulting services are also available. Its website contains links to checklists for selecting an appropriate school-improvement program as well as free downloadable publications on comprehensive school programs.

Project Zero
Harvard Graduate School of Education
124 Mount Auburn Street, Fifth Floor
Cambridge, MA 02138
617-496-7097
www.pz.harvard.edu/Default.htm

This educational research organization was founded at Harvard University in 1967. Its website contains information on current research projects as well as a bookstore of available resources.

Rethinking Schools
1001 E. Keefe Avenue
Milwaukee, WI 53212
414-964-9646
www.rethinkingschools.org

This urban-advocacy organization, established by a group of teachers in Milwaukee, supports a balance between educational research and classroom practice. Its website contains articles on current educational issues, and the organization itself publishes a journal called *Rethinking Schools*. This nonprofit, independent grassroots publication, started by teachers in 1986, provides articles that emphasize urban school and social justice issues. Its aim is to encourage teachers, parents, and students to become actively involved in supporting quality public schools.

Thomas Fordham Foundation
1627 K Street, NW
Suite 600
Washington, DC 20006
202-223-5452
www.edexcellence.net/

This organization supports educational reform by supplying grants for research, publications, and action projects, and has been instrumental in providing assistance to the urban school district in Dayton, Ohio. Its website contains information on many educational issues, including standards, tests, accountability, charter schools, school choice, teacher quality, and federal policies.

United States Department of Education
400 Maryland Avenue, SW
Washington, DC 20202

800-872-5327
www.ed.gov

This government organization oversees the U.S. education system, and its website provides a wealth of information on virtually all educational topics and issues.

Appendix A

⚬⬦ Glossary of Terms

Academic Emergency: Term applied to a school or district that is in danger of being taken over by the state. Other sanctions can include loss of funding and replacement of staff and administration.

academic freedom: Term associated with a teacher's ability to control curriculum and teaching within his or her classroom.

Academic Watch: Term applied to a school or district that has not made adequate achievement gains and is in danger of being placed on Academic Emergency status.

accelerated: Term applied to a curriculum system designed to allow students to complete a grade level's worth of study in advanced time.

accountability: Holding persons, teachers, schools, and districts responsible for student learning or other issues.

administrator: Individual tasked with supervising the curriculum, students, teachers, and facilities of a school. Another term used is *principal.*

Afro-centric curriculum: Curriculum designed to emphasize African American history and culture.

American Federation of Teachers: Teachers' union associated with the AFL-CIO.

America 2000: Program set up by President George H. W. Bush to improve America's public school system.

A Nation at Risk: Report created by President Reagan's National Commission on Excellence in Education. Widely distributed, it was critical of public education in general and urban education specifically.

annual appropriation: Term applied to a program that is funded by the government. Funding must be renewed each year.

assessment: Term applied to the process of gathering evidence and giving feedback to improve student learning and instruction.

at-risk students: Students who may not succeed academically due to social and/or economic factors. These factors may include having parents who did not complete high school, are unemployed, or are on welfare; not living with both parents; and having no health insurance.

block scheduling: System that allows a team of teachers in a school to rearrange the school day to fit the needs of the team. This may involve rearranging the time a class starts or increasing and decreasing the time spent in a class.

board of education: Elected or appointed governing body that supervises a school district or a state school system. Members make decisions that affect staffing, superintendents, curriculum, calendar, and budget concerns.

bond issue: Funding proposal used for a specific purpose such as building a new building or updating phone lines. Local voters must approve the bond issue in order to raise needed funds.

Brown v. Board of Education: U.S. Supreme Court case that ended legal segregation in public schools.

career ladder: Term that describes steps toward advancement during a teacher's career.

charter schools: Nonprofit schools associated with school choice. Parents are allowed to take the funding from the public school district to apply to tuition for the charter school.

Cincinnati Business Community: Local business organization created to influence political actions and education issues in Cincinnati, Ohio.

Coleman Report: Report published in 1966 that linked educational achievement to the socioeconomic status of students.

college preparatory: Term applied to a style of curriculum designed to prepare students for higher education.

Committee of Ten: Committee organized by the National Education Association in 1892 to develop recommendations for the public school system. These recommendations were implemented throughout most of the country.

common schools: Term that referred to the first public schools in the United States during the early and mid-1800s. Common schools were also some of the first schools to openly accept females into the student body.

consulting teacher: Lead teacher who serves as a mentor/evaluator for novice or new teachers in a district. May also be involved with intervention of a struggling experienced teacher.

creationism: Theory advanced by religious advocates proposing that evolution is controlled by a higher being.

curriculum: Term applied to everything that goes on in learners' lives both inside and outside the school, whether planned or unplanned. Curriculum thus includes the resources the students have or do not have; the quality of the teacher; resources such as chalk and computers or the lack thereof; the experiences of the students, whether planned or hidden; the culture, background knowledge, learning style, and multiple-intelligence strength and weakness of the students; what is taught or not taught including the books and resources used or not used, the content used or not used, the subjects taken or not taken; the sequence of courses; and, finally, objectives, standards, and interpersonal relationships.

curriculum council chair: Lead teacher who leads a specific subject area in a district, schedules and coordinates meetings, and helps set policy.

curriculum specialist: Lead teacher who serves as the curriculum expert in a specific subject area. May also lead curriculum committee for teachers in a district.

desegregation: Efforts to integrate racial groups into public schools.

educational vouchers: Private and public funding programs that allow the parents of students to send their children to the school of their choice, including religious schools. Funding associated with the student is taken from the public school district and applied to the tuition of the private school.

Elementary and Secondary Education Act (ESEA): Often referred to as Title I, this act is one of the many programs created under the Johnson administration as part of his war on poverty efforts. The program provides additional funding to schools and districts with a large number of students who live below the poverty line.

exceptionalities: Term that refers to the characteristics of nontypical students. Includes physical and mental challenges as well as giftedness.

excise tax: A tax applied to a particular item such as cigarettes, gasoline, and alcohol. Often the raised revenue is used for educational purposes.

Federal Department of Health, Education, and Welfare (HEW): Federal organization that oversaw health, education, and welfare issues and was instrumental in helping to desegregate school systems.

First Morrill Act: Created in 1862, this act set aside public land to be auctioned off for the creation and operation of public colleges.

GI Bill: Government program designed to pay for higher education for veterans of World War I. Although the program and its name have changed, the concept is still in effect for members of the armed forces.

Goals 2000: Educational plan advanced by the Clinton administration, based somewhat on President George H. W. Bush's *America 2000*.

Head Start: Program created as part of President Johnson's war on poverty, designed to prepare underprivileged students for school.

hidden curriculum: Term referring to a curriculum that is not specifically stated but is the conveyance of the culture of a school, in terms of knowledge or attitude expressed verbally or nonverbally.

higher-education institution: Term usually applied to a college, university, or trade school that is attended by students after graduation from high school.

high-stakes standardized testing: Term referring to standardized tests that affect retention of students, student graduation, and sometimes school and district funding. Results are often used to rank schools and districts.

Horn Book: Device used in colonial times by children in New England who were learning to read. It looked like a paddle on which a piece of paper was glued, with a thin cow's horn placed over the top to protect the writing. This writing usually included the alphabet and religious verse.

Individual Educational Plan (IEP): An individualized plan written for students with exceptionalities. The special education teacher usually writes the IEP using input from parents and regular education teachers. Both the school and the parents must approve the plan.

Individuals with Disabilities Education Act (IDEA): Legislation that sets guidelines and standards for the education and treatment of individuals with physical and mental challenges. In educational contexts it stipulates that the student will be placed in the least restrictive environment.

inquiry-based instruction: Curriculum utilized primarily in science that encourages students to study a topic that interests them. For example, teachers may create problem situations for students, who then attempt to investigate utilizing their background knowledge and present learning to try to solve the problems.

integrated arts: Utilization of art and music within the academic curriculum.

intelligent design: Term used to describe a theory maintaining that evolution is controlled by a higher being. Also referred to as *creationism*.

learning organization: Term referring to a setting—whether classroom, school, district, or college—in which it is postulated that all members are committed to the growth of all individuals in the organization.

magnet schools: Public schools within a district that allows students to attend a school that has a program of interest to them.

mentor: Usually an experienced teacher who spends time with a novice teacher, giving advice and direction.

mentoring: System in which an experienced teacher is teamed up with a novice teacher to offer guidance and advice.

merit pay: System that gives additional money to teachers who reach a set goal or standard. Usually based on the results of a standardized test.

Monitor schools: Schools based on the Lancaster system in which one teacher gives a lesson to a group of "monitors," who then give that lesson to the rest of the students. This system was popular during the early to mid-1800s due to its relatively low cost.

Montessori: Style of curriculum, advanced by Maria Montessori, that allows students to investigate subjects of interest and stresses use of manipulatives in early childhood development.

multi-age: Term referring to a classroom in which students of several different ages are taught together.

multiple intelligences: Theory advanced by Howard Gardner maintaining that students' intelligence can be expressed in several different areas such as motor or interpersonal skills.

National Association for the Advancement of Colored People (NAACP): African American organization started by W.E.B. Du Bois to look after issues affecting the African American community.

National Commission on Excellence in Education: Commission created by the Reagan administration that wrote *A Nation at Risk* report.

National Defense Education Act: Created by Congress in 1958, this legislation was designed to increase math and science proficiency, primarily in response to the Soviet Union's launching of Sputnik.

National Education Association (NEA): Largest teaching organization in the United States.

National Teacher Examination: Standardized test that most pre-service teachers must pass in order to meet licensing requirements.

neighborhood schools: Local public schools that accept all students based on attendance boundaries.

No Child Left Behind Act: Legislation initiated by the George W. Bush administration to reform public schools through mandatory standardized testing, teaching standards, and graduation requirements.

Northwest Territories Act: Legislation created under the Articles of Confederation that set parameters for statehood. Parts of this act comprised the first federal-level legislation affecting education.

Ohio Proficiency Test (OPT): Standardized tests that Ohio students must pass in order to graduate. Scores are used to rate districts and individual schools.

Old Deluder Satan Act: Legislation created in the colony of Massachusetts requiring towns to provide schools and teachers. The purpose of this legislation was to educate children in an effort to keep them from sin.

operational levy: Tax proposal that must be approved by voters in order to provide funding for local school districts. This funding is used for daily operations including salaries, books, building maintenance, and so on.

Paideia: Teaching style originally proposed by Mortimer Adler. Its three main elements are didactic teaching, coaching, and seminar.

Parent-Teacher Association (PTA): Organization made up of parents, administrators, teachers, and students that deals with school issues.

parochial schools: Private Catholic schools that provide basic as well as religious education.

Plessy v. Ferguson: U.S. Supreme Court case that legalized racial segregation based on the principle of "separate but equal."

PL 94-142: Law that stipulates how students with special needs are treated. The main mandate is that students must be placed in the least restrictive environment.

prepackaged or controlled curriculum: Curriculum that is teacher-proofed, in the sense that the teacher is told what and when to say and do.

program facilitator: Lead teacher who serves as the coordinator for a specific program in a school and who may model instruction and/or be responsible for disseminating materials.

school-wide lead teacher: Lead teacher who serves as the curriculum and policy coordinator of an entire school.

social promotion: Term that refers to the policy of promoting students who have not met the requirements for a grade level.

Sputnik: Launched by the Soviet Union, this was the first artificial satellite to orbit the earth. The launching caused the United States to increase its focus on math and science curriculum.

standardized test: A battery of tests that are given to a population at the same time and in the same way. Scores are normed according to the population.

standards: Official set requirements and guidelines that are to be met by a student, school, or district.

state-mandated curriculum: Term referring to a state's requirement that a district or districts use a specific style of curriculum. Most state-mandated curriculums are designed and implemented by an outside organization.

subject area leader: Lead teacher who also functions as the department head in a school. Departments may include math, science, social studies, and so on.

tax abatement: System that lowers tax requirements in order to entice private businesses to locate in a local area. As an incentive, the organization is permitted not to pay taxes for a set period of time.

teacher academy: Central location where novice and veteran teachers can receive professional development courses and sometimes college credit to improve their teaching.

Teacher Evaluation System (TES): Evaluation system put in place in Cincinnati Public Schools in Ohio. Created by the district and the teachers' union, TES evaluates teachers based on set standards and the creation of a portfolio of evidence.

team leader: Lead teacher who is in charge of a team of teachers. Team leaders also help facilitate team and school policies for the students who belong to that team.

tenure: A system that gives a teacher property rights to his or her job. Tenure is typically offered after a teacher has taught for a certain number of years and has attained a particular education level. Tenure systems vary from district to district.

Title I: Federal funding that provides additional money to districts with high numbers of students living below the poverty line. Also may be called *Chapter I.*

Title IX: A federal law that requires funding equity to ensure equality in sports between girls and boys.

unfunded mandates: Government laws that force schools and districts to make changes, but without providing the funding to do so.

urban schools: Term referring to schools that are located in a central city of a metropolitan area, or to schools that contain students who are socially or academically at-risk.

white flight: Term referring to the phenomenon of white citizens moving from urban centers to the suburbs.

year-round schools: Schools that operate year round rather than over the traditional nine-month period. Year-round schools typically operate for nine weeks at a time, with a three-week break between quarters.

⚬ Wright State University Teacher Leader Graduate Program

Dr. Grant Hambright
Program Coordinator

INTRODUCTION

Teacher leadership in today's schools is an essential function. Schools can no longer depend solely on the designated building administrator to sufficiently guide and manage the academic and supervisory duties entailed in running an effective and efficient operation. There exists a ready and capable pool of potential assistance with these essential tasks. Teachers, already the instructional services foundation, are the logical resource for this help through reconceptualized roles within their learning organizations. Katzenmeyer and Moller (2001) contend that teachers are leaders within and beyond their classrooms.

Professional development opportunities for teachers, concentrating on requisite training and knowledge, are essential as the traditional roles become altered to reflect current organizational needs. Training in skills such as team building, problem solving, and critical thinking will enhance the teachers' classroom functions in conjunction with aiding administrative duties. Knowledge is needed for emergent roles in which teachers could assist school administrators. These roles include, but are not limited to, mentoring new staff, participating in collaborative decision-making, designing and developing new curricula, and conducting staff development offerings.

The following describes our college's long-term commitment to provide teaching professionals with academic and leadership knowledge and skills essential to face the evolving structures and roles in the schools of today and tomorrow.

TEACHER LEADER PROGRAM OVERVIEW

The graduate-level Teacher Leader Program (TLP) at Wright State University is a data-driven and theory-based program designed for practicing teachers and other school-based personnel desiring an advanced degree. The curriculum consists of forty-eight quarter credit hours concentrating on: (a) organizational leadership; (b) philosophical and psychological foundations; (c) curriculum design and evaluation; (d) student assessment; (e) instructional analysis and management; (f) school law; and (g) statistical and research foundations in teaching. Relevant technology is a curricular strand woven throughout the program's tapestry of course offerings. Although substantive theory undergirds the coursework content, students are encouraged to readily apply their conceptual and skill-based understandings toward practical applications within their schools.

The TLP conceptual framework consists of overarching theoretical and experiential components. Ideally, program graduates obtain conceptual and practical understandings of theory and its relationship to teaching, learning, and leadership processes. Affective understandings aggregate as students learn and experience relationships between problem identification, action research, reflection, and the pursuit of continuous improvement of individual and collective professional practices. Critical theory, professional literature, and experiential histories provide lenses for students to scrutinize the multifaceted topics and issues found in educational organizations. An additional component of the TLP, student cohorts, affords program participants an inherent interaction dynamic, and, subsequently, exposure to colleagues with a variety of content-area, grade-level, and leadership expertise. The cohort structure also provides students with an authentic learning experience that they may deem an appropriate model to emulate toward building learning communities within their respective organizations.

Student cohorts, a structure facilitating emergent role-development, progress through the 12-term program. This programmatic format enables students to learn in a climate of cooperation and trust (Burnaford and Hobson, 1995). The cohorts remain intact and quasi-closed throughout their course cycle. The term "quasi-closed" refers to a limited availability for students in other college and/or departmental programs to enroll in a course offered at one of the off-campus sites. The "visiting" students request admittance to the cohort classes due to convenience (work or home proximity) or an on-campus course offering availability. Cohort size and other logistical restrictions dictate a "visitor's" viability toward enrolling in a TLP cohort site class.

Throughout the TLP students compile artifacts reflective of their acquired knowledge and skills. This progress and reflective portfolio is submitted to program faculty in lieu of a thesis or a comprehensive examination. Requisite components of the portfolio include: (a) a student's mission; (b) belief statements pertaining to education as a profession; (c) belief statements about children and their learning; (d) a professional development plan; (e) an ongoing professional dialogue journal; and (f) course artifacts with reflective entries assessing the projected personal or professional growth resulting from program involvement.

During the final quarter term, students present their self-assessing, self-reflecting portfolios in a formal exit interview with program faculty. In this setting, questionnaires are completed for quantitative data, and small focus-group interviews serve as qualitative instruments for overall program review.

Upon completion of the program, TLP graduates receive a master's degree in education with an emphasis in curriculum and instruction. At this point, program graduates may opt to remain in their current classroom settings or choose to continue pursuing other credential options. For example, the TLP curriculum is aligned with the National Board for Professional Teaching Standards (NBPTS). Although progressing through the program's courses, students are made aware of the standards' alignment with the curriculum objectives and activities. The TLP portfolio serves as a springboard toward meeting several NBPTS criteria. With additional assistance following program completion, students may apply their knowledge and skills toward obtaining this highly coveted credential. Other program graduates continue their university studies with the intent of eventually attaining additional licensure in supervision or administration.

TLP HISTORY

Historically, the TLP began as an off-campus professional development outreach program in 1976. Survey data indicated that area teachers wanted to take graduate-level coursework; however, travel, time, parking, campus and personal schedules, and family obligations presented constraints for the respondents. Based on these data, an off-campus course delivery system was envisioned. Classes were and are conducted in various sites scattered throughout the southwest quadrant of Ohio during early evening hours as a means of overcoming the cited barriers. The initial three cohort sites eventually grew to fifteen sites in 1988. By the mid-1990s, the program peaked with twenty-nine site offerings, and was the largest graduate-level program at the university (Kisch, 1996). Currently, the program provides classes at sixteen remote locations and retains its status as the campus's largest graduate program.

The program continuously evolves in response to internal and external input. Formative and summative data from program graduates, area school personnel, and program faculty and administration drive the program revision processes. In response to recent surveys and interviews, program changes include: (a) initiating an on-campus orientation for beginning TLP students for the purpose of acquainting them with program advisors, technology capabilities, research facilities, and miscellaneous perks afforded to all WSU students that were formerly unknown to previous graduating cohorts; (b) the initiation of the program's first "online" cohort that will receive a majority of its course offerings via the Internet; (c) aligning the TLP course objectives and activities with

NBPTS criteria; and (d) streamlining the TLP course offerings for smoother transitions into supervision and administration licensure coursework.

REFERENCES

Burnaford, G., and Hobson, D. 1995. "Beginning with the Group: Collaboration as the Cornerstone of Graduate Teacher Education." *Action in Teacher Education*, 17 (3), 67–75.

Katzenmeyer, M., and Moller, G. 2001. *Awakening the Sleeping Giant: Helping Teachers Develop as Leaders*. 2nd ed. Thousand Oaks, CA: Corwin.

Kisch, J. A. 1996. "Teacher Leader: A Program to Develop Teachers as Leaders." Unpublished study of the development of the Wright State University Teacher Leader Program.

Appendix C

☙ Interview with an Urban Principal

INTERVIEWER: How long have you taught and been an administrator in urban schools?

PRINCIPAL: I'm in my twenty-eighth year, about ten as a teacher and my eighteenth as an administrator.

I: Have you been with the same district?

P: Yep.

I: What are the positives and negatives of being an urban high school principal?

P: I can talk until next week on that. Positives: . . . Oh, challenging. Some people may see that as a negative, I see it as a positive. Ah, because it is rewarding as well and I don't think that you get the rewards if you don't have the challenges. I feel that what I do, what we all do in urban education is important, it is meaningful and it gives us a real sense of accomplishment. The negatives are some of the obvious ones: lack of resources, lack of parental involvement and by that I recognize that we have a number of parents that are actively involved, but I don't think you see the same level of involvement as you do in the suburban or the private or parochial schools. And most urban districts tend to be very large and when you have that you tend to run into bureaucracies and sometimes those bureaucracies and the politics and the unions and the civil service regulations and all those types of things . . . make it difficult to make the changes that are necessary.

I: Do you have any problems recruiting or retaining teachers?

P: I think recruitment is more of a problem than retention. In terms of retentions I don't know that we have any more teachers who leave and I can only speak of the buildings that I am familiar with. But in the buildings that I've worked in I don't think that we have any more teachers leave those buildings or leave the district or leave teaching than they do in other types of schools in other settings. I think retention is more difficult because of the perception that people new to the profession have about urban education. But once they overcome that perception or mis-perception and they see what it is really like and what they can or can't accomplish I think that they tend to stay.

I: Do you think recruitment or retaining is affected by the fact that this is a magnet school compared to a neighborhood school?

P: Certainly the quality of the schools that I've worked in urban education—there is no question about that. By the same token I know a number of teachers who have worked in neighborhood schools and even though they have had opportunities to move to alternative schools or magnet schools or other types of programs they have stayed where they are. So, well, those schools in the "city" might be a little more challenging and some of maybe the younger inexperienced teachers have bailed; I think that those who came to urban education and even in adverse circumstances realized that they could be successful and they could make a difference have stayed. Now statistically those schools have a little bit higher turnover rates. I would imagine they do.

I: This district has a lead teacher program. What are your thoughts about that program?

P: I think it is a step in the right direction. But I don't think that we've taken full advantage of it in order to really use that to improve instruction, improve teaching, improve the schools. There is so much leadership potential among teachers and so many skills, so much expertise, that we could use those lead teachers much more effectively and in a much broader sense than we presently are. So I think that the concept is good. I think we have taken a few baby steps in the right direction but we haven't fully taken advantage of that program.

I: This school has a teaching program for high school students. Do you think that program is successful? I mean, have you seen students who have been inspired to become teachers, especially urban teachers?

P: We've had a few that have gone completely through the pipeline and become teachers. We have each year, as that program becomes more established and more successful, more that are pursuing teaching degrees in college and so I would say that it is gradually becoming more successful and more effective in realizing its mission of preparing teachers to return to urban education.

I: Another issue is that this district has recently enacted a comprehensive teaching evaluation system. Any thoughts on the system itself?

P: I have two basic thoughts; one is in terms of establishing professional standards. The domains, the standards, the rubric language that says this is what your best and your brightest teachers do on a regular basis. All the standards and the rubric language I think is excellent because it gives a really clear picture to teachers, to administrators, to everyone in the district, that this is what good teaching looks like. So in terms of saying that these are the best practices and these are the ideals to which all teachers should be striving, I think that it is excellent. In terms of the evaluation aspect of it I think that it is exceptionally cumbersome, time consuming, too much of a paper chase, that it actually detracts from the job that administrators and teachers should be doing. And so I have real problems and concerns about how the evaluation aspect has been designed and implemented. So I really don't like how we are conducting the evaluation system right now. But in terms of saying these are the best practices, these are the standards, I love that. But in addition to all of the other problems it really causes you to look at the individual trees rather than the forest when you are assessing a teacher's performance and it almost seems that they have tried to make it administrator proof rather than saying hey, here are the administrators that we have hired and we are just going to have to trust their professional judgment, when they go into a classroom, to look at the big picture, and to use these standards, but just kind of give us the big picture of "Is this a beautiful forest or not?" rather than spend all this time and energy saying this is an oak tree with seventeen branches and fourteen leaves and therefore you know when you add all this up you have a good forest. Because from all the detail that is required, many times when you sit back you miss the forest because of all the details.

I: With stuff like the No Child Left Behind Act coming out, what are your opinions or thoughts on high-stakes testing?

P: You know, it's interesting that you ask that question right after we've talked about the teacher evaluation system because if anyone in this district looked at the teacher evaluation system and those standards and that teacher determined whether or not the student passed his or her course on a single paper-and-pencil objective test that was given at the end of the school year we would say that teacher is terrible and ought to be fired. And yet the politicians across the country at the federal level and the state level have decided that that is the best way to assess whether or not school districts are doing a good job; schools are doing a good job, teachers are doing a good job, and we are just not that smart to come up with a single test that we can administer one time a year that is going to tell us all that. It just is bad education and what is troubling is that we in education haven't stood up to the media, to the politicians, to all these people, and said this is nonsense. Should we have standardized tests? Sure, let's have standardized tests and let's look at the results as one measure of how students are performing, how teachers are performing, how principals and schools and districts are performing, but let's look at all the other stuff that we need to be looking at to make a final assessment as well.

I: You mentioned earlier about the bureaucracy and politics sometimes associated with urban districts. Has that affected how you perform as an administrator? Does that get in your way, or is it more of a help?

P: You know, it is interesting because there are probably many suburban districts where the politics are much worse than they are in urban school districts. In fact, sometimes the large bureaucracy can actually help you or works in your favor. Because you kind of get lost in that bureaucratic morass. But in response to your question: Yes, there are times when the bureaucracy or internal politics get in the way of what principals, teachers, and schools are trying to do and make our jobs more difficult.

I: You mentioned the politics of how this district is looked at as an urban district, with the politicians above up at the local, state, and national level. Do you think they get in the way of making true reform or trying to make progress toward achievement for students?

P: I don't know that it's a matter of how they look at urban education as it is that the vast majority of the people and the vast majority of the elected representatives do not live in urban districts. And so I think that's the politics that gets in the way of giving the urban districts the types of resources and support that they need; it's that the representatives that are voting on those bills or enacting those laws don't represent those districts.

I: If you could tell anybody why they should or shouldn't be an urban principal, what would you say?

P: It is, as I said earlier about working in urban education, very challenging; if you want a job where you will never be bored, where you are always going to be tested, this is a great job. And if you are successful and effective and you see some of the things you are achieving and accomplishing, it's incredibly rewarding. On the other hand, it is a relatively low-paying job, long hours, high stress level, and the rewards tend to be more intrinsic versus extrinsic and more personal—personally recognizing your achievements. You are not going to get a lot of public recognition for your achievements. In fact, I don't know, maybe it is just me in the way I do my job, it seems to be that you get much more criticism than compliments.

I: Do you think that the college teacher training programs properly prepare teachers for the urban environment?

P: Oh, absolutely not. I think some colleges in recent years have started to make a more concerted effort in that regard toward urban education and try to get their kids some meaningful urban experiences. But I think the problem is larger than that. I am not sure how good of a job colleges of education are doing in just preparing teachers. And again I know that there are some universities and colleges that are doing a much better job than others. But just making a very broad general statement I would say that the colleges of education aren't doing a very good job of preparing young people to be teachers. What is going on in the universities versus the classroom is too far removed from what is going on in the high school classroom. They need to give their students more practical real-life exposure and to the skills and strategies that are needed to be successful. And that would be especially true in urban education because we are dealing with more difficult children in many cases, more challenges, and so if they are not just in a general sense adequately preparing their graduates to be teachers, then even less so to be successful in an urban setting.

I: Given the recent ruling on vouchers and the No Child Left Behind Act and other things, any thoughts about the future of urban education?

P: All I can say is that I think in order for our country to remain strong and prosper we need a strong public education system. And I think we need strong urban centers. So we need those two things and it only follows that we need strong urban public school systems. So I think the cities and the country need strong urban public education. Have we as a country really supported urban education? I would say no we haven't. I think we have not done a very good job. Are some of these political decisions going to help urban education? From what I know and from my experience I would guess not. I don't know if they are necessarily going to damage it. I think regardless of those types of things it will survive and it won't be fatally harmed, but I guess the real negative is that people will be spending all this time and energy and limited resources on things that won't necessarily help us to become what we need to become. And so many of those political solutions I think are misguided and detract us from making the necessary repairs and improvements that need to occur.

I: Any final thoughts or recommendations, or anything else in general that you wish to say?

P: Well, I subscribe to the fact that problems and solutions to problems are best developed and implemented at the level closest to the problem. And so if you have to choose between a solution in the classroom versus the school, I would say a better solution is going to come from the classroom. If you have to look at the solution coming up in a school versus the district I would say that it should be left up to the individual schools. If it is going to be statewide versus individual school districts, again go to the district level. If it is going to be individual states versus the whole country, then the solution should come up at the state level. And I think that in recent years we've seen people attempt to come up with solutions in a more centralized level. The national government is going to solve the problem. The state is going to solve the problem. The district is going to solve the problem. The more you can get it down to the individual classroom or the individual school, the better chance you have of coming up with real meaningful solutions to problems that exist.

I: Last question, what is the solution? What is the fix for the perceived failure of urban education?

P: Students, good parents, good teachers. The reason I say that is that over time what has happened, for a number of reasons, is that good students and good parents have left urban school districts and good teachers have not necessarily been attracted to the urban districts. And so we have to bring all those people back so that the problems become manageable. If 10 percent of your students are special education and 20 percent of your students are below the poverty level and 30 percent of your students have academic deficiencies, then the problems in the school become manageable. When the good students and the good parents move away and now those percentages become 40, 50, 60, 70, 80 percent, now the problems become so large it becomes very difficult for an individual school to deal with those problems. Or an individual teacher in the classroom to deal with those problems.

I: Thanks a lot.

Appendix D

◆◆ Interview with a Practicing Urban Teacher

INTERVIEWER: How long have you been teaching in urban schools, and what do you teach?

TEACHER: This is my seventh year and I teach social studies. . . . I taught five years in a magnet school and two years in a neighborhood school.

I: What do you think are the positives and negatives of teaching in urban schools?

T: Well, there are a lot of internal rewards. You are certainly doing a service and you should be proud of it. Number one for being a teacher because that is challenging enough, then being a teacher in an urban setting; it takes quite a bit, and those who can stay more than a couple of years really should be proud. It feels good when you take a student who obviously needs you and needs your skills and bring them to the point that that student can succeed. Negative is the typical ones that most people see, such as the parental support; sometimes it seems that the society that the student comes from doesn't value education. And it is also the lack of stuff you need. The basic stuff like copy paper and money to buy films and computers that work and so forth, and that the students themselves can be a challenge. The place where the students come from is different than what people know, and when you have them in your classroom it takes different strategies to teach them. Not only teach them to do classroom management and all the kind of things like that. So now there is quite a bit, but again I think that the rewards, if you can take it, outweigh the negatives—provided you can deal with the stress.

I: Do you think that retention or recruiting of teachers is a problem?

T: I certainly do. I have seen a lot of first-year teachers come in and leave the district or leave teaching altogether. Our district I think . . . probably . . . turns over 200–300 teachers. Some of that is from retirement while others are from not liking the setting or not liking teaching to begin with. So I think recruiting and holding on to decent teachers is a challenge anywhere, but that challenge is multiplied in the urban setting.

I: What are your thoughts on the bureaucracy and politics in urban schools?

T: Well, unfortunately urban schools are a magnet for criticism anyway, especially with all the standardized tests. There are problems with the tests. . . . It seems that urban districts don't do as well on these tests; therefore, the criticism really comes down on urban schools. Some of that criticism is fair and a lot of it is not. Because urban schools have such a large student population, they get a lot of attention as well. And with education and politics, they have always been kind of married together, but it seems to be even stronger against urban schools. As far as bureaucracy, most urban districts are large. That is certainly the case in the district I work in and there are certain layers of supervision; some of it is needed and some of it in my opinion is not. Which makes it even a bigger target, especially with politicians, because it is larger than the suburban districts. There are more supervisors, more administration, but there are a lot more requirements in an urban district. With special education, vocational education, there are some urban districts that hire people just to do grants because they are so short on funding. So it can be large and I see some of the resources being spent on overhead instead of what is underneath the roof sometimes. But then again, if a lot of those people were not there we would probably feel it.

I: What are your thoughts on your teachers' union?

T: Well, that is somewhat mixed. We belong to part of the American Federation of Teachers and they are closer to a traditional union than I guess the other organization. And I see a need for it because you have to use some of those traditional labor tools to get a good contract, but that just draws more attention from some who don't generally like unions to begin with and when you bring in the fact that it is a teachers' union, we seem to be the cause of everything from the downfall of education to the plague. So I am kind of mixed. I pay quite a bit in dues, but I see that if it wasn't there that urban teachers would really have a harder problem.

I: What about your teacher evaluation system?

T: I'm against it. I think that teachers should be evaluated; they should be observed by practically anyone who wants to come in. I have no problem with anybody coming into my classroom to observe, from my building administrator to the superintendent to a parent. But the problem I have is that they try to apply these standards and they do a strict interpretation of them. I think that it is very unfair; for example, there is something in my evaluation system that says, "Do you provide a warm and caring classroom?" Well what the heck is that? If you go into a kindergarten classroom you would expect to see one thing. If you go into a twelfth-grade calculus classroom you would expect to see something else. And a lot of these things are subjective. And teaching is a challenge anyway. I know a lot of colleagues of mine who are spending so much time on their portfolio stuff that they have to turn in and they are making sure that everything is cleaned up and tidy and I think that they are spending less time on creativity as far as designing lessons and implementing lessons for their students. So I believe that teachers should be evaluated, but the current system that we have—when you are rubriced against this, that, and the other—is too much of a waste of time for the teacher and I think that the administrators are really catching it too. They have enough to do to begin with and you are talking about annual observations for every single teacher in the building plus comprehensive evaluations, which is six visits I believe between them and somebody from the district, so I think it is too much and I think that they are trying to measure the wrong thing.

I: You have a lead teacher system and a career ladder in your district. Do you have any thoughts on those?

T: I like the idea of a lead teacher, but to be honest with you I have not seen a whole bunch of benefit from it. I know that as a first-year teacher I benefited from having a lead teacher on my team, but I have known many of my colleagues as first-year teachers did not have that benefit and lead teachers did not seem to get around to them and did not make the time to help them out. Most of them answered questions if they were asked, but they should be given one or two free bells [class periods] a day to go around and help the teachers who are struggling, or being there to consult with other teachers to improve lesson delivery all the way around. So again I think that it is a good idea, but I don't think that it is being implemented well.

I: What about the career ladder specifically? Where you can get tenure or not get tenure?

T: I think that it is a good idea and I still believe in tenure to begin with. But I know a lot of folks out there who would like to see that eliminated. I think the career ladder is a good idea and needs to be very open, and obvious steps need to be taken to attain tenure or career ladder status or continuing contract or whatever it happens to be called in that district. It needs to be fair and for the most part I think ours is fair.

I: Do you have any other thoughts specifically on tenure?

T: Well, I think tenure is a good idea and a lot of my colleagues may disagree but there are some good things out of the legislation that is coming out that are requiring teachers to get additional education. I would like to see more of my colleagues get more technology training or more training on how to implement standards that we are being forced to use or maybe training on how to help students pass standardized tests. I think that it is good, but I see a possibility of abuse too.

I: What are your thoughts on your high-stakes tests and accountability system?

T: Well, I think that high-stakes tests are wrong. I think standardized tests are good in that every student in the same grade takes the same test, but it should be a tool. But now it is a weapon for conservative forces to beat up on districts, especially the urban districts. The tests themselves, as research shows, are written in a white, upper-middle-class style of language and in the urban schools I believe that that is a hindrance. I think that having a single test to determine whether or not a student graduates from high school is kind of ridiculous. Should that student know the information on that test? Certainly if it is a good written test based on standards that are in the district, but many of the tests are not. I know that the critics say that somebody should be able to pass a ninth-grade- or a tenth-grade-level test, but I would love to see some of these critics actually have to take the tests. I would like to take these to whatever state legislature creates them and require every member to take them and pass them. They should know this. From the horror stories, I can't really confirm them, but I have heard a lot of stories about children being so nervous that they are sick about having to take the test. The tests should be good, they should be well written, they should match the standards that are measured; but I think that the district should have the opportunity for the option of alternative assessment. And some students simply don't test well. I have a student who has a 4.0 average, but when she takes the ACT test she scores pretty much dead-center. I know that she is much smarter than what she is showing. She does not test well. On the other hand, I was in the military and when I take a standardized test I test very well. And in the military I was promoted past others who I knew didn't test well but were twice as good at their job as I was at mine. So again I think that standardized tests are good, but the high-stakes portion of it needs to be rethought.

I: Do you feel any pressure to teach to the test?

T: Oh, absolutely. A lot of teachers, and I probably fall into this group, feel that we owe it to the children; if the children have to pass the test in order to graduate, we have a responsibility to make sure that they graduate and make sure that they pass the tests. Schools are judged by the results of these tests. I think that there should be a lot of other criteria that schools are judged by, but we have to live with what is put upon us. They are judged, districts are judged, and it is kind of ridiculous. Something that maybe my colleagues will probably be against is if we are going to have a standardized test, in my opinion it should be a national standardized test. With the exact same standards seen all over the place. Now a lot of conservatives and liberals are against this because they want to keep the federal government out of it, but if the federal government is mandating high-stakes standardized tests to begin with, then I think that there should be national standards that are clear to the students, clear to the teachers, and we should go from that. But to answer your original question before I rambled on, yes I feel a lot of pressure to teach to the test and quite frankly myself and a lot of my colleagues shut down for about three or four weeks before a test just to ram, cram, and drill and fill until they are ready to take that test. It is probably nothing to be proud of, but my students do well on them; but again I think that it is because we spend too much time on test prep.

I: You said earlier that you worked at a neighborhood school and a magnet school. Do you have any thoughts on this?

T: As a teacher at the magnet school, I prefer the environment. Number one is that I know some magnet schools where the students are tested prior to admittance. Our particular school does not, but if you are going to test the students before you admit them, you know that they are already smart, so half the battle is that at least the intellect is won, you just have to work on the classroom management and guiding that student toward achievement. And even if not the tests, it is easier to teach in the magnet schools, in my opinion, because the parents care somewhat. The parents have to stand in line in some cases and sign their children up. If they are going to do that, if they are going to make the effort of looking into their children's education, then they care about it. When you call home they are much more responsive; they are going to take more interest in making sure that their children see success and that they do their homework and have the supplies they need. And I don't mean to knock the parents of neighborhood school children. I have known a lot of wonderful parents. But if you compare percentages of parents who are really dedicated, then the magnet school certainly comes out on top. And that makes it much easier, in my opinion, if you have parental support.

I: Along with that, you have been in a school for the last three years that has received payment based on the accountability system in your district, whereas other schools in your district have not received that payment, especially the ones that are in the neighborhood. Do you have any thoughts on that?

T: There's probably some unfairness to the system. I am not sure if the criteria are normed when comparing neighborhood to magnet schools. I believe it is based on the previous year's test scores and any kind of improvement on that. So I think that the neighborhood schools have a chance on doing that, but the challenge is much higher. On the other hand, a couple of the magnet schools are testing and the students who pass the test are admitted. People look at these schools and say what a wonderful job they are doing when the kids are so much higher level achievement-wise than the neighborhood school kids. So I acknowledge the fact that I don't donate the money that I get for being part of this school, but there is some soundness in the argument that it is not quite fair.

I: Do you have anything else to talk about?

T: I just find it sad that the people who want to jump on the bandwagon and criticize urban schools and slam the teachers, slam the students, slam the system and stuff like that are the same guys who never spend any time in these schools. Politicians do this and most of your politicians come from a different area of the state or the city and they have no real understanding of what is going on and they really need to spend some time to talk to the principals, the teachers, and above all else the students. And a group that I blame even more than politicians is the media. In my opinion, and I am ranting here, the media has lost its investigative edge. The media takes whatever is said by politicians and others at face value without doing any investigation. It would be wonderful if we had a camera crew follow around those students for a period of time and do some exposé kind of stuff on it. But that doesn't happen. They show up and have their cameras in front of the school and interview somebody and say "Back to you, Johnny." And they don't really delve deep to find out what is going on. Our urban schools are hurting. They are hurting from funding to direction, and to be honest with you there are some teachers who need to leave, there are some administrators who need to leave. I think that there is enough blame to go around, but it is not hopeless. The students who go to our schools deserve the best that we can give them. I try to do that; it is hard to do that on a daily basis, but I try to give them a decent education. As a society we know that it is a heck of a lot easier to pay for education than it is to pay for their prison cells. As far as money goes they are hurting. To be honest with you as an urban teacher I am paid pretty well compared to a suburban district. That doesn't hold true everywhere, but I feel that a lot of other teachers are paid a little bit more and I feel that their job is more challenging. But there are other needs in the urban schools. I hear a lot of especially conservative politicians attack urban schools because they spend more per child than a lot of affluent suburban schools; but they don't look at the big picture. You don't have the security concerns, you don't have the run-down buildings, you don't have the need for a higher population of special education students. There is a lot more to it. And a lot more can be done. I don't want to feel complacent and I don't think that urban teachers should hurt their arms patting themselves on the back, because I think that we can do more. But for a country to be what it should be, it should take care of the students who need the education services the most.

I: The final question, after all that, is where do you see yourself in ten years? Will you be in an urban school?

T: Good question. I've been working on my master's and I may want to eventually teach at the college level. It depends on how bad some of the challenges get. If we continue to have problems with the teacher evaluation program system, if we keep getting slammed by the media and by the politicians, we wouldn't be caught dead in an urban school. If we keep being slammed by those guys it is hard to keep getting yourself up in the morning, to keep fighting the good fight. But then again I feel that I am being useful; I feel that I am serving a better purpose. I am probably doing more good here as a teacher than I would have in a suburban and even a parochial school. I think that I am doing well by these students; at least that is my intent. I will chug away with it as long as I can stand it. After that, unless Led Zeppelin is hiring a drummer or something, I will probably be here.

Appendix E

❧ Children Get Left Behind When High Stakes Are Confused with High Leverage

Scott Thompson

The following article illustrates the harm of standardized, high-stakes testing.

Most everyone across the political spectrum would agree that the heart of educational improvement is the improvement of teaching and learning. Many would also agree that this progress must be viewed through the lens of equity. This is the purported intent of No Child Left Behind (NCLB). It seems to me that those who crafted this legislation and those who must grapple with its influence would do well to remember that even the best of intentions can lead to unintended consequences that may not be apparent in the short run, but that in the long run can be adverse, or even devastating, in their effects.

We need to take both a deeper and longer view and ask, where will an approach to educational accountability that is tied to annual standardized testing take us? One powerful set of lenses for gaining a deeper perspective on these issues is provided by systems thinking. The disciplines of organizational learning, systems thinking being chief among them, provide the concepts and tools for uncovering the underlying dynamics that cause complex human systems, such as school districts and multinational corporations, to behave the way they do. This way of thinking and taking action has been evolving over many decades, but it reached its widest audience with the 1990 publication of *The Fifth Discipline* by Peter Senge.[1]

SHIFTING THE BURDEN

Among the systems thinking tools are systems archetypes, which are patterns of counterproductive organizational behavior that are repeated in diverse contexts. Because these patterns play out under the surface, they are seldom recognized, which essentially dooms people and organizations to blindly repeat them. Systems theorists have identified at least a dozen systems archetypes.[2] One that is especially applicable with respect to test-based accountability in general and to NCLB in particular is called Shifting the Burden.

Daniel Kim, publisher of *The Systems Thinker*, uses an aspect of the Helen Keller story to illustrate this archetype.[3] Because of her blindness and deafness, Keller's parents had a tendency to rush to her aid with every problem she faced, and it's easy enough to sympathize with their inclination to help their daughter. But Keller may never have realized her potential had another person, with a very different approach, not become a part of her story. Keller's teacher, Ann Sullivan, saw that she must not allow her student's disabilities to prevent Keller from becoming self-reliant. Keller, of course, went on to graduate from Radcliffe College and to become an author and role model for people with disabilities and for many others.

Kim explains, "Helen Keller's story is much more than an inspirational human interest story; it illustrates a pervasive dynamic that is rooted in an archetypal structure. The well-intentioned actions of her parents shifted the burden of responsibility for Helen's welfare to them."[4]

Shifting the Burden takes place when an obvious solution is used to relieve what is perceived as a problem, but is actually only a symptom of the problem. Kim observes that "these symptomatic solutions have two specific negative effects. First, they divert attention away from the real or fundamental source of the problem. More subtly, symptomatic solutions cause the viability of the fundamental solution to deteriorate over time, reinforcing the perceived need for more of the symptomatic solution."[5] Shifting the Burden, in other words, is an approach that employs short-term remedies at the expense of long-term solutions.

THE TESTING BANDWAGON

This archetype, I believe, provides a map that plots the eventual destination of the testing bandwagon. Shifting the Burden, like all the systems archetypes, is a tool for probing assumptions. What are the assumptions at work in test-based accountability? It is assumed, correctly I believe, that on the whole and most acutely in areas of concentrated poverty our public schools are not enabling students to achieve at levels that will assure their success in life and work. It is further assumed that the basic problem is low test scores, or, if not the scores themselves, then a level of learning that can best be tracked by test scores. Other assumptions flow from these. If the problem is best described by low test scores, then we need regular testing both to spur and to monitor results on standardized tests. A whole system of accountability is then built around test scores.

The trouble is that the burden is being shifted. Test scores are the symptom, not the underlying problem. And while strategies aimed at raising test scores will probably result in higher test scores, the unintended consequences of this symptomatic solution will be harmful, if not toxic, to schools and students in the long run. Test-based accountability assumes that higher test scores equal better learning, but researchers have found that it is possible to raise test scores without improving the quality of teaching and learning in the classroom. In fact, it is possible to raise test scores by lowering the quality of teaching and learning.

The situation is perhaps analogous to farmers being rewarded or punished according to the annual weight of their animals. If the stakes were high enough, farmers would find ways to boost animal weight prior to the annual weigh in. It is not difficult to imagine how the short-term success of tactics for increasing animal weight could have deadly long-term effects both on the animals and on farm productivity.

Some research is finding increased student dropout rates attributable to high-stakes testing programs.[6] This is especially true for students who don't perform well on standardized tests, who are retained in a grade, or who are turned off by the test-prep, drill-and-kill environments that sprout like mushrooms wherever testing is overemphasized. We know how devastating the consequences of dropping out can be. In 1998, for example, the unemployment rate for dropouts was 75 percent higher than for high school graduates.[7] Those students who remain in school may well see their scores rise, but at the high price of receiving an education that doesn't begin to tap into their potential or to truly prepare them for living and working in a world that grows more complex by the hour.

Here is how Anthony Alvarado, Chancellor of Instruction for San Diego City Schools, stated the problem in an interview with Michael Fullan: "When you set a target and ask for big leaps in achievement scores, you start squeezing capacity in a way that gets into a preoccupation with tests, perhaps bordering on cheating. You cut corners in a way that ends up diminishing learning. That is the antithesis of [what we want]."[8]

It is argued by the proponents of test-based accountability that you can't make continual progress unless you measure progress. Fair enough, but why do we then assume that an annual standardized test is best suited to the task? Performance assessments can provide students and teachers with much more timely and relevant feedback that can be used for focusing and improving instruction throughout the school year.

What do standardized tests actually test? Do we know of living-wage jobs that require anything like test-taking ability? But high-quality jobs and civic participation in our democratic society often do involve solving complex problems, working on projects in teams, and the ability to perform tasks requiring analysis, synthesis, interpretation, communication, and imagination—things that standardized tests are least able to assess.

This is not an argument for the elimination of standardized testing. It is an argument for recognizing the limitations of such tests and their consequent inadequacy for being the sole driver of an educational accountability system.

So, if low test scores are symptoms and not the underlying problem, then what is the "real" problem? The fundamental challenge in public education, it seems to me, is that our nation is now calling upon our systems of education to accomplish a goal that these systems were never designed to address. That goal is to enable all students across the socioeconomic spectrum to graduate from high school prepared for college-level work or living-wage jobs in a rapidly changing economy. It is not possible to achieve this goal without systematically and systemically building the capacities of educators and educational leaders to accomplish what has never previously been accomplished in public education. Meeting this challenge in our nation's 80,000 schools will require fundamentally changing the policies, practices, and structures of school systems. Increasing the regimen of standardized tests, in and of itself, does none of this. In fact, if the stakes around standardized tests are high and if the accountabilities are exclusively focused on the tests, they can have the effect of pressuring teachers to narrow the curriculum and reduce their instructional practice to mere test prepping.

What may seem paradoxical, given my argument above, is that I believe standards, assessment, and accountability can be high-leverage strategies for tackling the actual underlying educational challenge of our times, but not as they are popularly defined in most political circles. As I have argued elsewhere, we need to distinguish the authentic standards movement from its "evil twin," which could also be called high-stakes, standardized, test-driven reform.[9]

AUTHENTIC STANDARDS-BASED ACCOUNTABILITY

What would be the characteristics of an authentic standards-based accountability system? I draw the following characteristics from actual school districts:

> Teachers, parents, and others have actively participated in developing common learning standards, and they continue to participate in the ongoing refinement of the standards.
> Student assessments are aligned with the standards, and students are given numerous opportunities on various kinds of assessments to demonstrate that a standard has been met. No single test or assessment is used to determine whether a standard has been met, whether a student can be promoted to the next grade, whether a student can graduate, or whether a school will be designated as "low performing." Assessments are used to diagnose students' needs and

to improve or adjust the instructional practice of their teachers. Multiple forms of student assessment in combination with other indicators are used to evaluate schools.

The school system is investing heavily in high-quality professional development for teachers and principals, specifically supporting their efforts to enable all students to achieve high standards of learning.

Persistently low-performing students are given the time, opportunity, and intensive, individualized support needed to improve their academic performance.

The school district is accountable for giving persistently low-performing schools intensive assistance aimed at building school capacity for continuous improvement. These same schools are then accountable for meeting the educational needs of their students, but if they continue to fail their students after intensive intervention, they should be reconstituted.

District resources are (re)allocated so that students who are most in need actually receive needed supports, including well-qualified and well-compensated teachers.

The school system gathers multiple forms of data to improve school-level and district-level decision making, the targeting of resources, and program implementation.

Parents and other community members are actively engaged at every stage of the district and school improvement process. This means that school system leaders are listening and responding to parent and community concerns and perspectives, as well as getting the district message out.

District-level and school-level leaders throughout the system maintain a laser-like focus on teaching and learning and vigilantly guard against whatever would shift energies and resources elsewhere.

UNINTENDED CONSEQUENCES

NCLB/ESEA is more sharply focused on closing the achievement gap than any previous federal legislation, and that focus is crucial. But the long-term unintended consequences of a remedy based on a misdiagnosis can be destructive. What concerns me is not only the adverse consequences that the "evil twin" of test-based accountability is already having on teaching and learning, but also its potential for undermining authentic standards-based accountability, which may hold the highest leverage for developing systems of public education where all students encounter a rich and demanding curriculum and the quality of teaching and individualized support they need to master it.

It is perhaps fitting to conclude with Helen Keller's own words: "Life is either a daring adventure or nothing. To keep our faces toward change and behave like free spirits in the presence of fate is strength undefeatable." Those words were expressed by a mind that was nurtured and developed through an individualized, not standardized, education.

NOTES

1. Peter M. Senge (1990), *The Fifth Discipline: The Art and Practice of The Learning Organization* (New York: Doubleday).

2. Senge (1990), pp. 94–113 and 378–390. See also Peter M. Senge et al. (1994), *The Fifth Discipline Fieldbook: Strategies and Tools for Building a Learning Organization* (New York: Currency Doubleday), pp. 121–150.

3. Daniel H. Kim (1992), *Systems Archetypes I: Diagnosing Systemic Issues and Designing High-Leverage Interventions* (Waltham, MA: Pegasus Communications).

4. Kim (1992), p. 22.

5. Kim (1992), p. 22.

6. See, for example, Maureen Kelleher (June 1999), "Dropout Rate Climbs as Schools Dump Truants," *Catalyst;* and Walter M. Haney (1999), *Supplementary Report on Texas Assessment of Academic Skills Exist Test* (Los Angeles: Mexican American Legal Defense and Education Fund).

7. Joshua Benton and Roy Appleton (May 20, 2001), "Through the cracks Texans who drop out face bleak futures defined by limitations," *Dallas Morning News.*

8. Michael Fullan (2001), *Leading in a Culture of Change* (San Francisco: Jossey-Bass), p. 63.

9. Scott Thompson (January 2001), "The Authentic Standards Movement and Its Evil Twin," *Phi Delta Kappan.*

◆◆ Index

❧ About the Authors

Kathy Adams, an urban high school dropout, has been an educator for over twenty years. She is currently an assistant professor at Wright State University in Dayton, Ohio.

Dale Adams, a retired army warrant officer, is currently an urban teacher in Cincinnati Public Schools in Cincinnati, Ohio, and a doctoral student at the University of Cincinnati.